Lyons at the Gate

Lyons at the Gate

Further Adventures of Judge Joe Lyons

Dermot Meagher

Also by Dermot Meagher
Judge Sentences: Tales from the Bench
Lyons and Tigers and Bears

With Robert Coles, M.D. and Joseph Brenner, M.D.
Drugs and Youth

Cover photograph, cover design and book design by Charles L. Ross
Drawings by Dermot Meagher

Photographs on pages 22, 58 and 296 courtesy of the Trustees of the
    Boston Public Library, Leslie Jones Collection
Photographs on pages 8, 44 and 98 courtesy of the Trustees of the Boston
    Public Library
Photograph on page 206 courtesy the Social Law Library
Photographs on pages 230 and 298 by Renato Cellucci

ISBN: 10:1481953907
ISBN-13: 978-1481953900

To
Renato Cellucci

For we are all packets of motives and never aware
of the sum total of our reasons for doing anything.

Louis Auchincloss, 2010

Nevertheless, the more intimate portion of his brain
was deeply engaged in those labyrinths of minor
provincial intrigue in which so many able intellects spend
themselves, for want of wider opportunity.

Edith OE Somerville and Martin Ross
Mount Music, 1916

CONTENTS

PRINCIPAL CHARACTERS
in order of appearance

Honorable Joseph Lavin Lyons
an appellate judge in Massachusetts

Angelo Bruno
inamorato of Joe Lyons

Josie Lavin
Joe Lyons' aunt and biggest fan

Larry
Joe's doorman, a spy

Dino Randozza
previous obsession of Joe Lyons

Giuseppina Randozza
mother of Dino and Bishop Rocco Randozza

Tom Murphy, Esq.
law school classmate, old friend and adviser of Joe Lyons

Sam Nemesis
right wing, reactionary, judge hater

Mary Alice Finnigan Jones, now Alice Jones, wife of Harry Jones

Hasan Nasser
Harvard University Kennedy School of Government student

Eleanore Emmett
Harvard Graduate School of Arts and Sciences student

Guido
restaurateur and owner of Guido's Back Bay Grille

Harry Jones, Esq.
ex-boyfriend of Joe Lyons, now husband of Alice Jones

Honorable F. Frank Wolf
aka "Wolfie", gadfly, wheeler dealer

Maureen Ronayne Randozza
niece of Dino Randozza, granddaughter of Giuseppina

JoJo Danieli
Maureen Randozza's girlfriend, a butch

State Representative Billy Meadows
an ambiguous good looker

Honorable Gigi Boland
colleague and erstwhile confidante of Joe Lyons

Miss Mary Margaret Managhan
Secretary to the Chief Justice

Carlos Colorado
recently of Santiago, Cuba

Patrick Foley
law student and legal intern

Trooper Rodney Banks
Patrick Foley's boyfriend

Franny Flynn
bon vivant, of Boston, Palm Beach and Provincetown

Bishop Rocco Randozza
brother of Dino Randozza, son of Giuseppina

Michael Nemesis
seminarian, son of Sam Nemesis

Mary Rose Quirk
First Assistant Clerk/ Magistrate, Boston Municipal Court

Austin Ignatius Costello
Clerk/Magistrate, Boston Municipal Court

Chief Justice Cesar Lopez
of the Boston Municipal Court

Trooper Horace Mulligan
Massachusetts State Police

In Pursuit of Madeleines

Joe Lyons and Dino Randozza did not last long as a couple.

The excitement of their differences wore off for each of them. Dino slipped away from Joe once he realized that the idea of being a gangster involved with a judge was exciting, but the reality was not. As a small example, Joe had to stay away from places where excitement might exist for Dino—such as racetracks, casinos or nightclubs.

And, in comparison to Dino, Joe had to wake up early because the court sessions started at 9:30 A.M. That was the official start of the court day.

The courts used to open at 10:00 A.M. but the *Boston Globe*, in one of its spurts of Puritan joy killing, pointed out that even bankers didn't keep bankers' hours any more. According to the *Globe*, the only people who still slept late were movie stars, gangsters and hookers. The courts should begin work at 9:00 A.M. like everyone else, the *Globe* insisted. Talk radio soon picked up this cause.

After consultation with his secretary, Miss Mary Margaret Managhan, who had a standing 9:00 A.M. hairdresser appointment every three weeks and who said "Don't give them everything," The Chief Justice changed the opening hour of the Court day to 9:30 A.M.

That Solomon-like splitting the difference was not satisfactory to the *Globe* and the talk radio hosts. They wanted 9:00 A.M., or maybe even 8:30 A.M., and wrote further editorials criticizing the court. As often happens with compromise decisions (viz. Solomon), nobody won.

The change didn't please the Justices either. A lot of their appointments, therapy of all sorts, yoga classes and gymnasium training occurred before 10:00 A.M.

The staff was similarly disturbed by the opening hour change. Some court officers had morning jobs. Many court employees, including some of the younger judges, had to deliver kids to school. One assistant clerk was the altar boy for the 8:30 Latin Mass every day at the Church of Saint Philomena. He had the most Catholic Justice from the Supreme Judicial Court, the other altar boy at St. Philomena's and a daily communicant, call the Chief Justice and intercede, dropping not so subtle remarks about creeping Secularism depriving Catholics of their religious civil liberties.

The Chief Justice gave the altar boy a dispensation so long as he stayed beyond his usual early departure for Parish League basketball practice three times a week.

Change was difficult for everybody. Had the prigs at the *Globe* ever thought of the repercussions of their righteousness? And what time did they start work at the *Globe*, by the way? Everybody knew about cigarette-smoking, hard-drinking reporters strolling into the press room in time for a beery lunch at the crack of noon.

It was merciful that Dino pulled away first because Joe had no idea how to get out of a romantic situation. He had been in so few. Joe's usual way of getting rid of unpleasantness was to hope it would pass soon, and letting it.

After the lusty honeymoon on East Fifty-First Street in Manhattan, in the shadow of Saint Patrick's, Joe and Dino got together in Boston a few times a week. There was usually a jump after Joe slowly removed his suit and tie in front of Dino naked in the bed, followed by supper at restaurants where they hoped nobody would recognize either of them. Dino knew lots of remote Italian places where the food was good, his privacy respected and the service perfect and unobtrusive. Dino would then drop Joe off back at his Beacon Street apartment just below the State House with a goodnight kiss and a grope in the car. They would tell each other how much they enjoyed the evening, sometimes whisper endearments, before Joe went upstairs to his apartment to read pastoral Irish novels.

Larry, Joe's doorman on Beacon Street noted these drop-offs in a little red book, just as he had noted Joe and Dino's departures. A man in a dark suit and red and black striped tie gave him $100 a week to do so.

After dropping off Joe, Dino stayed out to do business until the wee hours. He then awoke at the crack of noon, the same time as the hookers, movie stars and newspaper reporters, and had a double espresso.

Although they were very passionate at the beginning of the affair, that wore off. There was little else to keep them together.

Dino's solution was to disappear, a luxury that Joe, who had his steady judge job, did not have. Dino spent more time in Rome. During his pursuit of the missing page of *The Book of Kells* Dino had developed a pecuniary as well as aesthetic interest in illuminated manuscripts. One day while strolling through the Piazza Navona, one of Dino's favorite places in Rome, near Bernini's Fountain of the Four Rivers, with the rivers as bearish colossi in odalisque positions surrounding an obelisk, Dino met Monsignor Oliver Dunn from Tralee, who had become the acquisitions curator of the Vatican Museum. Monsignor Dunn was wearing civilian clothes, a tan suit in fact, and revealed his true self only later in the evening when he met Dino for supper at a little restaurant near the Piazza Farnese on the Via Monserrato. Dino's heart or maybe it was his prostate twitched at the sight of the tiny block of magenta at Monsignor Dunn's Roman collar.

Dino was able to help Monsignor Dunn add to the Vatican's collections. Dino already had the connections. He just hadn't known it until his interest in Art blossomed with *The Book of Kells*. The art business was full of people who did what Dino did.

Dino was no fool regarding Joe however. There was no abrupt ego-deflating break. Dino thought, *It's always good to have a judge in your Rolodex*. Besides, Dino liked Joe. He did not want to break off with acrimony, or even drama.

In the corners of the North End, East Boston, Malden, Revere, Quincy and other Italian-American enclaves around Boston there were young, handsome, Italian-American men who wanted older men, and pink and grey Irish ones at that. Previously they were Dino's competition. Now one of them would be his solution. That one was Angelo Bruno.

*   *   *

Joe met Angelo in the Starbucks at the Beacon Street end of Charles Street, down Beacon Hill from Joe's condominium. The Starbucks was the balancing weight to Panificio's coffee house at the other end where Joe had first met Dino Randozza after their computer introduction.

Unlike Joe's hookup with Dino, the meeting with Angelo was not preceded by any electronic romancing. Joe had stayed away from the computer's siren songs ever since Dino. At first he had no need, then he was in fear of what could happen if he were to answer another computer ad. Joe thought, *One close call is enough*. Joe limited his websurfing to the weather.

Joe's Proustian urge for madeleines one Tuesday lunch hour in mid-October, sent him to this Starbucks. He knew they sold madeleines, albeit wrapped in cellophane. Aunt Josie was coming up from Providence to stay the night and she had first introduced him to them when he was a little boy.

Joe was planning to walk over to meet Josie at the Back Bay Station after work. The plan was that they would stop somewhere for supper and then take a cab back to Joe's Beacon Street apartment. He would serve her the madeleines in the morning with her tea.

Joe's court still maintained an all judges, almost mandatory lunch in the cafeteria of the office building at One Beacon Street next door to the Courthouse. The exception was the very contrary Justice Firrfield, who always ate bean sprouts, peanut butter and tofu alone in his office.

When the Court was founded in 1972 (recent in comparison to other Massachusetts courts) it obviously had no history or traditions. Somebody thought that a public lunch with all the judges would be a good idea. Of course, the judges could not talk about cases lest some nearby lawyer, reporter or wag overhear them. So, day after day, they had strained conversations about children, vacations and teaching gigs, which soon bored neighboring tables. It also seemed important that the judges' camaraderie occur in a democratic setting, thus, the public cafeteria at One Beacon Street next door.

*   *   *

Joe walked down Beacon Street, past his apartment building, to the corner of Charles Street. This Starbucks had two entrances; both had doors opening out with glass windows two steps up from the street. As Joe went up one step and in on Beacon Street Angelo Bruno was exiting at the Charles Street doors. Angelo did a double-take mid-lintel at the sight of Joe.

Joe was wearing a dove gray, pinstriped, soft wool flannel suit, polished dark brown wingtips, a white pointed collar shirt and a navy blue polka dotted silk tie, a Brooks Brothers' staple. Angelo was more casually dressed in khaki plain front pants, a robin's egg blue cashmere three button sweater shirt and a tan jacket casually draped over his right shoulder. Angelo looked like he just stepped out of a fashion magazine. Angelo saw Joe coming in through the glass of the door but so bent on buying the madeleines was Joe, he missed Angelo completely. The twisted, ogling Angelo almost fell on the last step down to Charles Street but caught himself, turned left around the corner and came back into Starbucks by the Beacon Street doors, the same as Joe had just entered. Angelo espied Joe by the pastry counter and quickly searched for some excuse to put himself there. *Maybe it will become apparent once I see what's in the pastry case*, Angelo hoped. He stood to Joe's left as Joe talked to the *barista* in charge of pastry, who, in the hierarchy and patois of Starbucks is probably called something else like *patisserier*, except in mock Italian.

"I probably shouldn't tell you this," the counterman said, "but I am sure that the French Bakery in the Meeting House further up Charles Street sells fresher madeleines than our plastic-wrapped numbers. If you are going to buy a dozen, you'd do much better up there. Don't tell anyone I said this. O.K.?" That said, he winked at Joe.

Joe smiled back. "Thank you for your honesty. I really appreciate it. I'm buying them for my aunt, who's visiting from Providence. She will appreciate it as well."

"No problem, sir."

The "sir" almost killed the previous kindness. There is nothing an older man appreciates less than being called "Sir." It is too obvious an acknowledgement of the age difference between the speaker and the recipient. It also is sexless, except in some kinky sexual sports which did not interest Joe. But Joe was still smiling at the kindness and gentility of the counterman as he turned for the door, contemplating his route back to the courthouse at the top of

Beacon Hill now that he had been diverted. *I could walk up Charles Street, then climb up Mount Vernon Street after I buy the madeleines; it would be a nice walk,* Joe decided. *It won't be any more time. I'll be back in the office by two.*

"And how may I help you?" the clerk then asked Angelo.

"Oh, nothing, nothing. Thank you, very kind, I'm just looking," Angelo said. Right below him was an umbrella hooked onto the pastry case. "Did that nice man leave his umbrella here?" Angelo asked.

"Oh no, that umbrella has been there all day. We figure its owner will come back for it once she remembers where she left it," the *panifacatore* said.

"Oh, it must be that sweet man's umbrella," Angelo said oblivious to what had just been told him. "Where is that French Bakery you sent him to?"

"It's at Mount Vernon and Charles. You can't miss it. He's kind of cute—that old guy, No? I think the umbrella belongs to a harried Back Bay mother who came in here this morning with three wild kids. They each wanted something different and she was very distracted."

"I'm going to bring him his umbrella. It looks like it might rain," Angelo said, as if in a daze, paying no mind to the counterman's statement of ownership. Angelo was away from the counter like a shot.

Joe had walked up Charles Street to Branch Street. Angelo tried not to run, just power walk with big steps to catch up. He reached Joe at the next block, Chestnut Street, just after the Beacon Hill Bistro, formerly Rebecca's, formerly Sharaf's, the teenage gay hangout of the Sixties.

"Excuse me, I think you left your umbrella in Starbucks." Wisely, Angelo did not call Joe "Sir."

Joe looked at the umbrella, which was bright yellow with pink daisies, and then looked Angelo up and down, at first for the preposterous notion that a man dressed as seriously as Joe was would have such a frivolous appurtenance, then because he had not seen a man so handsome since Dino Randozza.

Angelo could've been Dino's son, maybe a brother or a nephew. Although he had the broad Roman nose, he wasn't one of the Italian-from-Italy Randozza relations; Angelo's clothes were too American, preppy almost but not clichéd. They showed knowledge of what made him look good. The pants hugged his bum. That soft, cashmere, Veronese sky blue sweater shirt open across the clavicle, exposed a chestful of black and occasionally gray hair, like a soft brush or a fur coat left Joe breathless.

Joe couldn't say anything. He just nodded his head negatively. But when he found his voice, after an embarrassingly long time, he whispered quietly, lying through his teeth, "Thank you so much. That is my favorite umbrella. How nice of you to retrieve it for me. Thank you. Thank you. You are such a kind man. Thank you!"

* * *

At the counter of the French Bakery Joe asked politely, "Do you have any madeleines today?"

"Marilyn don't work here no more. She works in Chelsea."

The French Bakery did not have madeleines. They have never sold madeleines as a matter of fact. The teenaged girl at the counter did not even know what they were. When Joe attempted to explain by a reference to Marcel Proust, she looked blank and then said, "We don't have them either."

"'Them' what?" Joe asked just a bit peevishly, as if the girl at the counter was a lawyer who had misplaced a pronoun in oral argument. Joe tried to restrain his irritation because he didn't want to appear mean in the presence of the handsome man now standing beside him at the pastry case.

"'Mahshel Proons,' what you just said. We got all kinds of croissants—chocolate, almond, ham and cheese. We got sandwiches too. Whatchou want?"

Joe gave up. Angelo smiled benevolently, both because he was amused at Joe's frustration and because he had some sympathy for the counter girl. Angelo wasn't sure what madeleines were either, although he deduced that they were some kind of French pastry. He tried to think what the Italian equivalent might be. If he knew, Angelo would have rushed to the North End, bought them, put them in a beautiful box with a ribbon and delivered them to Joe immediately. Angelo's mind went to *sfogliatelle* because they were the best tasting pastry he could think of. He was sure that the French had nothing superior, and he was about to offer it to Joe as a substitute.

Joe said, "I give up. I'll go back to Starbucks later. Right now I should return to work."

"I can walk you there," Angelo said not even knowing where "there" was or what Joe did for work. Whatever it was, Angelo liked the uniform—the suit, tie and wigtips. "Or I could give you a lift," he said. "My car is parked up on Beacon Street, just below the State House."

Uh oh! Joe thought, *not this again. A walk up Beacon Street with a handsome Italian man! This time in daylight!*

Joe began to plot the route, how best to cover the possibilities of being observed, *We'll have to take the back streets. We can go up Chestnut. Not many people walk there. Then cut across Walnut and it'll just be a few yards we'll have to walk on Beacon. If anyone has spotted us, they'll think we're coming up Beacon, not down it. The television cameras will be looking down the Hill. I hope there is nobody in the lobby. Larry, the doorman, won't let them in and he'll keep his mouth shut. I think I can pull this off. Oh dear! How do I get into these things? Concupiscence! The apartment's a mess. Did I make the bed? Do I have any lube?*

A Surprise Visitor

At 4:15 P.M. Joe's doorbell rang. His cellphone, the ringer of which was shut off in the left pocket of his pants hanging half off a chair and half on the floor in the living room, had been ringing as well, but of course Joe did not know that. The doorbell was ancient and had been replaced by telephone service from the concierge desk years before. Joe knew that something was peculiar when he heard that old ring, so he pulled his naked self away from Angelo and off the queen-sized bed in his, the larger of the two bedrooms, and went to the speaker attached to the doorbell apparatus next to his front door.

"Yes," he said impatiently into the box on the wall.

"I'm sorry to bother you, Judge. This is Larry downstairs at the front desk. Your aunt, Josie Lavin, is in the lobby and she wants to come up. She doesn't understand why I won't just let her. She says she has a key." Larry then added in a whisper, "I didn't tell her you have a guest."

Of course Larry had seen Joe come in with Angelo at 1:45 P.M. He had even noted it in his little pocket notebook for the benefit of the man in the dark suit. This guy wasn't Dino Randozza, but he looked Italian. No harm noting that.

"Oh Christ!" Joe said. "Can you delay her a bit? Thanks Larry."

"I'll do what I can," Larry said.

Joe had never talked about his romantic life with Josie, although he assumed she knew, just like his mother knew even though he had never talked to her about it either, except when Arthur Bruce died and Joe felt compelled to explain his perpetual sadness. At that time he'd said no more than, "A very good friend died from AIDS last Sunday." Joe assumed that his mother had talked about his "orientation" with Josie. The Lavin sisters kept few secrets from each other and although they talked in a kind of code, especially when talking about sex, their truths did out.

"Angelo, Angelo! Get up. Put your clothes on. My Aunt Josie is downstairs and she is coming up. Who can we tell her you are?"

Before that was decided there was a noise at the door of a key being put in the lock. Joe, who was able to put on his pants, shirt and shoes quickly, rushed to the door. Angelo grabbed as many of his clothes as he could and scooted into the bathroom.

At least he can wash around, clean up and comb his hair, Joe thought peevishly, as he tried to neaten his own thin white hair with his fingers. *I'm still stained with love.*

As he opened the door he said, "Josie, how nice to see you? Why are you so early? I thought we had agreed that I'd meet you at the Back Bay Station."

"That Larry downstairs is very officious. He's seen me here a hundred times. What's his problem? Does he drink? He wouldn't let me come up. Were you napping? You look like you just got out of bed. I took an earlier train. It was such a nice day I went to South Station and walked up here. Through the Common. So many pigeons! I still have the legs. They say they're the last to go. Can I make a cup of tea?"

Joe was stumped, but fortunately Josie didn't wait for an answer.

She headed for the kitchen which connected to the living room and which had a small passthrough out to it.

"This is a funny place for underwear, Joe. Right here on the counter. I didn't think you wore these bikini things. It's very Italian of you. Pina Randozza used to buy these for her sons, even the bishop. Did you pick this pair up in Italy? They do dress so well there, even the men. But why are they on the counter below the passthrough?"

Josie had lived with her brother for years so she wasn't offended by men's underwear. She instinctively folded the underwear and put it to one side of the counter. She remained curious, but said nothing more on the subject. Again Joe was stumped, but again Josie saved him when she jumped to another subject.

"Do you still get that Irish tea sent from Vermont? I'd love to have that. Where is it, Joe?"

Joe rushed in to the kitchen, quickly pocketed the neatly folded bikini briefs from the counter before Josie could check the size which was not anywhere close to his 40-inch waist. He found the Irish tea in the cabinet above the passthrough and put some water in a pan to boil. Josie had taught him long ago not to use a teapot, especially one that you filled through the snout.

"You can see what's in the pan. God knows what's crawled in one of those teapots or what's corroded inside," Josie had told him after he presented her with a beautiful Alessi Italian teapot. "Excuse me, but what do Italians know about making tea. They can cook everything else, but we know about making tea."

Just then Angelo appeared from the bedroom fully dressed (except for his underwear, of course, which was in Joe's pocket but Angelo did not know that.)

Josie looked startled, but said, "Oh, excuse me, Joseph! I didn't know you had company." She then turned to Angelo and said, "I apologize for bursting in. I'm Josie Lavin, Joe's aunt from Providence, and you are?"

It's a strange word to apply to someone in her late eighties, but Josie was cool. She could handle anything and anyone. You could take her anywhere. Maybe it was fifty years of teaching unpredictable kids that gave her this gift but she had been cool before the word had its present meaning. She didn't see what she didn't want to see. Sometimes, like today, she didn't see what you didn't want her to see either. Rather, for people she loved she didn't comment on what you didn't want her to see. That is not to say she didn't note it somewhere, and it was possible it would be brought up later, but only if it would be in your interest. The "you" in this case was Joe, her beloved Joe, the boy she never had, her sister's son, fathered by a man otherwise occupied with his head in the Greek or Roman skies. They, Joe's parents, didn't know what a jewel they had in Joe, but Josie did and their blindness didn't stop Josie from loving him, shaping him, spoiling him. Joe could do no wrong, even when he did. So, here was this handsome young Italian man, sculpted by Bernini himself, coming out of Joe's bedroom. What was he doing in Joe's bedroom in the middle of the day, a work day, a person, but not Josie at this time, might ask? If Joe was entertaining him, he must be alright.

Angelo became even more alright when Josie discovered that he was a fourth grade teacher. That was the most noble thing a person could do in Josie's mind, especially these days when educated young people thought the best place to work was in "Finance," whatever that meant—greed, probably.

"How long have you been teaching, Angelo?"

"I started right out of college when I was 21. That was twenty years ago. I taught the second grade for a while but the principal needed someone for the fourth, so I stepped in about eight years ago. It seems that kids are maturing earlier and earlier each year—particularly the girls."

"Oh, I had a terrible time with the girls, Angelo. The older they got the harder they were. I think it's the television that is ruining them. Such disrespect—and bad taste. In my day we wanted to be fashionable and elegant, now all they want is to look cheap and act rudely. I worry about them. It's a wonder they all aren't pregnant by the eighth grade. The boys are just stupid at that age, don't you think? They get led around by the noses by the girls. But the kids are teachable, don't you agree? They must love having a handsome, charming man like yourself as a teacher. I know I would have. Oh dear! Do they get crushes on you? Do you get mash notes?"

"I've had a few notes, even a couple from boys."

"Oh, that's o.k. They have a right to fantasy romance too. It's harmless. I'd worry about the ones that are falling in love but not sending notes. They are the ones who suffer. Don't you agree, Angelo?"

"I was on Facebook, but there was no privacy, no boundaries. One mother even sent me nude photos."

"I'm sure and I don't blame her. I hope that you didn't take it out on her child. How did you deal with the mother?"

"I called her sister, who I had gone to high school with. She said the mother was in a loveless marriage but that she, the sister, would take care of it. I know the mother's husband. I didn't want to call him. He can be a brute. I went to high school with him too. I guess that in a way I'm lucky to be teaching in the community I grew up in. It is strange to see kids whose parents I knew as kids. I could tell the kids some stories."

"But you wouldn't. You're a gentleman, I can tell, and you know it would be destructive. We all change as we grow up and it's usually for the better. I've been around long enough to have seen that proven. God bless you!" Then she added after a pause, "And how do you know Joe?"

That question came like a bolt out of nowhere. Joe and Angelo looked at each other. Joe jumped in, " Every May Day, Law Day, judges go off to speak in the schools. I was sent to Angelo's school last year. He was in charge of the presentation. They gave me a nice lunch and I met Angelo. He was coming into town today, so we arranged to have lunch. He was going to give me a ride to Back Bay Station to meet you. We tried to buy madeleines. Angelo tells me that *Sfogliatelle* are better and he was going to take me to the North End to buy some at the Modern Pastry."

Of course, that was much too long an answer to a simple question and they all knew it was a lie, but nobody was telling.

"That's lovely," Josie said. "Pina Randozza has taken me to the Modern Pastry. It's the best bakery in Boston. They are not too heavy with the sugar. Of course, in Providence we have wonderful Italian bakeries and even a French one. I love *Sfogliatelle*, almost as much as madeleines. Do you like the morning ones or the afternoon ones with the cream filling, Angelo?"

Angelo had heard of the Randozzas and of Pina. He read the newspapers, even the *Herald* sometimes. Dino had been pointed out to Angelo once in the now defunct Napoleon Club, the gerontophile bar, the "Wrinkle Room" as it was nicknamed. Angelo wondered what Josie might be doing with Pina Randozza, but he said nothing on that subject. You don't ask questions if you're Italian. Italians aren't boundaryless like the Irish, who, on first meeting, might ask who ended up with your mother's rosary beads.

"I like them plain with a little powdered sugar on top—the small ones. I forget which those are, afternoon or morning. We have a great bakery in Revere. I'll bring you some when we meet next." Angelo then stood up and said, "Speaking of Revere, I had better get home. I have to make dinner for my father."

Joe showed Angelo to the door. *Whether or not to kiss him good-bye? A hug will be O.K., won't it? Even straight baseball players do that.*

They hugged. "Call me," Joe whispered while in the embrace.

Joe shut the door slowly.

As soon as he got back to his chair, and Josie, Joe realized that he had never given Angelo his telephone number.

"What a nice man!" Josie said. "Cooking for his father! He'll make someone a great husband some day."

Of course, Josie knew that Joe was gay. Who didn't know that? It had been in the *Newport Daily News*, below the fold on page one, when he was nominated to be a judge. *Newport gay man named to Massachusetts bench*. The article named his parents and even his illustrious grandfather, which of course tipped the astute readers off to his many aunts and uncles and even more cousins. The word was out in Rhode Island.

But what did "gay" mean to her? They had never talked about that. Apart from an occasional reference to the man who did her hair, Joe had never heard her even approach the subject. They talked about Civil Rights for the Blacks, the Latinos and the American Indians, but never about the Gays. Joe had no idea what Josie thought about it or even if she thought anywhere beyond the word. Certainly, she had never told him what she thought about his gayness. Had she thought about what he did in bed, or wherever else he found a spot for sex? Did she know who put what where when?

Joe knew what he thought about being gay—more or less. It wasn't always so positive. It wasn't as benign as being in the Elks as Happy Tessler had told him to think about his homosexuality for the Judicial Nominating Commission. Gaiety defined him. Yes, his sexuality defined him even though one or the other of the shrinks he had seen every now and again had told him he shouldn't let it do that. Because straight people never really had to think about why they desired mates of the opposite sex they never pondered the matter of their attraction. Nobody had ever questioned it. Many of them thought gay people shouldn't do so either.

Just to remind them of the limits of their tolerance Joe loved to say, "I don't care what you people do. Just don't rub my nose in it," whenever straight people became too graphic about their sex lives. Sometimes the constant self assertion required to be a gay person got to Joe. *Why do I give a fuck what these straight people think anyway?*

At other times Joe thought, *What is the point of all this equality ideology if I'm not getting laid.* Horniness made Joe bitter and depressed. "Horny, Angry, Lonely, Tired." Sometimes he wanted someone so bad, but didn't dare make the first move. It had been that way with Angelo a few hours earlier.

But Angelo knew that and he made the first move. Angelo pushed Joe up against the wall as soon as they got in the door of Joe's apartment and he, Angelo, started taking off Joe's clothes, starting with the jacket and shirt, all of a piece. He threw them on the floor. This wasn't going to be a neat seduction. It was a willing one, however, and when Angelo got down to Joe's belt Joe helped with the buckle. Joe then unbuttoned Angelo's cashmere sweater and pushed it and Angelo's wifebeater undershirt over Angelo's head. He bit Angelo's left nipple—just a little—and then went at Angelo's khaki pants. Angelo had no patience for Joe's fumbling and he just pulled the pants down and neatly stepped out of them and his bikini briefs at the same time with a laugh. He kicked the briefs up with his right foot, caught them in his right hand and tossed them without looking while kissing Joe again.

Of course, the bikini briefs went through the passthrough and landed on the kitchen counter where Josie later found them. Angelo then picked up the whole bundle of his and Joe's clothes, minus the bikini briefs and Joe's pants which Joe had draped on the edge of a chair, and carried the bundle to the bedroom pushing Joe in front of him while admiring Joe's pink and white bum.

So, it intrigued Joe what Josie might be thinking about having caught him in the act—or at least right after it. He had never talked to her about gaiety at all—his or anyone else's. He had let the *Newport Daily News* bring him out and hoped that was all that needed to be said about it. He had no idea if Josie voted for politicians in Rhode Island who supported Gay Rights (even though he, before he was a judge and when he could contribute to political campaigns had done so generously.) He had even given money for supportive candidates in Rhode Island, to help them attract his relatives' votes, but he could not bring himself to call the very same relatives, not even Josie, who loved him without reserve, or his parents, and ask them to vote for the good guy candidate.

He hoped that his lesbian cousin, Lizzie, was educating them. Was it Irish reticence—Joe and Josie never talked about straight sex either—or just another instance of gay shame? Here he was, the openly gay judge, and he couldn't say, "Don't let them destroy me," not even to the people who supposedly loved him.

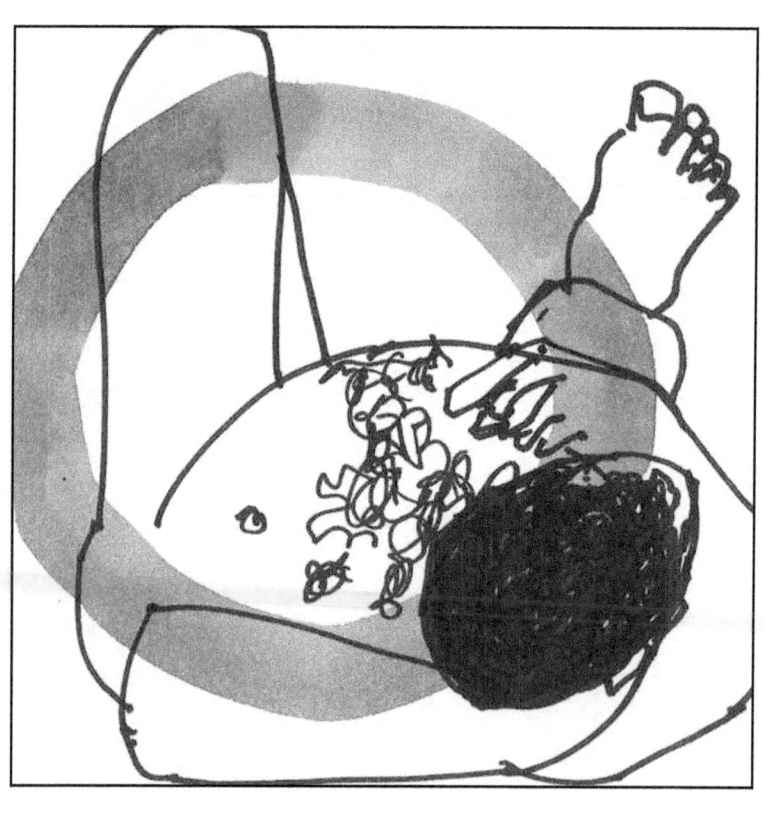

The Fig Leaf

Where did this fascination with, some would say obsession for, tawny, beautiful Italian men with classical torsos and hairy chests come from? Was it Joe's memory of Benny and his sons, his grandfather's gardening crew? Joe remembered looking out the window at them as an eight year old, trying to decide if Benny's son Mike or Lou, the younger son, was his favorite, just as Blessed Mother blue was his favorite color and violets were his favorite flower in the Spring. In the Summer he favored zinnias. Joe had to have a favorite among the sons, but it was difficult. Lou was darker and taller, but Mike was hairy chested, more muscular, and winked at him.

Of course, there had been Arthur Bruce, who was half Italian and where it counted. He wasn't tawny, but he was perfectly pelted with curly dark hair across his chest and in a fine line down his stomach. Joe had fallen hard for him. His departure led to Joe's crackup.

There had been other Italian men before Arthur, longterm tricks actually, but Joe would have liked them to work out. There was the Vietnam veteran he met on the riverbank one sunny afternoon who told Joe his name was "Danny D'Agostino. Yeah, like the bread company. That's my uncle's," Danny lied. Of course, "D'Agostino" wasn't his name. Even though Danny had been fearless, even wounded, in Vietnam, he was still afraid of being found out to be gay.

Like Arthur Bruce, there was another half Irish, half Italian man where the Italian won out. His name was Mike Tucci and he had the Irish virus, alcoholism, to detract from the Abruzesse good looks. That courtship didn't last long because Joe couldn't keep up with Mike's drinking.

Prior to Dino Randozza, Joe's most significant Italian was Paolo DelAmore from Revere.

After Joe's crackup/breakdown/Valium withdrawal in the mid-seventies, after Arthur Bruce left, after they let Joe out of McLean's Hospital, when he only had to drive out there for morning therapy sessions, Joe would spend afternoons at the L Street Beach in South Boston. This was the incongruously city authorized, public men's nude beach in the heart of what was reputedly the most conservative section of Boston proper, or proper Boston. The L Street Beach was a well known secret, not only to the residents of South Boston but also to most gay men in those days, although not many went there.

Recently on Haulover Beach in Florida, another public nude beach, Joe met a man named Al who had grown up in South Boston a few blocks from L Street. In the mid-fifties when Al was 17 he told his father that he was going to the L Street Beach. His off-the-boat Italian father paused, then said, "Don't get queer, Al! Don't get queer!"

At L Street there was a long brick bathhouse that paralleled the shore line, then wooden fences perpendicular to the shore that extended into the water and separated the Men's section from the Women's section on the left and the open K Street Beach on the right. "Fags stay away!" was painted in big white letters on the fence between the Men's section and the K Street Beach.

In 1976 before he was able to find a job again, Joe went to L Street on every sunny day. He knew the perils of being gay there. Even if he saw other gay men he knew, Joe only nodded discreetly at them and sat by himself. They did the same. They all knew the rules, but there was something very exciting about being surrounded by naked men even if you couldn't touch.

On the beach the old Jewish men sat together as did the aged Armenians, Italians, Lithuanians, Syrians and Poles. It was a gerontophile's delight. Who else but retirees and the unemployed could sit out in the sun all day?

Public employees seemed to be the answer. God knows how many cops and civil servants, even an occasional judge, stripped down on the sand. And there were Catholic priests (from out of town) as well as one high church Episcopalian who had mastered the subway and bus route all the way from Isabella Stewart Gardner's Church of the Advent at the foot of Beacon Hill. Unlike the Roman priests, who disguised themselves in civvies, the Anglican arrived in his clerical collar and black suit, to the shock of no one. Some of the oldtimers swam in the chilly water year round and were televised running into the sea on New Years Day. They were called the "L Street Brownies" because they also took the sun all year round, albeit from a protected solarium on the roof in the winter.

Most days there would be an old grouch at the front door handing out a patch of cotton, which was called a "fig leaf." It was a triangle of unbleached cotton with strings attached at the three points of the triangle. There were no instructions as to how to tie it, but if worn correctly, it went on like a modern-day thong. You were supposed to wear it over your privates, but most of the time you did not need to wear it at all. Some people just tied it around their waists with the triangular patch dangling at their hip. Others draped it on their leg. Most men ignored it.

Joe had been warned by a gay elder that there was another mean old guy with a feather on a stick, who patrolled the beach and tickled those who did not wear the fig leaf. However, Joe never saw the man and believed he was apocryphal.

Most of the time Joe stayed naked, his clothes rolled up as a pillow at the end of the towel. Following his mother's advice, "Go in the water; you'll feel better," he usually swam a few laps from fence to fence. Otherwise he just lay there saying the rosary, counting on his fingers, to quiet his still racing-from-Valium withdrawal mind, or he walked the beach by the shoreline sneaking peeks at the men lying down on the sand. Joe pretended to look serious, as if pondering some weighty issue of the Law in case any of his old colleagues or a judge were there. They never were.

From his towel Joe plotted the best route to the outdoor showers where he could see handsome men stretching and washing themselves. One day as he walked down the boardwalk, towards the handball courts and to the shower, he was preceded by two beautiful young men with white Irish bums below strong, freckled backs and above sturdy muscled legs. One had dark, almost black hair cut long, as was the fashion in those days, and the other was a short-haired redhead. Neither should have been exposing his pale skin to the burning sun, and in fact the redhead's back was peeling.

They were walking very jauntily about ten feet ahead of Joe. Joe was certain that they didn't know he was behind them. Joe also believed that if they did sense his presence, they had no idea of the lust they aroused in him. The redhead looked around, side to side, then looked back towards Joe. Then he said, in an Irish whisper, to the dark haired one, "Geez! There are a lot of hot dog inspectors here today. You'd think this was the NEPCO[1] factory."

---

[1] NEPCO, New England Packing Company, the maker of the Fenway Frankfurter, sold at Red Sox baseball games.

Joe quickly stepped off the boardwalk and headed to the water. On the way, about 15 feet from the shore, Joe espied two men lying down on adjacent, towels, not too close, but close enough so that at the least you knew they had come to the beach together. Joe recognized the man furthest from him from the gay bars. He didn't interest Joe, except as a fellow traveler. The other man Joe had never seen before. He was a handsome, well-built man lying on his back with olive skin, wavy, sandy blond hair, green eyes, beautiful body hair distribution like a pelt across his chiseled pectorals and a treasure trail leading down to a big uncut cock draped over his left leg.

How did Joe catch all this in one glance?

Gay men early on develop the all encompassing look. Sometimes they can even see through clothes. Joe also noticed that this beauty was reading a book, the cover of which said, among other things, "YOGA" in big letters. He was holding the book straight out in front and above his puffed chest, modeling his well-knotted biceps, triceps and forearms to their best.

Joe continued on into the water and redid his two laps across the beachfront. He exited just about where he began and walked a few feet up the beach towards the bathhouse until he was at a 30-degree angle, maybe ten o'clock, from the beautiful man's view, beyond the left side of his YOGA book.

Joe sat down on the sand, no matter its roughness, and looked out to sea pensively. He then stood up, turned around so that he faced the prince, bent forward, dug a little larger-than-head-sized indentation a few inches into the sand, then piled up the contents on the forward side. Joe descended to his knees, all the time keeping the Italian within his sight. He was pleased by the knowledge that the object of his desire was regarding him from around the side of his yoga book.

Joe clasped the fingers of both hands together, put them in

the hole back side down, leaned his head in onto the palms of his hand, arched his bum into the "downward dog" position and walked toward his hands. At just the perfect moment, when his back signaled "Go!" to his feet he slowly push/pulled first one leg, then the other vertically up into the air, executing a perfect headstand. He held it for what he perceived to be a reasonable amount of time, came down slowly to his knees again and raised his head.

"Jesus, that was a beautiful headstand!" said his heart's (and prostate's) desire.

Joe smiled faux bashfully and said, "Thanks. How's the book? Did I do it right?"

"You were great. I wish I could do that. Maybe you could teach me. Not here, not today, but sometime. My name is Pauly, Paolo DelAmore. Sicilian."

Paolo's companion looked up briefly then rolled over onto his stomach, the next best thing to taking a walk, while Joe and Paolo pursued their courtship.

Joe said, "My name's Joe, Joe Lyons. Sure, sure, I'll teach you, but I warn you it's really the only yoga position I know."

"I've been going to the Sikhs, the Golden Temple at the corner of Newbury and Mass. Ave. They have a yoga session beginning every even hour from eight in the morning until eight at night. Have you heard about it? It's great." Paolo said.

"No, no, I haven't," Joe said. "Though I know where the Golden Temple is. I've been to the restaurant. I'd like to go do yoga sometime," Joe said.

"We can go tonight. What time is it? 3:30?" Paolo asked. "We probably can't make the four o'clock session. What about the six? Are you game?"

"Sure, I just have to stop at my house in the South End to check my messages. I'm looking for a job." Joe intentionally mentioned the South End, which at that time was just "getting queer." That geographical hint would give Paolo another clue to Joe's gayness, as if he needed one.

"Alright, let's leave now. I'll follow you to your house. This is my pal, Alex. He lives in the South End too. Alex has his own car. Alex, we're leaving, going to yoga. I'll talk to you later," and Paolo patted the face-down Alex on the shoulder. Alex didn't even look up. He just lifted his right hand and waved goodbye.

* * *

Joe arrived first. He had given Paolo his address and Paolo professed to know how to get there. Joe got out of his battered navy blue Volkswagen Beetle and waited on the stoop. Paolo pulled up in a little forest green MG convertible with the top down. He got out of the car and tugged on his white tank top, a "wifebeater," as the shirt was sometimes called. Joe gasped as he saw Paolo raise his muscled right arm through the shirt's opening after he had looped the left arm through the other side.

Joe wanted to say, *Why bother? I hope to have that and the rest of your clothes off as soon as we get inside,* but they were still playing the game that this was simply a quick stop for Joe to check his messages before yoga at the Sikhs' Golden Temple.

They went up the stairs of the brick row house to the parlor floor level, though Joe also lived in the street level and it would have been easier to go in the door under the stairs. But Joe thought that the parlor floor was grander and would make a better impression. Also there was a bed in the back parlor, a big brass bed that Joe had inherited from two old bachelor cousins. Joe fantasized that he used the bed like they would have wanted to. Joe was feeling very feisty. He hadn't been this energized in months, since Arthur

Bruce had left, in fact. Seduction excited him. Or maybe it was still the Valium withdrawal.

Once inside the back parlor, Joe wasn't too sure what to do next. Besides, the answering machine was downstairs and to complete the ruse about going home to check messages Joe would have to go down to check it. But Paolo didn't need the intrigue. As soon as he came in the door he was wide-eyed. He walked around the bed to the back bow window and said, "Wow, this place is great! You got a parking space too, and a little garden. Any tomatoes? Any basil? What's in front?" Paolo marched to the front of the house through the large opening that contained two etched glass-windowed pocket doors separating the front from the back parlor.

In the front parlor there was a couch and some side chairs, a big original mirror in a carved wooden frame over the fireplace, and a mural of naked gymnasts on the long right hand wall painted by an itinerant painter/dancer/actor to whom Joe had turned over the floor in a period of lust and extreme depression after Arthur Bruce left.

"This place is great! Look at those acrobats. I could do that," Paolo said as he peeled off the tank top, revealing again his perfectly pelted chest. He mimicked the pose of the bottom acrobat with arms upstretched to catch the top guy,

"Hey, let's try that. I'm strong. I bet I could hold you. I'll lie down on my back on the rug and you try to balance on my hands. If you think you're going to fall, lean sideways so you'll fall on the couch. Come on," Paolo said as he tugged at Joe's shirt.

"But those guys are naked," Joe said with a sly smile, nodding to the mural on the wall.

"O.K., I'll take off my pants. We've just been at the nude beach. There's nothing you haven't seen of me…and I saw what you got." Paolo took off his Levis and white briefs, smiling at Joe all the while.

Joe did not follow right away. Paolo grabbed at Joe's belt, trying to unclasp it. The belt had a monogrammed silver belt buckle that slipped over the belt and then clamped it down—very stylish for Ivy Leaguers from the Sixties, but not the easiest belt to remove. Joe had to help Paolo get him out of his khakis.

Instead of Joe going up into the air, they both went down onto the rug, Joe on top of Paolo at first.

* * *

After, Paolo said, "That was wild! What time is it? I promised my wife I'd be home by 6:30. I gotta cook the pasta. We'll do the yoga next time."

There was a next time, actually three or four of them, equally exciting as the first. After the second time at Joe's house Paolo took Joe in his MG convertible with the top down up to the Don Orione Home and the giant statue of the Blessed Mother who looks over East Boston, Winthrop, Chelsea and Revere. Paolo made Joe light a candle for their relationship. Paolo then brought Joe up to Saugus to meet his wife and two kids, a boy about nine and a girl five. The wife was a peach. She and Paolo had been high school sweethearts. Paolo cooked the pasta and she served Joe dinner. Joe couldn't figure out if she knew what else was going on with Paolo. He never asked Paolo, who just said, "She loves me a lot. I'm good to her. We're good to each other."

They also eventually did go to yoga at the Golden Temple, one time before sex. With his big, beautiful, slightly lascivious smile, Paolo said he wanted to loosen up first, to be able to get into new positions.

However, Paolo and his delights were too magnificent to be contained by Joe and his monogamous rubric. One day Paolo called Joe and said, "I got a problem. You know your friend Tom Murphy. Well, he keeps calling me. You're better sex, but he…he takes me places."

Joe, who at this time hardly had enough money to keep himself fed, never mind wine and dine Paolo, said, "Paolo, you're a beautiful man, but I can't let you come between me and my friends."

Tom Murphy had been Joe's friend since law school. He was an anchor for Joe those days; Tom listened to Joe's travails, was helping Joe find a job and had even lent Joe money.

That was not the right response for Paolo, who soon stopped seeing both Tom or Joe. He jumped into the gay fast lane in Boston.

Eight years later Paolo was one of the first to go when the epidemic hit.

Dolce far niente

It was two days after the 16th anniversary of Joe's being appointed a judge and it was a beautiful day—one of those days in Boston when winter suddenly turns into summer, bypassing spring altogether. Joe decided that he could not bear sitting in his office reading cases and lawyers' briefs on a day like this.

Joe called the Chief Court Officer to say he would not be in, mumbled something about springtime allergies (which wasn't entirely untrue) and went back to sleep for an hour. He did not do this easily. He had a work ethic which, at the least sent him to the office, even if he only read the advance sheets of appellate decisions nationwide and "conferenced" or gossiped with the other judges.

The rationalization today went something like this. *Two days ago was the 16th anniversary of my appointment as a judge. I have 77 unused sick days. The Legislature hasn't voted judges a raise in eight years, and God did not make this beautiful day without reason. It would be a sin to spend the day among those dusty old books and nitpicking colleagues. I'll be able to think much better on the Esplanade (or "the Espionade," as Georgie, an old friend and occasional bedmate, used to say). My decisions will be all the more pellucid for having cleared my head today in God's good air.*

Joe noticed how often he invoked God in this rationalization, which made him have less and less faith in it. However, he was not so without faith that he gave up the enterprise—rather the lack of enterprise, more correctly stated.

Joe lounged around his apartment in a big Japanese bathrobe, a *yukata*, patterned with fat carp with Escher-like scales in indigo and white. The robe made him feel international, part of a larger world than the one he lived in—small-town Boston. In the mornings Joe drank Darjeeling tea with whole milk and ate raisin toast with lots of butter. Today was no different, except that he put seedless raspberry jam, made by the Trappist monks at Saint Joseph's Abbey in Spencer, Massachusetts, on the toast as a special treat. He couldn't justify the butter, except to say that he was Irish and the Irish ate butter.

When will I get out of the house? Joe wondered. The good weather outside was his reason for skipping work. He'd better get it together before the weather changed. This was New England, after all, and the weather could change in the next half hour. Joe felt very alone right then. If somebody would only call, it would break the isolation. He couldn't think of anyone he wanted to hear from or anyone he would have liked to talk to. They would have been at work or would wonder why he wasn't. Aunt Josie would think he was sick and would take the train up to care for him.

The fling with Dino Randozza had been exhausting, unreal, almost as if in a dream. *It was too much excitement for a man my age,* Joe thought. He had these moments when, without any evidence but the calendar, he decided that he was an old man, a few steps from the grave. It was self pity, in one of its myriad forms, one of Joe's worst character defects. In reality Joe was pretty healthy. Although his father had recently died at age 87, Joe's mother was still alive and prospering as was the beloved Aunt Josie.

Without knowing it, Josie had been his companion during Joe's tempestuous fling with Dino Randozza. She had gone with Joe to Ireland where they met Dino Randozza's formidable mother, Giuseppina. Pina and Josie hit it off like schoolgirls. Pina took Josie to Venice and Rome and involved her, as if she were family, in the consecration by the Pope in Saint Peter's itself of Pina's son Rocco as Bishop. Pina opened new doors for Josie, who prior thereto had shuttled from her apartment in Providence to one or the other of her sisters' houses in Newport. Occasionally she visited Joe, her favorite nephew in Boston, but those visits were becoming fewer and further between.

Joe was glad that his romance with Dino Randozza was over. It had long been time for a sensible and appropriate romantic partner. Angelo Bruno, the schoolteacher from Stoneham, who he had met on Charles Street, seemed to fit the bill, Joe thought. Since they met they had seen each other every weekend and as many nights during the week as Angelo could negotiate with his sisters.

No formal declaration of the status of their relationship had come from either of them yet. Joe knew the dangers of trying to put a name on "it." He knew gay men who had been together for twenty years, who married when recently allowed to, but had side affairs all along and would continue to do so. He also knew people, who, if asked, would say they were "only dating," but were monogamous. Joe knew that the label on his relationship with Angelo Bruno did not matter, yet he was burning to call it something. In Massachusetts, where same-sex marriage so recently had been legalized by the Supreme Judicial Court, the pressure to attach the spousal label in one of its many forms (husband, wife, spouse) to a gay relationship was now great.

Angelo was six feet one, 195 pounds, dark, slim of hip and wide of shoulder. Except for his larger prick than the ancient Greek ideal, he could be the model for one of the Greek bronze warrior statues found in the Ionian Sea, the beardless one of the *Bronzi di Raice*, now housed in a museum in Calabria. For Joe Angelo had perfect body hair distribution, like eagle's wings across his chest, a thick expanding trail like a Christmas tree down to his navel, and then a "treasure trail" to his big uncut cock, which got hard as marble and stayed that way even after ejaculation.

For years Joe had been a "top" because it was expected of him. He was the older man, the successful one. When it became more difficult for him to rise to the occasion, Joe willingly gave it up to Angelo. Angelo enjoyed sex, and he was good, ever anxious to keep Joe pleased. Angelo liked Joe to come first and then lay back as Joe worked his charms on him.

Angelo had visited the night before, hitched up Joe's new laptop, and made love to him. Joe played the coach and Angelo the quarterback, complete with shoulder pads and jockstrap. After putting the jockstrap back on (to protect his privates from the spattering of the sautéed *broccoli rabe*?) Angelo cooked dinner. Angelo later lay his head in Joe's lap while they watched mindless television with the sound off until Angelo had to return home to get up to teach the fourth grade in Revere in the morning.

Angelo lived with his father, who was 89. Angelo was the youngest child and although he had three older sisters, they each were married with children of their own. Somebody needed to be with Papa. Angelo didn't mind—until he met Joe. Then he really would have preferred to live with Joe. This was a problem, but Angelo's sisters helped out. The nights Angelo went to be with Joe one or more of the sisters cooked for their father and sent one of their older kids over with food to eat and sit with Grampa until Angelo came home. The kids liked it because their grandfather let them smoke and didn't care what they watched on television or how loud they played it. He was more than a little deaf. There was a third bedroom where they could sleep if Angelo came back too late. They always knew that he would return sometime. Also they liked Angelo. The nieces thought him handsome, sexy and well dressed and the nephews thought he was "cool." They and their mothers thought that he had a girlfriend in the North End or maybe a number of girl-friends, and they didn't mind that they didn't know the particulars. The sisters also knew that if Angelo left their father's house, one of them would have to take up the slack or move their father in with them. So, they didn't pry.

That morning Joe continued to sit and pondered the contem-porary gay definition of "partnership," listing all the attributes he did not want in a man, while dreamily looking out the window. Joe then stood up, his *yukata* billowing like a spinnaker as he rose and walked to the window facing Beacon Street and the Boston Com-mon across the street in order to water the tumescent amaryllises on the sill. Joe was trying to give some purpose to this lovely day in May away from work. He hoped to do so without continuing to feel guilty. Busy young men and women passed below him, crossing Beacon Street on their way through the Boston Common to State Street and the Business District on the other side. They look so ea-ger, Joe thought, noting sadly that he had not been eager about work in a long time.

Because he was over 65 and had served the Commonwealth as a judge for more than 15 years, Joe was now eligible to retire at the maximum rate, 75% of his annual salary on the day of retirement. He thought about retiring a lot in recent years, but decided to put off the decision until the Legislature voted judges a pay raise—which raise would also increase his pension.

The Great and General Court, which is what the legislature is called in Massachusetts, had been dicking around with the latest proposed raise (which was *less* than the raise proposed three years before) for almost a year now. On this day it was in a conference committee as part of a supplemental budget, but no one knew when the committee would send it out for a vote. And even if they did pass the raise, there was the penny pinching, Republican millionaire Governor and his veto to worry about.

Joe was feeling taken advantage of, put upon, and sorry for himself. Self pity was not a good place for Joe. This frustration with the other branches of government morphed into a day off, albeit guilt-ridden, lonely and wistful so far.

"We'll have to do something about this," Joe said aloud to himself as he plopped into his chair and began reading *The Uncrowned Queen of Ireland*, a life of Kitty O'Shea, Charles Stewart Parnell's mistress and, some claimed, the reason Ireland had to wait almost 30 years more for its freedom. But Joe realized that it was too nice a day to sit home and read and revive old resentments at British colonialism.

Joe stood up dramatically, dropping the *yukata* from his shoulders onto the living room floor. He strode into the bathroom naked, stately, pink and plump, his body covered with grey and white hair. He looked in the mirror. Not too bad for 66, he thought. Then he showered. After the shower he shaved and put some Kiehls moisturizer on his face. The Kiehls was his concession to men's cosmetics. He consoled himself with the knowledge that some people, some men, most pertinently some handsome, younger men liked old, husky, hairy bears. It didn't matter that Joe didn't understand this, or that Joe didn't go for men who looked like himself. As Pierre Loti supposedly had said, "I am not my type."

Joe then put on a gray-blue suit, a light blue shirt and a small patterned pale and dark blue tie—a workday costume designed to put the taxpaying snoops and any "media" types he might bump into, or the ever vigilant snoop, the judge-hating Sam Nemesis, off the scent. If he was dressed for work, they might think he was indeed working. Joe hated having to use this subterfuge. It was undignified, among other things, but Boston is a very small town. There are noses everywhere, beginning with his neighbors, most of whom lived off trust funds they hadn't earned themselves. They would begrudge the hardest working of civil servants a day of leisure. And then there was Sam Nemesis.

Sam Nemesis was a non-practicing lawyer who made a lot of money developing shopping malls in wetlands, until he was stood up to by the environmentalists. They had appealed a local zoning board decision in Sam's favor to the Massachusetts Supreme Judicial Court, and won. Sam was also a born-again Catholic, *Opus Dei* probably. He had recently moved his family of seven daughters and two sons to Still River, Massachusetts, the headquarters of the more-Catholic-than-the-Pope, *Slaves of the Immaculate Heart of Mary*, otherwise known as "Feeneyites" named after their founder, Father Joseph Feeney, S.J., a former chaplain at Harvard who had gone reactionary and anti-Semitic in the 1950s and gotten himself and his followers excommunicated. They had recently been reconciled to Rome. Sam had liked them better when they weren't.

And there were always the news reporters with nothing better to do than catch public employees taking a day off. During one witch-hunt of judges, Joe was photographed leaving the Courthouse by a *Boston Globe* photographer without his knowledge. When the picture was published along with those of three of his colleagues on the first page of the City/Region section, grainy and distorted by the long-range lens, Joe realized just how vulnerable he was. One of his colleagues said, "You look like they caught you leaving the whorehouse," while Joe's wonderful Aunt Josie had said, "You certainly are better looking than those other men." Joe didn't want to be in the papers again, no matter how good he looked.

Joe walked down to the first floor of his building, stopped at the mailroom, opened his mailbox, quickly examined his mail and took the one non-commercial, Palmer method hand-addressed letter and put it in his pocket. He also took out a stamped, triple folded piece of paper, sealed with a green paper disc, a flyer, from Ganymede Farm. *They always sent interesting stuff*, Joe thought, as he opened it.

It was an invitation from Ganymede Farm, a gay commune in Apollonia, Massachusetts, about fifty miles west of Boston, in North Central Massachusetts for a 35th Anniversary Party on June 9th. After a recent class report from Harvard, in which Joe had listed Angelo as his partner, Joe received an email from one Neal Freedman, a college classmate Joe had never known. The email said, "I remember you from our college days, although we never met. If you and your partner, Angelo, ever get out this way, please call and visit. I am one of the founders of a gay commune begun in 1972. I read about your appointment as the first openly gay judge in Massachusetts when it occurred and meant to write you then. I don't want to let the opportunity slip by twice."

Joe and Neal maintained a correspondence and seemed to enjoy each other. They had not yet met. Joe thought the idea of going to the 35th Anniversary celebration in western Massachusetts might be interesting. Most of the other summer traffic would be heading the other way, East to Cape Cod, or North to Maine and Vermont. It might be a kick. Joe made a mental note to talk to Angelo about it.

Joe did not open the letter. Joe refolded the flyer and then folded it in half and put it in his other jacket pocket. Joe didn't want to be bothered by the world today. He would read the letter at his leisure once he found a refuge in the Public Garden.

Joe then puffed up his chest and marched through the lobby of his apartment building, past the doorman's booth. Joe nodded to the doorman, Larry, cheerily, went through the open right side of the double wrought iron over glass front door, took a right on Beacon Street and walked down the hill in the direction away from the Courthouse.

At Spruce Street he crossed Beacon and entered the Boston Common past the ugly *bas relief* to somebody's Puritan forebears, for one of whom, Governor John Winthrop no less, James Michael Curley, Boston's Irish rogue of a mayor, at the time of its erection in 1930, had lent his visage. Joe always smiled at the well turned butt of the Indian brave scantily draped in a clinging breechcloth on the furthermost left side of the relief. Somebody who worked on this statue had a "skip to his hip," Joe mused. Was it the blueblood Yankee architect with the three last names? Or the Italian sculptor? Or the unnamed Department of Public Works guy in charge? Or all three?

Joe walked jauntily down the paved path inside the Common that ran parallel to Beacon Street. He already felt better. If he had an umbrella, he would have twirled it. Joe crossed Charles Street at Beacon to enter the Public Garden, walking purposefully as if he had somewhere to go. It was his intention to cross most of the Public Garden, and just before the cherry trees, which arched over the main path and the oval-shaped rose garden, to veer a little to the right onto a lesser path, which led to the Ether Monument. The main path continued past a cherubic fountain to a gate, which was often closed but which had two smaller gates on either side that opened out onto Arlington Street at the beginning of Common-wealth Avenue, the *Champs Elysees* of Boston.

Joe had intended to sit on a bench behind the Ether Monument, read the Palmer method beautifully addressed letter for the first time and the Ganymede flyer once again, then watch the world go by and feel grateful for his life, healthy and prosperous at late middle age in Boston, beautiful in the spring. The Ether Monument was a Neogothic and Classical (at the same time) memorial to the accidental discovery of the anaesthetic properties of ether at the Massachusetts General Hospital after its use by some thrill seeking medical students later in the Nineteenth Century. The monument was being repaired and was not much visited these days. In the mornings old Chinese people came over from Chinatown on the other side of the Common and did even slower than usual *Tai Chi* alongside the statue. Otherwise the Ether Statue was not up there in the pantheon of public statuary in the Public Garden. Joe liked the site because from the bench behind the statue Joe could have a panoramic view of the north side of the Garden, yet be isolated and largely unseen. He also liked the figures on the top, a turbaned, bearded old gent offering solace to an unconscious young man draped in his arms.

However, before he could turn off to the path to his favorite bench, about 25 feet from the cherry tree arch, Joe was interrupted by a hearty hello from a woman coming from the other direction, from fashionable Newbury Street.

His caller was Mary Alice Finnigan Jones, a woman Joe never enjoyed seeing—not even when he wasn't skipping school. Mary Alice, who was so grateful to have married so that she could drop the too Irish "Finnigan," was the recent wife of Harry Jones, Esquire, an estate planning lawyer, also, although not many people knew it, one of Joe's romances from the Eighties. In fact Harry was Joe's first gerontophile, the first man Joe knew who pursued older men. Of course, in the Eighties Joe wasn't that old, but he did have white hair, was becoming portly, and wore a suit and tie every day. That was enough for Harry Jones, Esquire.

Mary Alice always assumed a superior attitude when she talked to Joe, perhaps because she was the one who ended up with Harry. Of course, Mary Alice could never specifically acknowledge that Joe and Harry had a romance because that would make Harry at least a wee bit gay, but she referred to the fact in certain oblique ways. Mary Alice would say, "When Harry lived with you…" or "When you and Harry lived on Revere Street…."

Joe didn't have the heart, or was too polite, to tell Mary Alice that she was welcome to Harry. Joe had never really been all that interested in Harry in the first place, but was only responding to Harry's blandishments because it had been a dry time in Joe's love life and he welcomed a man's attention, even if Harry was too pale in every sense of the word and not the man Joe really wanted. *What else would I be doing?* Joe asked himself when Harry first pursued him, *Feeling sorry for myself?* After a year Harry Jones dumped Joe because, as Harry put it, he "wanted to socialize more, to go dancing."

As Harry's offhand termination notice indicated, the romance was not deep, nor were the two of them into soulful communication. This was not a "sharing and caring" kind of romance. Harry and Joe had become a habit. Harry wanted a social life and Joe was a stick in the mud. Joe reasoned that if you wanted an older man, at least let him act older and eat at home. Joe had no desire to be a "disco queen" or a gourmand in the latest restaurants. So, bye bye, Harry! Good luck! Through some twisted circumstances, Mary Alice was the result—although Joe had never seen her dance. She too had some years on Harry. Maybe Harry treated the sexes equally in his gerontophilia.

Mary Alice Finnigan and Joe were about the same age and both were Irish-American Catholics from Newport. However, Mary Alice's family had been brought down by her parents' alcoholism. It got so bad that at age ten Mary Alice was taken in by two old schoolteacher aunts. Mary Alice worked through high school in a women's clothing store. She then went to the University of Rhode Island where she studied languages. From there she enlisted into the Army. She was sent to a base in England where she took some more language courses in a special program for GIs at Oxford in order to become a translator.

Mary Alice was never the same after Oxford. You would think that, like Rose and Joe Kennedy's daughters, she had been presented to the Queen. She did not re-enlist after Oxford but went to New York, became an ad executive, and lived in a small apartment on the Upper East Side. At a cocktail party in the Seventies she met a homely, aged, but very rich, Protestant pork heir from Kansas City with an ugly German name. She married him at the Marble Collegiate Church, Norman Vincent Peale's church, in Manhattan. Her now old schoolteacher aunts back in the Fifth Ward in Newport, still quite Catholic, anguished about going to the wedding and finally stayed home. Mary Alice produced a son, who became the apple of her husband's eye. Because her husband's name was so ugly to her Mary Alice kept her own name during this marriage. Women were beginning to do that in those days. The husband died when their son was eleven.

Financially Mary Alice and the son were all set after her husband died. Mary Alice moved to Boston, to Mount Vernon Street on Beacon Hill to be specific. Mary Alice met Harry Jones at the Church of the Advent, the most high Episcopal, if not Anglican, church in Boston, more Catholic than the Roman churches. Somewhere along the way Mary Alice had become just "Alice." Perversely, Joe always called her "Mary Alice," perhaps to remind her where she came from and that he knew her when. She never objected.

Harry and Mary Alice married in a discreet ceremony in the Lady Chapel at the Church of the Advent—which was kind of a concession to Rome, Joe thought, since most Protestants did not give the Blessed Mother any attention at all. Joe was invited, but did not attend. He would have seen Harry dance, albeit with Alice, at the reception at the Ritz Carlton on the edge of the Public Garden, if he had accepted the invitation.

It was about this time that Joe started calling her, but not to her face, of course, "Mary Alice, the Apostate." He soon regretted doing so because the name was picked up by other Irish-Catholics, and Joe was not mean, as a rule. But as any reader of Joyce knows, the Irish love a nickname, particularly one that cuts, especially for somebody who gets too uppity. Samuel Johnson said, "The Irish are a fair race; they never speak well of one another." The name stuck even after Joe abandoned it as being too mean spirited.

Anyway, here was Mary Alice Finnigan Jones, ambling down the Public Garden path, walking a corgi and dressed in a Barbour jacket, like Elizabeth II, or at least Helen Mirren, with the Barbour pin still on up by the collar in case you thought the jacket was a knockoff. It wasn't raining and they weren't in a misty heath, but there was the Barbour jacket. At least Mary Alice wasn't wearing her usual faded pink baseball hat with the image of Nantucket outlined on it, Joe thought. That would be too much in the early springtime soft sun. And even she knew that it was too early for her to be carrying her Nantucket basket handbag with the little carved ivory scrimshaw whale on top.

"Having a day off the bench are we?" said Mary Alice. Joe was going to ask her what governor made her a judge, but resisted. Fortunately, Mary Alice didn't wait for a reply before adding, "I just left Harry at the Back Bay Grille. He has a business breakfast. I thought we were going to have some rain. Poor Windsor thought so too. Didn't you darling?" she added leaning down to snuggle the drooling, smelly old dog.

Windsor? Joe thought. *What's your connection to Windsor, Mary Alice Finnigan?* "Nice to see you," Joe said instead, doing a feint around Mary Alice's right side. "I have to run." However, Joe could no longer pull off to his bench behind the Ether Statue. It would be too visible. He'd have to take a little walk, perhaps through the Public Garden Gate, up the Commonwealth Avenue Mall and then circle back on Marlborough Street when Mary Alice was out of sight. Joe did glance back as he approached the Public Garden Gate at Arlington Street. Mary Alice was chatting it up on a bench with some tweeded old dame who was patting Windsor. Joe's walk would have to be longer if Mary Alice didn't leave the Public Garden soon.

Mary Alice was very good with Beacon Hill old ladies. A lot of these venerables came out to walk in the Public Garden once winter passed; others slogged through it all year long. They could let down their tightly coiffed hair with Mary Alice. It was like confiding in the maid; they knew she wasn't one of them, although she had studied them very well and knew what made them tick.

After Joe went through the opening to the left of the Public Garden gate, he looked to his right to check the traffic so that he could cross Arlington Street to the *allee* of elms and locusts on the Commonwealth Avenue Mall.

Joe was gently bumped from the left.

A beautiful young dark man dressed in a well-made grey pin striped suit and a gorgeous violet (to welcome the Spring?) necktie, walking with an equally good looking long haired, blonde young woman dressed more casually in a peasant skirt from the Sixties,

Joe's era, stopped and said. "Oh, please excuse me, sir. I wasn't looking where I was going. Are you alright?" He solicitously held Joe's forearm as he spoke as if to prevent a fall. The blonde woman stood back a bit bemused, perhaps because she too, like Joe, had noticed that the bump had been very slight and did not warrant the continuing presence of the hand on Joe's arm.

Joe enjoyed the touch so he replied slowly after a pause, "I'm fine. You hardly hit me. I'm a tough old bird. Are you lost?"

"As a matter of fact we are. I'm taking my friend, Eleanore Emmet, to her brother's office on Dartmouth Street, but I must confess I rarely get to this side of the river and I don't know where it is. I haven't told her that yet." His accent was British, but not fruity and English. He turned to the blonde and smiled. She smiled back.

"I can show you," Joe said. "You're in the only logical part of Boston. It's ironic that you should get lost here. The streets in much of the city, at least downtown, were cowpaths and they wander aimlessly. From here the streets go up on a grid alphabetically. Arlington, Berkeley, Clarendon, Dartmouth, all the way up the alphabet to Hereford," Joe waved broadly from side to side at Arlington Street in front of them. "We can cross here and I'll walk you up to Dartmouth Street. I have an appointment in that area myself," Joe lied. "The Mall is very beautiful this time of year. You'll notice the magnolias in bloom all the way up."

The three of them crossed Arlington Street and entered the Commonwealth Avenue Mall. The young dark man stopped and held out his hand to Joe. "I am Hasan…" Joe could not hear the last name, "and this is my friend Eleanore Emmet. We're both Harvard graduate students. I study at the Kennedy School of Government and Eleanore is at the Graduate School of Arts and Sciences, studying late 19th and 20th century Irish Literature."

Joe responded, "I'm Joe Lyons. I'm a…a lawyer in Boston. It's very nice to meet you both." Joe never revealed his occupation to strangers, and he was in fact a lawyer, so that was not a lie. All Massachusetts judges are lawyers, although a law degree is not legally required for most of them.

"What Irish writers are you interested in, Eleanore?" Joe, who loved all things Irish, asked, having acquired some knowledge of Irish Literature himself, first as a Harvard undergraduate in Professor William Kelleher's famous course and later as his life went on.

"I'm writing my thesis on Edith Somerville and Martin Ross," she said.

"They were a pair of ladies, and fun too. What a great subject!" Joe said. "I take great solace in the *Memoirs of an Irish Resident Magistrate." Could this beautiful girl be a lesbian, like Mss Somerville and Ross*, Joe wondered.

Eleanore said, "You're the first person I've ever heard say that."

"Oh, things haven't changed much from late 19th century rural Ireland to 21st-century Boston, particularly in the court system in Boston. As a matter of fact, the people working in Boston's courts are probably descendants of Somerville and Ross' characters. I can see more than one Mrs. Cadogan among them."

"That's fascinating," Eleanore said. "We'll have to talk more."

" Eleanore, are you related to Robert Emmet?"

"As a matter of fact, I'm descended from Thomas Addis Emmet. You know that he came to New York where he practiced law before his brother was executed," Eleanore said.

"I do remember reading that. What a great heritage you have," Joe said.

In front of them was the first of the Mall's statues, the Alexander Hamilton monument, with the three faces of Washington, Jefferson and Hamilton on the front in *bas relief*.

"If you've not been here before, would you like me to play tour guide?" Joe said with a little smile.

"Oh, please do," said Eleanore.

"Yes, that would be very kind. We're early for Eleanore's appointment," added Hasan.

As he walked just a few steps up the Mall, at the statue of Alexander Hamilton, Joe realized how fond he was of Boston. He had never thought of himself as sufficient an insider to be explaining any of it to anyone. Today he thought, *Perhaps these people need my quirky point of view about Boston—a little Irish resentment tempering the affection. Eleanore Emmet would understand this tone.* Maybe Eleanore's revelation of her Irish interests inspired his offering of himself as a guide. His resentment wasn't much different than Irish attitudes towards England, attitudes that Joe's ancestors had come to America with. They transferred the same attitudes to the Yankee Protestants, who, like their English cousins, made life hard for the Irish in Boston and New England.

Joe began, "The inscription says 'Thomas Lee, a citizen of Boston,' like men used to be 'citizens' of Athens or Rome, 'gave this statue to the city.' He was a noble man in the best sense of the word and his descendants have been likewise. One of them, with the same name I believe, served for many years on the Boston School Committee during its most troubled time of racial integration of the schools. Apart from George Washington, I am not certain who all the men in the *bas relief* in front are. Perhaps the second is Jefferson, but who is the gent with the hooked nose?

"Of course," he pointed out, "Nobody notes that these granite monuments were quarried in Quincy and Vermont by Irish immigrants and carved by Italian stonecutters. There are no markers on the monuments indicating the people who worked on them. You would think they sprung fully chiselled from the head of...Priscilla Alden. With a couple of exceptions, this mall is a testament to the Yankee Protestant Ascendancy of this city—a people whose time has long since passed, I suggest. Where on this Mall will they put statues to the recent immigrants—the Latinos, the Chinese, the

Southeast Asians, the Russians—never mind the Italians, the Irish, the Jews or the Lithuanians and the Poles, who arrived over the past 160 years?"

As they walked onto the next block, Berkeley to Clarendon Streets, Joe was on a roll, a roll he did not even know he had in him. "Some of the purists, the real and the would-be descendants of those Puritan Bostonians, were in an uproar recently when a group of merchants from Newbury Street, one street over, and some of the more recently fashionable people of Boston, the *parvenu*, but more traveled, urbane and cosmopolitan people, thought it would be 'fun' and 'pretty' to put lights on all these trees, the trees in this *allee*, at Christmastime. The Puritans, you might recall, didn't celebrate anything, leastwise Christmas. Anyway, their successors, both real and 'wannabe,' protested, but the…new, 'happier,' Joe searched for the inadequate word, "people won out. Commonwealth Avenue is modeled after the *Champs Elysees* after all. There is no need for Yankee restraint here."

Eleanore smiled at Joe's rant and Hasan tried to follow it all very seriously, with furrowed brows.

"But Mr. Lyons, I had no idea there were such disputes among the classes and ethnicities here in the United States. I was born in Egypt, in Alexandria, another city of many ethnicities, and I thought we had a complicated social structure."

"Perhaps it's only in Boston, my friend. The rest of the States are a little more homogenous than we are." Joe said, not too welcoming of the interruption. He quickly continued his tour guide rap, "This hearty lad is John Glover of Marblehead, a Revolutionary War hero. I'm not sure why he's here, on the Commonwealth Avenue Mall in Boston, but he does add a certain dash, doesn't he? Particularly, with his foot on the cannon. It looks like he's ready for something— if not everything."

At the next block Joe noted the bench on the right hand side of the walk in memory of David Brudnoy. "The man to whom this bench is dedicated could only have achieved affection in Boston. He was a conservative, a libertarian radio commentator, who was also gay and who died of AIDS. Even people who didn't like his politics, or his sexual orientation, admired his civility and humor. Thus, this bench.

"In front of us is a bust of Patrick Andrew Collins, 'born in Ireland, always her lover.' Isn't that a beautiful thing to say? If you look at the sides, you'll see a larger than life sculpture of a full-figured, busty, sleeveless woman in sandals holding a harp with Irish interlacing on it and a branch of some leaves, which I do not recognize. They are too big to be shamrocks and don't seem to be serrated enough to be oak leaves. It's an interesting notion of Ireland—not your usual shawlie, *Kathleen ni Houlihan* or Dark Rosaleen, *Roisin dubh*. I wonder who dreamt her up. The American girl on the left hand side is much more classical, more respectable looking even."

"I thought you said the Irish weren't represented on this mall," Hasan said.

"I said the Irish and Italian laborers who quarried and cut the stone for these statues, who prepared the stone for the sculptors weren't represented here," Joe said tetchily. "This statue is a nod to the Irish, a token. It's interesting that it was erected just as the Irish were getting political power here. There is another Irish monument in the city to John Boyle O'Reilly, a Fenian, a writer and a poet. It's by Daniel Chester French and is up in the Fenway. Again there is a representation of Ireland as a woman, but she's not the hardy, barefoot lass we see here. Unfortunately, because of its location unless you're walking in the Fens, you can see only the front of the statue when you're stopped in traffic."

Joe thought for a bit, thought better of his testiness, realized that he wasn't in a courtroom and that these people were not lawyers appearing in front of him. He then said, "Perhaps I was hasty in my judgment about the lack of Irish representation on this mall. The next statue is also a monument to some men who were Irish-American—nine firemen who were killed in a fire at the Hotel Vendome, now a condominium building, diagonally opposite on the left hand side of Commonwealth Avenue. Many of their names are Irish. It was a terrible fire in June of 1972. I remember standing just about here and watching the embers." Joe paused for a while in remembrance.

He began again and said, "Well, here we are at Dartmouth Street. What number are you looking for?"

"Number 46," said Eleanore. "It's a former townhouse."

"That would be to the right, away from Newbury Street towards the river and on the right hand side. I'll walk you over."

Joe had hoped to learn more about Eleanore's family. It wasn't every day that one met a descendant of Robert Emmet. "*When my country takes her place among the nations of the earth, then, and only then, let my epitaph be written,*" he had said in court before he was hung. Emmet's speech from the dock was an old standby of Irish-Catholic schoolchildren declamation contests in this country. It had stirred Joe at twelve when his Aunt Josie first recited it to him and still moved him.

Joe was also interested in Eleanore's studies. In his day, Harvard would not have allowed a student to take seriously Edith OE Somerville and Violet Martin aka Martin Ross, two late 19th, / early 20th-century women of the then crumbling Irish Protestant Ascendancy. About a hundred years earlier, in 1803, their English overlords had executed Robert Emmet—hung, drawn and quartered him as a matter of fact. Somerville and Ross, who were in fact cousins, as well as coauthors, chronicled with great insight and humor Irish country life around them. Today Irish gay activists have decided they were lesbians. Joe wanted to learn more. However, Hasan had edged up next to Joe, and Eleanore, who appeared to be a shy one, lagged behind.

They arrived at 46 Dartmouth Street. Eleanore thanked Joe politely. She added, "Hasan can tell you how to get in touch with me. I would like to hear more about your court system's similarities to the English resident magistrate system in Ireland. You could be a big help to me." She shook Joe's hand and then kissed Hasan, sisterly, on the cheek. Joe thought that Hasan was going in the building with Eleanore but he stayed on the street, next to Joe, smiling.

"And where are you going?" Joe said.

"Well, back to Cambridge eventually, but I thought I'd just wander around Boston before returning. As you can tell, I very rarely get over here and it's such a beautiful day."

Joe thought fast, then said, "I'm going to have a little breakfast. Would you like to join me before you begin your tour?"

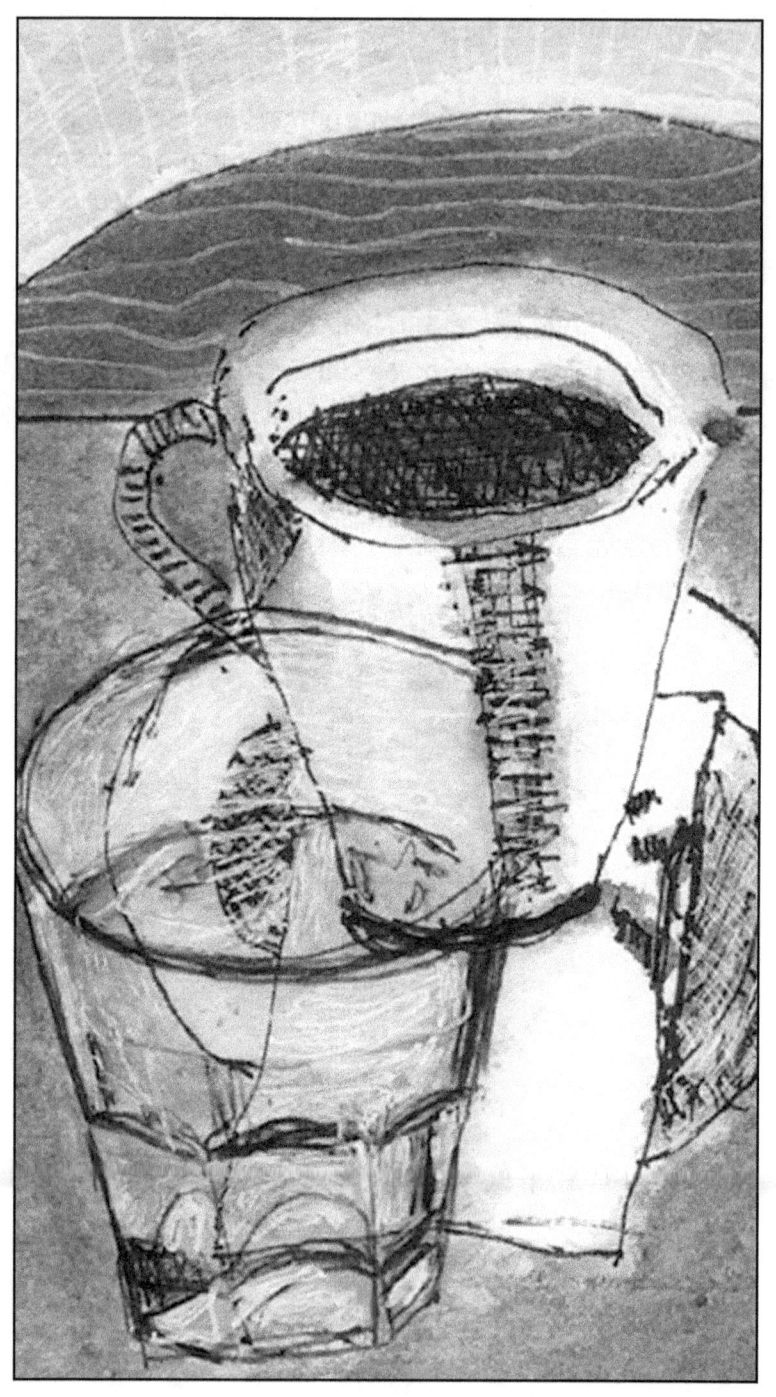

A Very Busy Brunch

As fate would have it, Guido's Back Bay Grille was just down Newbury Street, between Dartmouth and Clarendon Streets. Guido and Joe had been flirting for years, although they had never done anything about it. Joe liked the idea of appearing at Guido's with an unknown handsome, well-dressed, exotic young man. It might make Guido jealous to see Joe in such good-looking company.

As fate would further have it, Guido was at the front door. He greeted Joe with a kiss, not just a European buss to the cheek, but a little more effusive a salutation than Joe wanted to receive in front of the stranger, Hasan. However, Joe accepted it graciously and even returned a peck to Guido's well shaved and moisturized cheek.

"How are you, Joe? What brings you here on a weekday?" Guido asked.

Another taxpayer, Joe thought. *I liked him better when he was a busboy.* "I'm taking a day off, Guido. Now don't call the *Herald,* like you do when movie stars come here to eat." Joe then remembered that he didn't know Hasan's last name and, although he disliked the modern practice of introducing by first names only, Joe had no choice. "Guido, this is my friend, Hasan. Hasan, meet my old friend Guido, who owns this wonderful restaurant."

They shook each other's hands and smiled. Hasan said, "It's indeed a beautiful room," as he looked around the walnut-paneled, comfortably upholstered restaurant.

"Thank you," said Guido. His "thank you" was chilly. Maybe he was a little jealous. Not looking at Hasan Guido added, "Would you like a drink, Joe?"

"Oh no, it's much too early for me and someone might see me. It's sinful enough being here on a workday. How about you, Hasan?"

"As a matter of fact, I'd like a Mimosa," Hasan said, nodding in Guido's direction without looking at him, as if Guido were a pesky butler. Hasan knew how to respond to unwarranted rudeness.

Joe was surprised by Hasan's request. *Isn't "Hasan" a Muslim name? They don't drink, right? And it is pretty early in the day. Mimosa is a girly drink, isn't it? Well, what can I do—rescind my offer?*

They sat down at a table two rows back from the window so as not to be seen. Guido provided large, well-upholstered armchairs for his guests, many of whom were also well upholstered. Joe looked around to see who was there. Guido's Back Bay Grille was the place where powerbrokers, politicians, government relations types, public relaters and other "players" met to work out "arrangements" away from the brightly lighted State House, downtown offices and commercial salons.

Politics made strange bedfellows—and *vice versa*. Joe saw some evidence of that as he took in the room. Starting from the front, near the window, was "Wolfy," a retired judge of the Family Court, even though he himself had never married, now well into his eighties, with the District Attorney and one of his more handsome male assistants, who had just won a difficult double murder case, and Harry Jones, Esquire. Joe had been forewarned by Mary Alice that

Harry would be at Guido's, but not in this company.

Although Joe knew all four of them and some of them, like Harry and the D.A., he knew very well, their greeting was not very cheery. They each looked up at him a little shocked, and said, "Hello Judge." That was it; the greeting was as terse as that.

Usually one or more of these guys is all over me like sauce. What's this about? Perhaps their chill is because I'm here during the work-day but it seems more serious than that, Joe thought. However, his first concern was to be seen with and entertain Hasan. Joe did not spend much time worrying about the chilly greeting but he did mull it over.

And what is Harry doing with this crew, Joe wondered? *Harry is a lawyer but he mainly does estate plans and inheritance work. He has no interest in, or knowledge of, Criminal Law. Why is Wolfy here? Well, he is a wheeler dealer, probably trying to work something out with the District Attorney. Is Harry chasing Wolfy now, or vice versa? Or is Harry after the District Attorney, a good-looking older Irishman, albeit the happily married father of six daughters, who still wear white First Communion dresses at election time? Harry wouldn't be after the handsome assistant D.A. He's more Joe's type. Harry likes the oldtimers. Wolfy would also like the humpy assistant D.A., who, according to another assistant D.A., has the biggest schlong Boston.*

That's another mystery we'll have to work on. More will be revealed, Joe said to himself but he wanted to figure everything out right then and there.

Wolfy lived in the Back Bay with his sister and his doll collection. He frequently went to New York. "To go to the theater" is what he told people. The theater was usually The Gaiety on 46th near Broadway, but Wolfy didn't say that. Joe knew because he himself had been there on a few occasions, in the days before he'd been appointed a judge, and he'd seen Wolfy. Wolfy had seen Joe as well. They never talked about it. The Gaiety had a side room for lap dances and $300 dollars bought a private dance at your hotel. Wolfy thought nobody knew of his inclinations, but, of course, everybody knew.

At Joe's swearing in, when Joe, in his last speech as a civilian and first speech as a judge mentioned the historical significance of the first appointment to the Massachusetts judiciary of somebody openly gay, Wolfy, who was sitting towards the back, said quite loudly, within the hearing of three rows of Joe's friends, "Why do you have to tell them that?"

At the next table in the restaurant was Joe's old pal and advisor, Tom Murphy, Esquire, laughing it up with a beautiful dark-haired woman who was the lobbyist for various gay causes. Tom gave Joe a quick nod and a wink. The gay lobbyist, Marlene Weinerman, who knew Joe from the old days of Joe's gay activism, when the political strength of the gay community had yet to be recognized by most politicians, quickly smiled at Joe. She knew the boundaries imposed on Joe by his job and would do nothing to compromise him. For her, Joe was one of the victories in the struggle for gay

equality and Marlene, a real pro, was not going to jeopardize his position by being too effusive in her greeting. You never knew who was watching.

Also by the window were four middle-aged women, two of them painters, the third an art dealer and the fourth, Madge Mellon, a stockbroker whose clients were some of the most powerful women in the city. She was also one of the famous wits of Boston. Madge gave Joe a little fluttery wave with her free hand between bites of Eggs Benedict—and gossip.

Way in the back of the room, away from the windows, was the newly elected Speaker of the House with two men in dark suits, whose backs were to Joe, and a good looking, young black woman, also in a dark suit, who was taking notes. In this place, if you were in politics and you were working out a compromise, your importance sometimes was measured by how *far away* from the windows you were seated.

Oh, to be a fly flitting around these tables! Of course, Guido would never tolerate flies in his Back Bay Grille. What plots are being hatched here? Maybe at a certain time, like 11:15 A.M., everybody will switch tables and get the deals done.

There did not appear to be any reporters in the room. Guido would have told him if there were, even though Joe, being on the "Anonymous Court," the Appeals Court, would probably not have been recognized anyway. If the press came in the restaurant, Guido put them out of earshot, on the far right away from the action, near the kitchen. He waited on them very slowly and forbade the use of cellphones, as well as cameras in the restaurant. As a result, reporters rarely visited Guido's Back Bay Grille. Some photographers did stand outside sometimes, however.

Should I tell Hasan what's going on here, and who all these people are, Joe wondered? No, I don't know enough about him, and that silly, girly morning drink worries me. I'll wait and see what he's all about.

"How did you come to go to the Kennedy School, Hasan?"

"I was raised in Dublin."

That's the accent, Joe realized—*that beautiful clear Dublin diction.*

"My mother teaches Archaeology at Trinity College and I studied Government there. I thought of entering Government service but I'm too westernized for Egypt these days. The era of the American or European educated civil servant is over in the Arab world, I'm afraid. So, I thought I ought to capitalize on my exoticism and come to Harvard. The States may find a use for a 'Wog' like me. Besides, I was feeling very restricted in Dublin. It's a small town to begin with and this tawny face makes me even more recognizable."

"What's a 'Wog'?" Joe asked.

"'Westernized Oriental Gentleman'. It's a British term, from the days of the Raj, I suspect," Hasan said.

"Oh yes, I think I remember reading it in Somerset Maugham."

"Probably, it's something one of his characters would say."

"And how do you know Eleanore Emmet?" Joe asked.

"She studied at Trinity as well. She's a dear. Her family is from New York, a very distinguished family there, and in Ireland, as you discerned," Hasan added, taking another sip of the Mimosa. "We're best friends. She just started at the GSAS, the Harvard Graduate School of Arts and Sciences, I mean."

"I knew what you meant," Joe said with a little smile.

"Did you study at Harvard?" Hasan asked.

"I did. I was an undergraduate back in the olden days, in Adams House, the theatrical house in those days." Joe knew that "theatrical" could be a euphemism for gay and was testing Hasan to see if he knew that as well. Joe remembered that the first time he went to Dublin in 1969 the Irish referred to the gay bar, Bartley Dunnes, as a "theatrical" pub.

Of course, things were different now. People could say the word "gay." Some even shouted it, but this little dance, this "Is he or isn't he?" an exercise much more common in Joe's salad days thirty years before, was still being played. Men didn't just come right out and say they were gay then. One looked for signs, "dropped beads," in the gay vernacular. Joe noted that Eleanore was a "dear friend," not a girlfriend or a fiancee. He also noted the violet tie, the beautiful blue English shirt, the well-made bespoke suit and very good shoes, Peels perhaps.

This was a game and Joe knew it. At bottom, Joe wasn't really that interested. Hasan was a little too…too refined for Joe. But Joe would keep playing, at least through breakfast. Besides Angelo kept Joe happy and even though he enjoyed doing it, Joe had no need to flirt. It was not likely that Joe would do anything if the flirting was reciprocated.

"Oh yes, I've heard of Adams House," Hasan said. "They have an indoor pool."

"Yes, there used to be nude male swimming in that pool. I don't know what happens now that the houses are co-ed."

"Co-ed?" said Hasan.

"Yes, co-educational, men and women living together. Is it only an American term? How do you know about the Adams House pool? Have you swum there?" Joe was diving in for the pearl now.

"A friend of mine told me about it. He's a music tutor in Adams House."

"Oh," was all Joe could say. A music tutor in Adams House was a giveaway, a shiny bead indeed, at least it used to be. There weren't many straight music tutors in Joe's day.

"What will you have to eat?" Joe asked. "The Eggs Benedict are very good here." And in case Hasan did not know, they are also the gay national breakfast dish, Joe did not say.

"That's what I'll have, then, the Eggs Benedict," Hasan said smiling, adding another point to the "yes" side of the gay ledger that Joe was running in his head.

"Do you like the Kennedy School?"

"It's very interesting—much more earnest than Trinity. I'm not certain that I want to be a civil servant in this country. My classmates get all excited about the strangest things—like flowcharts and caseloads. They're very big on Economics at the Kennedy School. 'Efforts flow to the quantifiable,' said James Q. Wilson in the one course that really requires me to think. It's called *Bureaucracy*, which is a very daring title for a course. It almost invites rejection. Perhaps the Foreign Service would suit me better—if I could find a country to represent." Hasan laughed. "Maybe I'll go 'private,' as they say here. I do have a unique set of skills and knowledge. How many Irish-Egyptians educated in America does one meet? I feel that I would be more valuable with a little more knowledge—perhaps International Law, but I don't want to spend another three years in law school."

"Yes, school can go on forever. Maybe you just ought to test the waters after the Kennedy School."

"I've sent out C.V.s already, but no returns thus far."

Perhaps Hasan has a visa problem. So long as he stays in school he can stay in the country, Joe thought. "I may be able to help," he said. "Give me your phone number or email address, if you want." Joe pulled out the well-addressed envelope he had retrieved from his mailbox earlier that morning to write on.

Just then there was a little hubbub at the door. A party of three women came laughing through the entrance. One of them was Maureen Ronayne Randozza of all people, who Joe hadn't seen since the previous year in Ireland, where she had been studying at University College in Cork. She was the niece of Joe's tempestuous, penultimate paramour, the source of his recent (and future) discontent, Dino Randozza. *Why is she here?* was Joe's first thought. *What table will she be sitting at?* was the second.

Maureen Randozza was no longer all dressed in black, the color she wore so often that her grandmother, Giuseppina, now the Countess of Trapani, often told her, "Youth is wasted on the young." Instead today she wore a lilac, full-skirted, cotton dress, very girly and frilly. It set off her long, thick red hair nicely, and it was timely. Lilacs were still blooming in the Public Garden, and at the Arnold Arboretum Lilac Sunday had recently passed. *Congratulations to Maureen*, Joe said to himself. *She's finally grown up.* One of her companions was similarly dressed in a darker shade of purple, but the third, who was built like a fire plug, had on a man's gray suit, with a white shirt, a red and blue striped tie, and clunky tan tie shoes. This manly ensemble was accessorized by a little gray fedora, *a la* Pinky Lee of days gone by.

Either exercising a lady's prerogative of keeping a hat on inside, or ignorant of the gentleman's requirement that it be taken off, the fireplug pulled her hat down tighter as she came through the door and, with a courtly wave of the arm, let the two "girls" precede her to the table where Tom Murphy was chatting up Marlene Weinerman, gay marriage advocate.

En route, Maureen looked over, saw Joe and waved. Joe waved back. She made no attempt to talk to Joe. *Perhaps I'm not supposed to see the company she keeps*, thought Joe.

"Who's that? I think that I've seen her before." Hasan said transfixed.

Joe hesitated, then said, "The Redhead? Well, she studied in Ireland last year, at Cork. She's the niece of a…a friend of mine. She's related to a number of people both here in Boston and in Ireland. Her mother was from Dundalk. I'm not sure what she studied in Ireland or what she's doing here, I mean back in the States. Is any of that a jog to your memory?"

"Not yet, but I'm sure I've seen her before, Of course, there's no shortage of beautiful red-haired women in Ireland, as you know. I'd like to meet her again. She's very beautiful."

Those unwelcome comments added points to the other, the straight, side of the ledger running in Joe's brain about Hasan's sexuality, but the gay company Maureen was keeping today, albeit a shock to Joe, made the romantic success of an introduction difficult. It was ironic to Joe that as Hasan was leaning to straight, Maureen seemed to be tipping the velvet.

"I'll see what I can do. They appear to be all business at that table this morning."

"I'll remember her soon, I'm sure. I'll remember before we leave here. I'm usually very good at this. That's one reason I'm interested in politics," Hasan said. "I can always put a name to a face and usually I can tell just where we met."

Joe was relieved that Hasan might be straight. Joe wouldn't have to rise to this occasion of sin. He wouldn't have to complicate his life and his romance with Angelo Bruno. Flirting was fun, but as his friend Donald used to say, "The Game is usually more fun than the Get."

There was a time in Joe's life, in those halcyon gay days before AIDS, when every possible romantic challenge had to be won. Old age, good sense, or both made winning less necessary, or desirable, these days. Not that Joe was going to rest on his laurels or live in his memories. Joe agreed with another friend who often said, "Sex and possibility, sex and possibility. That's what keeps the heart pounding."

Angelo Bruno was providing possibility, reality and sex these days, and had done so as recently as last night with the touchdown *tableau vivant*, but this little diversion, this feeling-out flirtation with Hasan, was fun for Joe—fun and nostalgic.

Meanwhile things were very busy at the other tables. Tom Murphy, Esquire, was huddled with the four women, three femmes and a butch. Every once in a while Tom would lift his head and look back at the Speaker's table, trying to figure out who the men in the dark suits were whose backs were to him. He didn't have to wait long because soon the two of them stood up and walked towards Joe in order to leave the restaurant.

One was Billy Meadows, the very handsome and urbane member of the Great and General Court. Billy was a usually liberal Democrat representing a rural and outer rim suburban area up near the New Hampshire border. The other man was Monsignor Patrick Owens, the Chancellor of the Archdiocese.

Contrary to everybody's expectations, Billy Meadows had recently voted to send the proposed Anti-Same-Sex Marriage Constitutional Amendment to the electorate for a popular vote. And the Archdiocese of Boston, with Monsignor Owens as its spokesman, was the chief proponent of that effort.

Not a very good combo for our side, Joe thought, as they walked by his table. Billy Meadows, who was also a lawyer, said, "Good morning, Judge."

Joe replied, "Hello, Representative."

After the men passed, presumably to the door, Joe and Tom looked at each other across the room with concern. Not so with the four women at Tom Murphy's table. They bounced up from their table and rushed the Speaker's table. Maureen winked at Joe as she passed him. Tom Murphy, Esquire, followed behind, stopped, looked at Joe and held up both his hands as if to say, *What can I do or say? These women are very determined.*

Joe heard the Speaker greet Maureen by name and also heard Maureen introduce her companions to the Speaker. "This is Trixie Pellegrino of Plymouth Street. Her father is Vito and her mother was Angelina Russo. Her uncle is Vinny Saraceno. You probably know her aunts, Pixie, Dixie and Mixie as well. And this," Maureen directed her attention to the woman in the gray suit by putting her hand on her shoulder, "This is *my* good friend, JoJo Danieli of Parmenter Street. Her mother was a Gritti from the old West End. JoJo's mother lives at the Nazzarini Senior Center. She's one of Josie's girls. You know, she gets out the vote."

Joe thought, *this girl's got it. She knows what to say to a politician. She just ran her connections to about 250 constituents by the Speaker in eight sentences and 35 seconds. In a small district, like that of a state representative, those 250 votes can mean the election. Putting JoJo's mother at the Nazzarini Senior Center, the 150 residents of which, mostly women, voted in a bloc early in the morning on Election Day, was the best.* Comforted by Maureen's political acumen, Joe leaned back towards Hasan.

There are a couple of unwritten rules about brunch at Guido's Back Bay Grille. One is, "Don't eavesdrop, but what you do hear, keep to yourself." A second is, "Never ask anyone why he or she is there." And a third is, "You can come to conclusions based on who you see with whom, but don't take it to the bank." Rules one and three were in operation today.

Guido himself never approached a table during a conversation. His clientele depended on discretion and he didn't want to be known as the source of leaks. The waiters were all Argentine.

They also were very handsome. Presumably they did not know the characters in the play that was acted every weekday morning at Guido's, although one time the *Boston Herald* had sent in a ringer waiter for a day or two. Fortunately it was during the summer and all he was able to report was that the president of a very large Boston bank was having a Bloody Mary breakfast with a branch teller of the same sex and that they were very "coochie coo." Guido figured out who the rat was and fired him the next day. Guido knew that if there were leaks, he would soon have no customers.

Hasan's Extracurricular Course

"What's going on back there?" Hasan asked as the laughter became more raucous from the tables behind.

Joe thought about explaining the intricacies of the situation as he perceived it, but he still wasn't sure if he could trust Hasan with his knowledge and wisdom. So he stalled by saying only, "The man in the back is from the North End of Boston, an Italian neighborhood. So are three of the women who just sat with him. I suspect that they are laughing over old times."

"And the other woman, and the man who nodded and winked at you, who are they?" Hasan asked, indicating that little had escaped his attention.

Joe paused and then said perfunctorily, "They are not from the North End," paused again and then added as a detour, "How long have you lived here?"

"Since September. Why?"

"Do you keep up with local news?"

"I read the *New York Times*."

"Oh, well this particular Massachusetts issue has even hit the

New York Times."

"What issue is that—gay marriage?" Hasan asked.

"Yes," said Joe, glad to be able to stop being coy. "Let me give you a little history. Stop me if you know what I'm talking about.

"In April of 2004, unexpectedly, the Supreme Judicial Court, the highest court in Massachusetts, decided that 'Equal Protection of the Law,' a right guaranteed by the Massachusetts Constitution, requires that people of the same sex be allowed to marry. It was a four justice majority decision.

"The Court made wonderful, revolutionary statements that would appear to be self evident but they had never before been applied to gay people in this context. The majority said, 'The Massachusetts Constitution affirms the dignity and equality of all individuals. It forbids the creation of second-class citizens.' One judge added, 'We share a common humanity and participate together in the social contract that is the foundation of our Commonwealth. Simple principles of decency dictate that we extend to the plaintiffs, and to their new status, full acceptance, tolerance, and respect.'

"The case in which the court ruled was the result of the failure of the state legislature to take up the issue of domestic partnership in a timely manner. That obstruction was mainly the doing of the then Speaker of the House of Representatives. The man behind us is his successor.

"As you can understand, all hell broke loose at the decision. Some people even called for the removal from office of the majority judges. One man hires Piper Cubs to fly over the justices' houses and over the city of Boston with banners trailing behind calling for the impeachment of the four judges who favored gay marriage. In the meanwhile some ten thousand same-sex couples have married in Massachusetts.

"People speculate about why those particular four judges voted for gay marriage. The notion that Massachusetts Constitutional

Law and fair play required it does not seem to be enough for them. It doesn't really matter what the justices' unconscious or less than conscious motivators were, but I'd suggest that it was because they knew some gay people, maybe in their families or among their friends."

Hasan nodded as if he understood.

Joe continued, "Barney Frank, the very articulate and witty congressman from Massachusetts, says that the greatest political act a gay person can do is to come out of the closet. It's hard to be hateful to someone who is in your life.

"I suggest the vote of the four justices of the Supreme Judicial Court proves this point. An equally interesting question is why the other three judges voted the other way. I have theories, but they are speculation only.

"The most recent effort of those opposed to same-sex marriage is what's called an 'Initiative Petition.' That would amend the state constitution by putting the issue to a popular vote, a vote of all the people at an election. The Constitutional Amendment would prohibit same-sex marriage or anything that looked like it, including civil unions, which grant all the rights and burdens of marriage, except the name. In order for the Amendment to pass, the two branches of the Legislature, the Senate and the House of Representatives, sitting as a 'Constitutional Convention' as it is called, have to approve the petition—but only by ¼ of the votes of all 200 of them, or 50 votes. And they have to do this twice, in two separate sessions—two separately elected legislatures. Is this too confusing yet?" Joe asked.

"No, I think I follow it. It was very difficult for me to realize how much power the individual states have in this country and how varied their procedures can be. We in Europe are used to thinking of you as a monolith, one country, one government. But I have a very good friend at the Kennedy School, himself a state legislator from Alaska, who explained Federalism to me. As a matter of fact he used the differing attitudes to gay marriage as the example."

"O.K., but stop me if I'm boring you," Joe said insincerely. He loved teaching Law to the layman. "There has been one vote on the Initiative Petition already. Remember that all that is needed are 50 votes in favor. There were 61 votes in favor during that first vote! If that happens again in a second vote with this new session, the matter goes to the voters. Many people think that the voters will strike down same-sex marriage.

"However, some things have changed since the last vote. Four of those who voted in favor of the amendment were defeated in the last election. So it comes down to changing eight votes, eight legislators whose votes have to be turned, plus making sure that two new legislators who are running in special elections are also opposed to the amendment. Are you still with me?

Hasan nodded affirmatively.

"The man who passed us, the very good-looking man with the priest, is one of those 61 who voted in favor of the amendment, one of the eight whose minds must be changed."

"He looks gay himself. What's his problem?" Hasan said abruptly.

Joe was startled at the frankness of Hasan's observation, although, in fact, he thought similarly. He said, "That's what people are trying to find out. His looking gay may be the problem. He may not want people to think he's gay."

"Are you trying to find that out? He seemed to know you. Are you one of the four judges who voted for same-sex marriage?" Hasan asked.

Joe knew that Hasan had probably heard Billy Meadows call him "Judge" so he wasn't going to get coy now and ask Hasan, "How do you know that I'm a judge?"

Joe said, "No, I'm not that important. Yes, I am a judge. I'm a member of a court below the Supreme Judicial Court. They don't let us play with such important issues as same-sex marriage. There are 25 judges on my court. Most people, except lawyers who go to court, 'barristers' you'd call them in Ireland, like Representative Billy Meadows sometimes does, don't even know who we are. We're known as the 'Anonymous Court' and I like it that way. I can have a private life—most of the time."

Hasan said, "All this is very interesting, but why does everyone want to talk to the Speaker of the House, including my beautiful redhead?"

"Well, he is important. The Speaker of the House of Representatives controls the votes of almost all the Democratic members, who are the majority of the House by far. He's opposed to the Anti-Same-Sex Marriage Amendment, if that's not too many negatives. In other words, he would allow same-sex marriage. He's brought along most, but not all, of his members in the House. Representative Billy Meadows, on the other hand, voted against the Speaker's wishes. That's why it's a surprise to see Billy here today—and with the Monsignor, who is the Chancellor of the Archdiocese. That they are together and that they are talking to the Speaker are not good signs, unless the Speaker laid out to Billy what is expected of him."

"Maybe they are a couple," Hasan said with a mischievous grin, again astonishing Joe with his candor.

Joe pretended to be unfazed. He continued, "Billy may have brought the Monsignor for protection. The Speaker is Italian, and, unlike most of the Irish politicians in Massachusetts, he is not afraid of the clergy. There's a healthy anti-clericalism among Italians, you know. They were dominated by the Church temporal for years back in Italy. There were even the Papal States. In Ireland the Catholic clergy were often defenders of the poor, not feeding off them. That's why priests still get some respect from the Irish. Also the Speaker is divorced and remarried. The clergy haven't said anything but they don't have to."

"Yes, I understand that," Hasan said. "You forget that I grew up in Ireland. We studied Parnell and Kitty O'Shea and we read *The Portrait of the Artist as a Young Man*. They even teach James Joyce in Catholic secondary schools these days. He's a national treasure. All Dublin celebrates Bloomsday on June 16th. It's a tourist attraction."

"Sorry, I forgot. I can get carried away with myself," Joe said, belaboring the obvious. "As a student of politics you'll agree that this is a wonderful case study and that it goes well beyond the usual boundaries we see regarding legislation. Have you talked about 'The Margin of Indifference' in Professor Wilson's course, or elsewhere at the Kennedy School? That's the theory that most people, and that includes most legislators, are indifferent regarding most issues, and that someone who is not indifferent about a particular matter can lead them his or her way. Hitler in the Reichstag is the most dramatic example of this principle.

"Well, the margin of indifference is small on this issue—not very many legislators are indifferent about this subject—and, as you can imagine, the factors behind people's strong opinions go back centuries, and also laterally into the very families of the legislators. One legislator who opposes same-sex marriage did so over the outspoken pleas of her sister, who is, as the newspapers say, 'a professed lesbian.' It has split the family in two, with the mother supporting her gay daughter. People have been coming out of closets all over the state."

"And you, where are you on this issue?" Hasan asked.

"Ah, my friend, I am a judge in Massachusetts and not allowed to voice my political opinions, and this subject is still considered a political matter by people who can make my life difficult, so I'll decline to answer that question. I can be disciplined for doing so. Some people would not even let us have political opinions. Former Justice William O. Douglas of the United States Supreme Court wouldn't even vote. That was too political an act for him, he said, even though he kept on hoping to be called off the bench to run for President or Vice President. We Massachusetts judges give up our freedom of speech when we 'take the silks,' as you say in Ireland, except our robes are made of polyester these days, though no less expensive than silk."

"In Ireland all barristers 'take the silk,'" Hasan noted quietly.

"Well, they don't here. Only judges get to wear robes. I wish we could dress up some of our barristers. One appeared in front of me last week wearing a pink blazer, with vulgar imitation brass buttons and a fake crest, khaki pants, his tie at half mast, no socks and boat shoes. I asked him where he 'parked the yacht.' My colleagues thought I was being fresh. Maybe he'll report me to the Judicial Conduct Commission. Oh well, he won't be the first one."

"I thought judges were elected in this country," Hasan said.

"Not in this state. This is another aspect of Federalism. In a lot of other states judges are elected, but not here, thank God. We're appointed by the Governor after a complicated search process and we serve until age 70—or death, whichever comes first. Federal judges aren't elected either."

"And how old are you?" Hasan asked.

"I'm 66 and I've worked more than 15 years as a judge. If the Legislature passes a raise, I'll be out the door. I'm eligible for the full pension right now but if there's a raise coming, I want to benefit from that. I haven't told that to many people, so keep it to yourself," Joe added with a small smile, as he looked from side to side conspiratorially.

Just then the people at the Speaker's table behind them stood up with much laughter. The Speaker walked ahead. He stopped at Joe's table. The others stopped behind. Joe began to stand.

"Don't get up, Judge. I hear you're getting old and thinking of retiring. You don't look so old," the Speaker said with a grin.

"I'm young enough to continue to work until you sweeten the

pot," Joe said boldly, taking strength from the ribbing to confront the issue of the judicial pay raise.

"Oh, don't worry about that. We'll take care of you soon. Just tell your judicial brothers and sisters to behave themselves until we can vote a raise. No yelling at lawyers. No dancing on tables late at night. And who is this young man?" Hasan had stood up and was standing by with a pleasant smile.

"This is Hasan Nasser, a student at the Kennedy School. Perhaps he could come visit you and see how legislation is made," Joe said, quickly making up Hasan's last name.

"Like sausages, Judge. You know that. Bismarck said it first. They must teach that at the Kennedy School, Mr. Nasser. Nobody should see how legislation is made. Call me, Mr. Nasser, and I'll take you around the State House. We're very proud of our government in Massachusetts. Your name is Egyptian. Are you from there?"

"I was born there, but I grew up in Ireland, sir. My mother teaches in Dublin. My father was Egyptian and my mother is Irish"

The Speaker said, "You're an unlikely looking Irishman, but you're in good company. Do you know my friend Maureen Randozza? Her mother, God rest her soul, was Irish, a Ronayne from Dundalk, I believe. I knew her father. He grew up with me in the North End."

Maureen extended her hand and smiled. Hasan could not believe his good fortune.

"I'm very pleased to meet you, Maureen Ronayne Randozza," Hasan thickened the brogue for his introduction.

The Speaker moved on after saying, "Just keep your colleagues out of the newspapers, Judge, and you'll be able to leave soon. Perhaps you'll go back to Ireland and work the farm."

Maureen Randozza and Tom Murphy sat down at Joe's table. Marlene Dinerman, JoJo Danieli and Trixie Pellegrino all walked out of the restaurant behind the Speaker.

Maureen said, "Uncle Dino is still in Rome, Joe, with that prissy

Monsignor Dunn. How is Angelo Bruno? Isn't he a doll?"

Before Joe could answer Tom said, "Things went very well here, Joe…I mean Judge. These women are spectacular. The Speaker had no idea of the support they could muster for…or against… him. Of course, he played it very cool. When I came here this morning with Marlene and saw that he was talking to that turncoat, Billy Meadows, and Monsignor Owen, I asked Marlene what we could do. It didn't look good."

Tom added, "The Speaker is tired of talking to either Marlene or me. We had to come up with something or somebody fresh, some damage control. Marlene went to the Ladies room, got on her cell phone and called up the lesbian equivalent of 'Queen Control.' Within minutes Maureen and company appeared. You saw them. You'd think the whole North End was gay- friendly after listening to them. You did a great job, Maureen."

Maureen said, "Didn't Tip O'Neill say, 'All politics is local?' It's particularly local when you come from the North End, which is really a small town south of Rome. He may be the Speaker for the entire state, but in order to get there, first he has to be elected in the North End. Everybody there has one gay cousin—at least. The Speaker knows the district, but he didn't know everything. He's always been good on this issue, although I think it was more from his heart than his counting the numbers. Like a lot of politicians he didn't realize that we are everywhere. We gave him some cover. Now I hope that he doesn't tell my grandmother about me and JoJo, though I suspect she already knows something. She's rarely seen me with a man."

As this conversation progressed Hasan's smile faded.

"We have to find a way to get to Billy Meadows, Joe…uh…I mean, Judge. I have to find a way to get to him." Tom said. "You, of course, can't do anything political."

Maureen interjected, "Billy Meadows is too good-looking to be all straight. I'll find out about him. Remember, I used to work in the South End. I have lots of friends there. He must go to a gym. We'll do a 'Queen Control' search of the gym trainers and masseurs."

Tom Murphy said, "Marlene thinks that's the problem, that people think he's too good-looking to be straight, so he votes against us to prove he's straight. Of course, a closet queen would do the same, and there are a few of them voting against us. We're dealing with them, but Billy Meadows has aspirations. A Democrat can't get anywhere in this state without the liberals and we're the liberal cause this year—at last, I hope. We shouldn't be discussing all this political intrigue in front of you, Judge, and we're probably boring your friend from India."

"He's from Dublin, Tom," Joe said. "Dublin, in Ireland! Didn't you hear me say that to the Speaker? Say something Irish, Hasan. Sing *The Wild Colonial Boy*. Do anything to prove your Hibernian *bona fides* to poor Mr. Murphy," Joe said laughingly.

Tom Murphy did not like to be embarrassed, but he was quick to recover. "Pardon me. I've heard of Black Irish and even known a few, but I've never met such a tawny Irishman, and one so handsome, I might add."

Joe quickly jumped in, "Hasan, let me apologize for our banter at your expense. It's just the way we…communicate. I've known Mr. Murphy for a long time. We've been through a lot together," Joe added patronizingly.

"As you just mentioned, Milord, Your Honor, Sir, I'm from Dublin. Your banter is but a pale descendant of ours. You've read your Joyce. You've listened to Oscar Wilde and Sean O'Casey. And you in Boston have Edwin O'Connor, George Higgins and J.G. Hayes, but Mr. Murphy is refreshingly direct and astute. Although I'm known as 'The Fair but Tawny' amongst my friends in Ireland, how could he expect me to be Irish? 'No offense intended; no offense taken.'" Then Hasan gave Tom Murphy a big warm smile, rousing in Tom

Murphy the same carnal hopes that Joe had so recently let go of.

"That'll show you, Joe…I mean Your Honor, Milord, Sir," Maureen said with a grin.

Joe decided that he would leave these three to themselves for a minute. He stood up to go to the men's room. Besides the fact that the conversation was getting close to being political, he really did have to pee. The men's room was in the back on the right hand side. Joe went through the first door. To his left was another door with a sign on it saying "Staff Only." Joe assumed that it was an office or a broom closet. Bumps and bangs and crashes were coming from there. In spite of those noises Joe was going to continue through to the bathroom until he heard a moan. Joe thought someone might be in trouble.

He turned the knob on the "Staff Only" door, which quickly opened.

There were Guido and Billy Meadows shirtless, locked in mad embrace on the handsome black rug with the ochre and Pompeian red Greek key border. Billy's right hand was moving down the inside of Guido's pants. A number of thoughts went through Joe's mind, not in any particular order. They were:

Oh my! What do we have here?

Can I tell anybody about it?

Will Billy's proclivities turn Billy's vote?

Will the knowledge that other people know his proclivities change Billy's vote?

What do I do with this information?

"Shut the fucken door, Joe!" Guido said.

"Oh, fuck!" Billy Meadows said, as he looked up and saw Joe. He then buried his face in the rug. He indeed was handsome shirtless, even with his chest shaved, not Joe's usual preference.

Joe shut the door, but he still had to pee. That's the way it is with old men. He also had to think. He went into the men's room and did his business.

The dilemma for Joe was what to do with what he had just seen. *The Canons of Judicial Ethics* forbade him from being involved in politics.

But was this issue—the civil right of gay people to marry, their "human right," as it was so eloquently called in the Goodridge decision—above politics?

Joe recalled his African-American colleagues who attended NAACP Legal Defense Fund dinners and the Million Man March. Didn't they think their issues were more noble than mere "politics" and didn't they justify their presence at such political advocacy events? And weren't they correct? Of course, nobody had questioned them. If anyone had inquired, his black colleagues would have made short shrift of them.

And didn't some of Joe's Jewish colleagues go to a lunch at the American Jewish Congress Social Justice Committee once a month? Wasn't that an advocacy group? Couldn't their presence be perceived as lending their title to political causes?

Finally, what about all the judges who processed in morning suits into the Cathedral of the Holy Cross for the Cardinal Archbishop's Red Mass every year and then went to a breakfast where some more Catholic-than-the-Pope yahoo worked them into a frenzy about abortion, the "Gay agenda" and "the New World Order."?

Would all this precedent allow Joe to use his discovery of Billy's *peccadillo* for the same-sex marriage cause—to convince Billy Meadows to turn his vote? Joe had to think this through and he wasn't going to be able to do that over Eggs Benedict, croissants and fresh squeezed orange juice at Guido's Back Bay Grille, especially while Tom Murphy, Hasan whatever-his-last-name-was and Maureen Ronayne Randozza played flirtatious Tic-Tac-Toe in front of him.

Joe's head hurt from all this intrigue and excitement. Joe decided that it was time for him to go to his office at the John Adams Courthouse. This lark of a day off in open view was not going to work. His office was the safest and best place for Joe to ponder this situation. It was designed for contemplation. He could look off into space and be working. He was supposed to mull and ponder there. *What would John Adams have done? What would Massachusetts Chief Justices Oliver Wendell Holmes, Lemuel Shaw or Stanley Rugg have done?* This situation was a dilemma only because Joe was a judge. It was not inappropriate to work it through on the clock in his office, Joe even more scrupulously decided, should the Judicial Conduct Commission require him to account for his *pensees* or the "Media" be able to read his mind.

Joe returned to the table and solemnly fibbed, "I just received a call from my Chief Justice. Justice Firrfield is sick and he was supposed to preside over a three judge panel at 11:00 this morning. I have to get to the Courthouse. I have to sit in. We'll talk later, Tom."

They hardly acknowledged his departure. Tom Murphy was busily engaged in attempting to charm the pants off Hasan, who in turn was trying to snuggle up to Maureen. Maureen, no fool she, saw all of this intrigue, laughed while eating Hasan's Eggs Benedict, the first good meal she'd had in days. Joe's presence was not going to be missed.

As Joe left he passed Wolfy's table with Harry Jones, the District Attorney, and his handsome assistant. They each looked up as Joe approached but only Harry stood up.

Harry whispered in Joe's ear, "I'll call you later, Joe. We have to talk."

Joe, still deep into his dilemma, nodded and said, "Yes, Harry. Call me."

* * *

Just as Billy Meadows' perfect Roman nose was not authentic, Billy Meadows was not his real name. Billy was born William Walter Medovski, the son of Walter Medovski, Jr. When Billy was five years old Walter Junior changed the family name to Meadows. Walter Senior, a Polish immigrant, had just died and Walter Junior was tired of being the immigrant outsider in Grayston, the small Yankee Nativist farming town fifty miles outside of Boston.

Walter Senior had arrived there as a farm worker from Poland in the early 20th Century. At that time there were a lot of farms which had been abandoned by the original Yankees because they no longer made any money as the country expanded westward. Immigrants ended up owning most of them. Little by little, Walter Senior accumulated almost 200 acres. Up until the end of World War II he farmed most of those acres. He grew vegetables, had a farm stand, and a couple of trucks for delivery to the city, as well as chickens and some dairy cattle.

After the War, when housing was scarce, and as the suburbs moved further away from the nearby cities, Walter Senior, and later Walter Junior, developed the land and constructed increasingly expensive houses. The first houses were near the new highway that had also been built in the Fifties to accommodate the suburbanites. But they saved the best land for themselves, giving it up slowly only for the most expensive homes.

Walter Junior had endured the taunts of his Swamp Yankee schoolmates in grammar school, but by high school he was stronger and handsomer than most of the other boys. He was also sexually precocious and in his first year of college in 1965 he knocked up and married a pretty blonde cheerleader he had been dating since high school. The result was young William. Five years later Walter Senior died plowing one of the last fields still left for farming. Walter Junior had finished his football career and business studies at Boston College and was working at the construction company his father had founded to build houses on the farmland.

It was time to become American. "Meadows" wasn't too great

a leap from "Medovski." Young Billy should not have to suffer the discrimination his grandfather and father had endured. Walter Junior's wife, Anne, nee Parkman, agreed. She didn't want to be some "Polak's wife." She aspired to be restored to the Yankee gentry she fantasized that her family had been before being wiped out by the Great Depression of 1929. She even wanted to join the Greystone Hunt and Golf Club which had sprung up, like Venus from Zeus, in the early Fifties as if it had been there since the Revolution began in nearby Lexington and Concord.

Billy inherited his maternal grandfather Parkman's long, thin, crooked and disapproving nose, and hated it. So, when he was twelve, during the summer vacation, his mother took him to Boston and he had the nose fixed—nothing dramatic, just straightened and widened a bit. Billy's mother had been a patient of the doctor's for similar purposes.

The next school year he went to Oxham Academy, a second-rate prep school in the foothills of the Berkshires where Billy learned how to dress like a preppie. He was close enough to Grayston so that his mother could visit him, but far enough away to develop a life of his own. And he did.

Billy went to one of the skiing colleges up North, which had pretensions of being Dartmouth but wasn't. That was where Billy learned that he couldn't drink, however. One Sunday morning, after a drunken Saturday night in the fraternity house, Billy woke up in bed with his American Literature professor. Billy had been adept enough in the sack, but was wracked with guilt the next day. Billy didn't want it to happen again. The professor, somewhere in his forties, dark-haired, handsome and a former football player, the very embodiment of manliness, wasn't anxious for a repeat either. The professor feared exposure. He usually played in Manhattan.

Billy's guilt did not stop him from returning to the professor, however. The professor, contrary to his better judgment, proving once again that, besides not having a conscience, a stiff prick makes no sense, jumped into bed with Billy each time.

The professor did not want a love affair with a student and Billy did not immediately grasp the concept of a fuck buddy. Billy had a girlfriend who was the captain of the cheerleaders (like father, like son). Billy was not going to give up the campus status that dating the hottest girl in the college gave him.

After college Billy went to a commuter law school in downtown Boston. He returned to Grayston and practiced law, mostly real estate, but some criminal trial work as well as a few appeals. He never gave up the Beacon Hill apartment he lived in during law school. When Billy won a seat in the House of Representatives, the Great and General Court of the Commonwealth of Massachusetts, Billy lived there, whether the House was in session or not. His legal residence was back in Grayston, of course. In the handout local magazines, glorified bar rags, Billy soon became known as one of *Boston's Most Eligible Bachelors.*

Billy curbed his hetero photo ops after a certain young man of the lavender persuasion, to whom Billy had not permitted a third visit, saw his picture and threatened to write a letter to the editor telling him what Billy really liked. That all was taken care of, or took care of itself. The gay heart can be fickle. A return visit followed by Billy's paramour's "chance" meeting with a State Police trooper, kept Billy's closet door shut.

Billy even married. It was a very pretty wedding at Emanuel Church (Episcopal) on Newbury Street in Boston. The bride was from New Jersey, one of the horsey towns, and the wedding made the *New York Times.* It was not a Catholic wedding, which years before would have upset both Billy's grandparents and his constituents, but Grayston and the Meadows had become sufficiently secular to let it pass.

Joe, who read the *Times* wedding pages to find the same-sex marriages and to see how many people with Irish surnames got married in Protestant churches (as if that were an indicator of the homogenization of America's upper classes) saw Billy's wedding announcement and took note.

Billy had appeared before Joe some years before. Joe had no particular memory of Billy's legal talents, but Joe remembered Billy's good looks. Billy's appearance before Joe was just about the time when Billy had won his first term in the Legislature. The Legislature decides Judges' salaries and Joe remembered legislators who appeared in front of him.

Billy, as well as other good-looking young male lawyers appearing in front of Joe who knew Joe's story (and female lawyers who didn't know his story, or who thought they could overcome his predilections with their dubious charms) flirted with Joe on the bench and did so again on those occasions when they met him by chance on the street. The flirting didn't mean the lawyers were gay; it just meant they would do what they thought they had to do to win a case, either the one they were arguing or the next one, or it meant that they liked attention from whatever source.

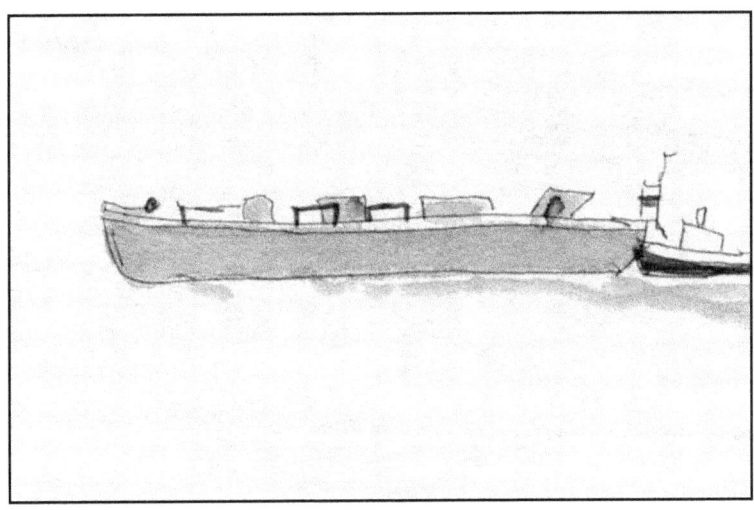

Life at Court

Joe climbed into a cab on Newbury Street and told the driver that he wanted to go to the John Adams Courthouse. The Russian cabbie, whose identification tag was hanging backwards, and was thus unreadable, even from the rear view mirror said, "Vich court-house is that?"

Joe, who thought that he had more serious matters to think about, exclaimed, "What? It's the one behind the Statehouse. Go down Beacon Street and let me off at Bowdoin." Then he added, "Please." There were now four courthouses in downtown Boston after all and nobody could be expected to know which was "vich," Joe realized. Many lawyers seemed not to know which one they were supposed to be in. At least that is what they told the judges when they arrived late. Some judges had been assigned to three of them in as many years.

The cabbie drove up Newbury Street, a few blocks more than necessary, before turning across to Boylston with all its red lights—the meter computed time as well as distance—to go around the Public Garden to get onto Beacon Street.

Once on Beacon Street the cabbie said, "You a judge? What you do at the Courthouse?"

Joe was surprised but not shocked; he'd ridden cramped Boston cabs with nosy foreign drivers before. Joe replied, "I'm a janitor. What's it to you?"

"You look like the judge that took away my speeding ticket. That bastard cop! He's on my ass all the time! You fixed him. You ride for free!"

Oh, what do I do about this? Another ethical dilemma, Joe thought, as they approached Bowdoin Street. Of course, Joe, being on the Appeals Court, had nothing to do with the driver's ticket. But the cabbie perceived him to have done so. All the white-haired Irish judges looked alike to the foreign stranger's eye. When the cab turned and stopped just into Bowdoin Street, Joe threw ten dollars at the front seat (for a six dollar ride; Joe had no change) and hustled down Beacon Street to Somerset Street and the back entrance to The John Adams Courthouse. *Peril lurked everywhere for a judge,* he said to himself, wiping his brow at the door.

He couldn't see the humor in his situation until he stepped through the door onto the black and white diamond tiled marble floor of the second floor of the Courthouse and remembered the story about the excited young typist who ran up to the then Reporter of Decisions, a tall drink of water with thick steel-rimmed glasses, slicked hair and bow ties, the last of the Yankee retainers at the Supreme Judicial Court. The young secretary was soaked down the right side of her skirt and blouse. She said, "I just slipped on the marble floor! The roof leaks onto the floor!" The Reporter of Decisions looked her up and down and then said deliberately in the flat tone common to his type, "I had no idea life at Court could be so perilous."

Joe walked up the stairs to his office on the next floor. The 1890 French Mansard courthouse, modeled after the Hotel de Ville in

Paris, had been renovated a few years before to the tune of $150 plus million dollars. Its name was changed from "The Old Courthouse" to "The John Adams Courthouse" as the result of a recent, popular biography of that cranky old worthy, which was written by a pal of the then Supreme Judicial Court Chief Justice.

Unfortunately, the Legislature, for reasons best known to its previous Speaker (the predecessor to the man in Guido's Back Bay Grille) had expanded the Appeals Court from 14 to 25 justices while the renovation was going on, and the justices of the Appeals Court, Joe's court, had only been allotted space for 14 judges in the renovation. So, they had to take up the slack. Thanks to Bill Gates, recent technology, namely personal computers, the Internet and email, the judges could stay home, do research there, communicate online with their law clerks, colleagues and editors and send in their decisions.

Many of them did just that, but propriety demanded that each have an office in the Courthouse. In addition, occasionally the dreaded "Media" and the judge-hating Sam Nemesis, took a head count of either the judges in the courthouse or their cars in the parking lot. Even when not physically present (as in the doctrine of transubstantiation) the judges were working, the Chief Justice told the Press. Presumably, the housebound justices wore their robes while pondering and padding around their houses in slippers and pajamas.

Because Joe had seniority he was assigned a good office, and because he lived nearby he used it. He rarely worked from home. However, the newer judges were not so lucky. Many of them did not even get windows in their offices. And the law clerks, one for every judge, two for the Chief Justice, had to sit in cubicles in the corridor. Seniority has always governed the interactions amongst judges. Besides, it was the easiest way to handle the *prima donnas*.

At the main door Joe passed the surly court officer, who barely looked up from his *Herald*. "Hello, Mr. O'Brien. How are you?"

Joe had learned long ago not to wait for an answer. There never was a reply. O'Brien was the brother-in-law of a long ago President of the Senate and he didn't think he had to talk to any judges except the Chief Justice, for whom he ran errands. Besides, talking hurt his hungover head.

Joe passed through the law clerks' corridor, greeting them each by name, received cordial replies, and then punched in the code to the Judges' Lobby next to the door to that *sanctum sanctorum*. The code was a joke because everybody on the floor, secretaries, court officers and even janitors had the code and "the Staff," as they called themselves, had no shyness about walking through the Judges' Lobby past the open doored judges' offices on their way to a lunchroom on the other side. Joe had tried to organize the justices to stop this procession; he got "the Irish chill" from the staff for months.

One day when nobody else was in the Judges' Lobby Miss Managhan slipped into Joe's office and told Joe that "the Staff" were not servants with separate entrances, that working at the Court was "public service" not slavery at some hierarchical law firm, and that just because people stood up when he entered a courtroom that did not mean he was anyone special. Most of "the Staff" had been there long before he was appointed and would be there after he left. All this was punctuated with lots of "your Honors," "Judge, Sir" and even a "Mister Justice" or two.

As a result of the chill Joe decided to dictate his own opinions to his law clerk who quickly learned the format and helped him with the mechanics. Joe then did the editing.

Across from Joe's office was that of the beautiful and brilliant Gigi Boland, the *Madame de Pompadour* of the Massachusetts Court system and the belle of the Appeals Court. If you wanted to get something done, you went to Gigi. She would either do it, or she would show you how to do it. Most likely she would do it her-self because she understood that power was only good when exer-cised. She didn't help just anybody. Over the years she had built up a coterie of favorites based on a lot of factors, friendship, ethnicity, sex, good looks, style and a host of intangibles which only made sense to her.

When Joe returned Gigi was sitting behind her desk. Gigi was very tall, five feet and ten inches, and thin, with long silver wavy hair that touched her shoulders. Her black, almost too-thick-for-a-girl eyebrows were her pride. They served her well as a judge by making her disapproving scowls even graver. She had been gray since law school and always wore metallic colored clothes that complimented her hair, pale complexion and trademark very red lipstick—Jungle Red. Gigi looked stunning in her judicial robe, which was lined in red, the same as her lipstick. The robe was fas-tened with one button just at her bustline, unlike the robes of the other women judges who chastely zipped themselves in from na-vel to chin. Most of them looked like crows next to Gigi. Yet they were not jealous of her. They liked her and admired her ability to get her way.

Even the Chief Justice of the Supreme Judicial Court, the Chief-est of Judges in Massachusetts, respected Gigi. She wasn't sure if she liked her, but she did respect her. The Chiefest of Justices may have reigned like the Empress of all the Russias, but in reality she was only *Prima Inter Pares*, like the Archbishop of Constantinople, the first among equals with the six other judges on the Court. She may have been their mouthpiece as well, but she could not push too far, as she learned early on. To the uneducated she was the top, and her title as "Chief" would seem to indicate that, but in reality her powers were circumscribed by the Constitution, statutes and custom.

Without *any* formal power, Gigi, who had only her wit, charm and striking good looks, knew how to manipulate the system and get things done. Everyone wanted her as an ally, including the imperial Chief Justice.

Off the bench Gigi was often photographed on the social pages or in the tabloids with one or more of her "boys," high-flying gay men who went to all the smart parties and charity events. Gigi never married and was not known to be involved with any one man—or woman. That added to her allure. The bigger shots she manipulated each thought they could win her.

Gigi said, "Joe darling, I was about to call you at home. Are you feeling O.K.? I was worried about you until I got a call from Madge Mellen, who saw you at Guido's. Were you working on the raise with the Speaker? Madge saw him stop and talk to you. I hope he's not going to leave us hanging again. A police patrolman doing road duty at construction sites earns more than we do."

You can bet that Madge told Gigi who else Joe sat with and talked to. *She didn't miss a trick, that Madge,* Joe thought. Madge was the stock broker/raconteur/wit at the table at Guido's in front of him with the lady artists. Joe decided that he wouldn't offer any information about anyone else unless asked—and that even then he might lie. He still hadn't entirely sorted out what to do about what he saw Billy Meadows doing in the "Staff Only" room with Guido. He didn't want Gigi's advice on this subject—yet. Besides, it was a "man thing," "a gay man thing," and although Gigi was no homophobe, whatever her orientation, she probably would not react well to the particulars of gay sex. And Joe felt some sisterly pull to protect Guido and Billy, the gay players. *There but for the grace of God, go I,* Joe thought. He had been in some dangerous clinches in his day, and there were times that he could have been exposed if someone had opened a door, looked in a closet, under a bed, or in the bushes.

Gigi was okay with the "gay thing" in all other respects. Some of, if not most of, her best friends were gay. Years before in 1964, Joe had seen Dolores del Rio, the Mexican movie star, whose beauty secret was to sleep fourteen hours a day (a fact that Joe envied) at a party in the National Palace in Mexico City on the *Quince de Septiembre*, the anniversary of Father Hidalgo's *Grito de Dolores*, the beginning of Mexico's War of Independence from Spain in 1810. Dolores del Rio moved through the Palace's rooms in a beaded green evening gown with a train at a hurried pace followed by at least ten men of all sizes and shapes, rushing to catch up to her. That was what Gigi was like with her "boys." She whirled them around like yo-yos. Joe knew some of the "boys" but he kept his distance. Good fences make good neighbors, he had learned.

"As a matter of fact, the Speaker was positive about the raise," Joe said. "He said that we should stay out of the papers and we'll see it soon. I hope there's not going to be another scandal about a grop- ing judge in the Trial Court. That lesbian locker room incident after the courthouse softball game out in Northampton never made the papers, thank God! The Trial Court Chief Justice is doing a good job. He got the offender to resign. Of course, the Empress helped. Ev- eryone likes an audience with The Chiefest of all Chief Justices. The offended probation officer is quite happy working in Jamaica Plain. She had a choice of there or Somerville. Jamaica Plain had the bet- ter softball team. So, that's really all I have to report, my dear Gloria Grace." Those were Gigi's real names.

"I didn't know about that *scandale*," Gigi said. "Why didn't anyone tell me that story?"

"You have to keep your ear to the ground, Gigi, particularly with the goings on out West, beyond Route 128. 'Beyond Dedham lies the West,' as your old property professor, Cornelius Moynihan, and the late J.P. Marquand used to say. You spend too much time in Beacon Hill salons and Back Bay ballrooms, Gigi. You have to mix with 'the people' sometimes," Joe said.

"Is that why you were sitting with those Sisters of Sappho at Guido's this morning?" Gigi said, just a little miffed at Joe's critique of the insularity of her social life.

"Oh, Gigi, Madge shouldn't let her imagination run away with her. She's just mad that I didn't give her an introduction. Which lesbian did she want to meet?" Joe said.

"And who was the Arabian Prince that your pal, Tom Murphy, Esquire, left with?" Gigi said.

"Really Gigi, I have to do some work today."

"Well good luck!" urged Gigi. "Your phone has been ringing for the last fifteen minutes. Somebody really wants to talk to you. And there's a very thick large vermilion envelope on your desk, addressed to you in beautiful script. It was delivered by hand this morning to the front desk by a very good-looking, very earnest young man all dressed up in a navy blue suit. I saved Dotty the walk and brought it into your office. Of course, I was really curious and green with envy. Nobody sends me mail as beautiful as that—not even the fancy shops where I buy my clothes. Are you communicating with the Vatican, Joe? Your mail today looks positively ecclesiastical. If it's an invitation to a swell event, even one in a church, I'd like to know about it. You know what they say about me. 'She always loves a party.'" Gigi added. "Oh, back to speaking of work, Firrfield is going to dissent on the libel case we heard last week."

"Dissent! Dissent? He doesn't even know which way we're going to rule!" Joe said.

"No matter, he thinks we're part of the Irish Conspiracy and he's decided that whatever way we rule will be the result of that," Gigi said. "He as much as told me so this morning after he came in with the *Globe* article about the latest priest pederast, whose last name is, to Firrfield, suspiciously similar to mine. Firrfield thought that he was being cute. He held the article behind his back and then asked if I was related to a Monsignor Bowen. I'd already read the *Globe*, and I'm on to him, so I said he was my first husband. That's when Firrfield announced his dissent as he slapped the article on my desk. Do you know Monsignor Bowen, Joe? He really wasn't into children, was he? Most of those priests liked them to have at least hit puberty," Gigi added. "Firrfield will be in to see you next. I suspect that it was you he was looking for in the first place."

Joe laughed. Firrfield seemed to hold Joe responsible for every pederast priest with an Irish name, of which there was unfortunately no shortage. After a while Joe didn't mind because Firrfield also confronted the black judges with Mike Tyson's latest antics and the Italians with John Gotti, the Randozzas of the North End and gangland slayings. Joe was tempted to make some cracks to him about Eliot Spitzer, Anthony Weiner or even Woody Allen, but he desisted for the sake of collegiality.

Joe left Gigi's office to cross over to his own. He opened the red envelope with the beautiful 18th-century script. It was lined in Florentine paper and contained a letter, a résumé, and a headshot of a very handsome dark-haired young man named Patrick Foley, about to be a third-year law student at Boston College Law School. Young Mr. Foley wrote that he wanted to work for Judge Lyons as an unpaid legal intern starting immediately.

The typed letter gushed over Joe's courage at being the first openly gay judge in Massachusetts, highlighted Mr. Foley's gay activist activities and was signed in the same beautiful script as addressed the red envelope. *Well, this is novel,* Joe thought. *I've never received a headshot in a job application before. And it is pleasantly contrary to the current politically correct trend of age, sex and race blind applications. Does the head shot list his characteristics—height, weight, eye color, dick size on the back?* Joe wondered as he turned it over. *This sending a headshot is very bold, quite unorthodox for a job seeker in the judiciary, but he does have my attention. Didn't Ned Rorem, the then scandalous, very handsome gay composer, do that in the Fifties? Ned Rorem did young Mr. Foley one better. He sent shirtless photos to people he thought could further his career. Well, so what if the young beauty is not original. And Mr. Foley's grades are very good. Maybe I'll have him come in for an interview. I'll read the writing sample later.*

Just then Joe's phone rang.

"Hello, Tom," Joe said after he checked the caller ID. The Court had recently installed phones with caller ID after the Chief Justice had picked up a call from the irate mother of a drug addict, whose conviction the Appeals Court had just overturned. The mother had suffered the consequences of her son's addiction long enough and wanted the son locked up until he got clean, and if that took the rest of the son's life, all the better. She had been robbed, lied to and put upon long enough.

After he calmed down, and on the advice of the more technologically informed Miss Mary Margaret Managhan, the Chief Justice decided to let technology solve the personnel problem. He was nearing retirement and had no stomach for controversy. When it came to internal management and personnel matters, the Chief had been led around by the very formidable Miss Managhan for quite a long time. She was one of the three women who ran the courthouse. The three women all were single, wore wool suits and sensible shoes, had seams in their stockings and very tight perms, lived with one or both of their parents, were in their sixties, knew where all the skeletons lay, who was related to whom, and they knew how to get anything they wanted done.

Their bosses, all men except one, had become so dependent on these women that they dared not contradict them. The "Misses," as some of the courthouse wags called them, had seen judges and chief justices come and go. They were the closest to permanent employees that the Court system had. The judges had to retire at age 70 by order of a constitutional amendment but the "Misses" could stay forever. They had "sisters" who had gathered similar powers in the other branches of government.

All this is not to say that they interfered with judges' decisions or opinions; they really did not care in most instances, but they were in charge of housekeeping, which bureaucrats might call "court administration," and their sympathies were with the staff even as they said, "Yes, Judge," and "Anything you want, Judge" and "Your Honored" the judges all day long.

But back to Tom Murphy's call.

"Why didn't you tell me that that Hasan guy is straight?" Tom said.

"Why do you assume that any good-looking man I'm with is gay?" Joe replied. "What happened?"

Tom said, "Well, I offered both of them, both Maureen Randozza and Hasan, a ride home. I was going to drop her off first. Hasan was all over her like sauce. I guess he'd read about the sexual fluidity of our lesbian sisters. She was cagey, but when he finally got around to asking her to lunch next week, she said she was very sorry but that she'd be camping in Vermont with her 'partner,' JoJo, that little fireplug butchie she introduced to the Speaker. And as if Hasan and I didn't know who she meant, she described JoJo to us as the 'girl in the sharkskin suit and the porkpie hat.' Why can dykes get away with calling women 'girls?'"

"Don't explain, Joe," Tom added. "I don't need that sexual politics scholarship now. Just tell me, what's the story on Hasan? Does he 'swing both ways,' as we used to say in 1965, or is he an 'avowed' heterosexual?"

"I don't know, Tom," Joe said. "I had the same hopes you did about Hasan until he started panting after Maureen. He's very interesting. I don't know why I should be surprised by an Egyptian Irishman. The world is shrinking. Who better to teach Archaeology than his Egyptian mother, although I think he said she is the Irish parent. The Egyptians have got the pyramids, mummies and hiero-glyphics and all that archaeological stuff.

"Never mind Hasan," Joe said. "We can talk about him later. He's not a gerontophile, I'm certain, at least not for us. He's very well brought up and polite, but I'm sure he's as nice talking to his Aunt Mary—or Aunt Fatima. I need to talk to *you*—as a client to lawyer. Do you get what I'm saying—confidential! I won't lead you astray, like I did the last time with Bishop Rocco Randozza at Holy Cross Cathedral. You'll have to put on the purple stole of the confession-al as well. This is really top secret—so far. When can I see you? It should be soon," Joe said.

"I have a date tonight and I'm not inclined to give that up. Is to-morrow night alright?" Tom asked.

"Oh, who? No, it's none of my business." Joe said. "Tomorrow will be fine."

Joe was playing around in his jacket pocket while he talked to Tom Murphy. He pulled out the envelope that he had received that morning on the back of which he had written Hasan's contact in-formation. He transferred the information to a card for his Rolodex. Although Joe had called Hasan "Hasan Nasser," Hasan had not giv-en Joe a last name, just an email address and a phone number, so Joe filed the card right in the beginning of the "H" section.

While he had the envelope out Joe decided to open it. For the first time he saw that there was no return address. Inside there was a piece of white $8^1/2$″ x 11″ business paper folded in three so that it had to be opened to be read. Joe unfolded the paper.

"Repent! You filthy somdomite," it said. "God is watching you—always." All this was in cutout letters, like a ransom note, mostly red. Of course, there was no signature.

This wasn't like the notes that threatened Joe last year, the notes he got with the Teddy Bears from Dino Randozza. Joe was curious who sent the note, however, and his mind wandered over those possibilities for a while. The similarity to the Marquess of Queensberry's note to Oscar Wilde was noted by Joe. He hoped there wouldn't be a similar result.

In the meantime Joe reached into his other jacket pocket and pulled out the flyer from Ganymede Farm. Joe thought he'd like to go to their Thirty Fifth Anniversary Party on June 9th in Appolonia. He'd take it up with Angelo later.

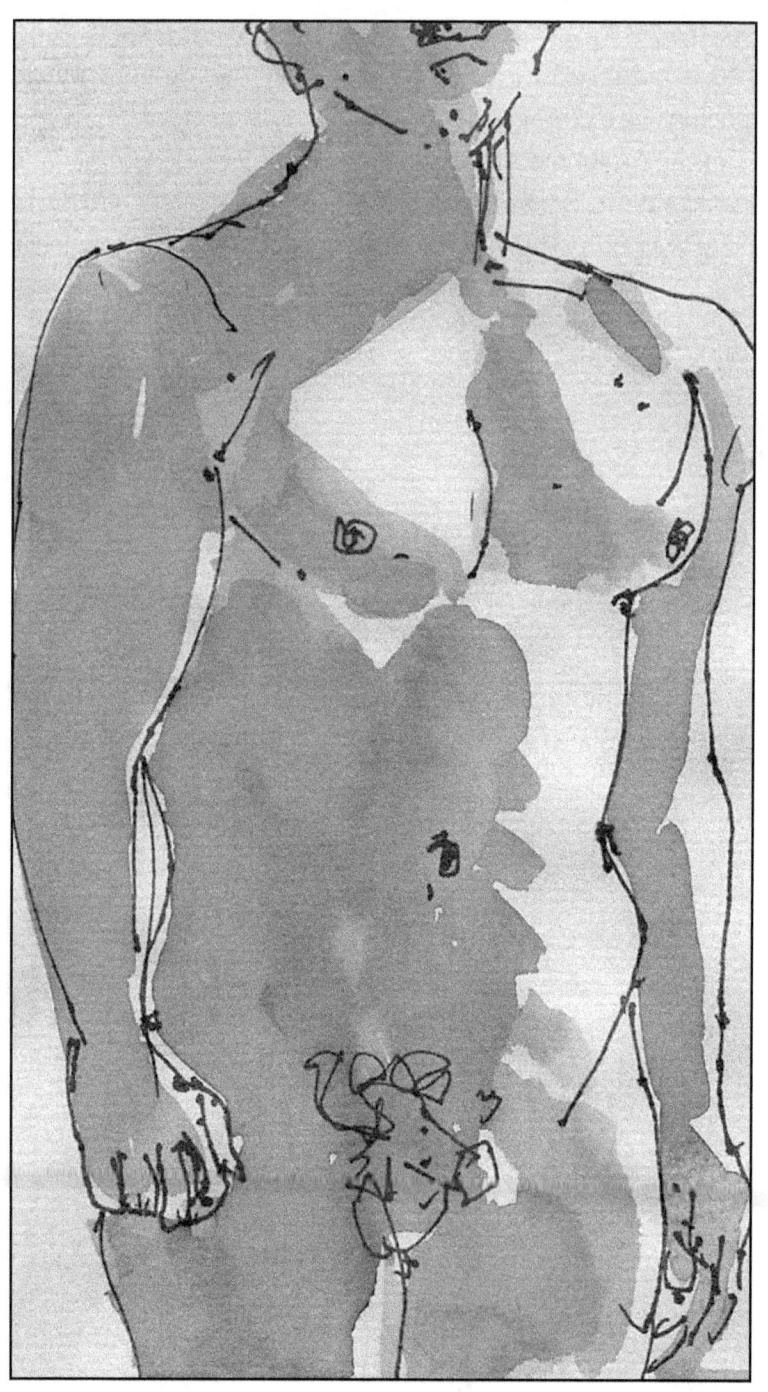

A Side Trip to Fort Viagra

The next night Joe met Tom Murphy at their usual spot—the Victoria Diner in Dorchester on the Roxbury, South Boston, South End line.

Joe moved the salt and pepper shakers around the table nervously before beginning. He said, "I tried to be cool about it. You may remember I had to pee. I got up and headed to the men's room. In that little hallway just before the men's room there's a door marked 'Staff Only.' All of a sudden I heard moans coming from behind the door, as if someone had been stabbed or something. Obedient to the sign I paused, but the moans continued—louder. I twisted the door handle and right there, right in front of me—it must be Guido's office because it was very well decorated—right there on the fancy Greek key rug were Guido and Billy Meadows, shirtless, pants unbuckled, making out. Billy was on top of Guido and when they heard the door open Billy rolled off, his hand still down Guido's pants. 'Shut the fucken door!' Guido screamed. Billy said, 'Oh Fuck!' and buried his face in the rug. When he saw that I was the intruder Billy knew he was undone. But I don't know what to do with this information. I mean that I cannot do anything with this information."

Joe told Tom about what he perceived to be his ethical dilemma—that as a judge he, Joe, could not engage in political activity. Joe went on a little too long for Tom on this subject, counting—and naming—the angels on the head of the pin, and their judicial precedents.

Tom finally interrupted Joe and his scrupulosity, saying, "You should've been a fucking theologian. How do you get out of bed in the morning? I heard what you had to say. I'm your lawyer. I'll take care of it. Stop worrying, for Christ's sake."

Tom added, "Why don't you and I go to Fort Lauderdale for the Memorial Day weekend? I know it'll be hot there, but Provincetown is full of lesbians that weekend and although I love my Sapphic sisters, they kind of put a damper on manly activities—for men—that weekend. I need a rest, and from the way you sound, you do too."

The previous winter, Joe and Tom Murphy had gone to Florida for a week in late February to break the back of winter. They stayed in a guesthouse in Fort Lauderdale a few streets down from the beautiful Fort Lauderdale Beach, off of Terramar Street. It was called *The Fig Leaf*. It was a very discreet place surrounded by ficus trees, other foliage and a high fence. It wasn't cheap—$300 per night at the height of the season. It had a pool, of course, and the obligatory hot tub, which seemed busiest at night. The pool area was, *comme se dit*, "clothing optional" and Tom took everything off immediately, almost before dropping his luggage in their room.

Joe, ever discreet (except when he wasn't) didn't know what tabloid photographer might be hiding in the bush, or if the long nose of Sam Nemesis may have followed them to Florida, so he kept his navy blue nylon boxer bathing suit on as he tried to do laps in the too-short pool.

Tom said, "The Fig Leaf is less than half price at this time of year.

We can have a good time. There'll be lots of sexy South Americans escaping their winter and the usual Southern belles escaping their closets."

Joe agreed, and on the Thursday before Memorial Day they were off. They again stayed at The Fig Leaf. Joe didn't see any vacationing South Americans, whom he was looking forward to, but there was an abundance of Southern men hanging around the pool and the hot tub. Tom seemed to have scored in the tub. At least he came back to the room late and took a shower after having bathed in the hot tub, which seemed redundant to Joe unless Tom had had sex in the tub, which was likely.

On their second day, Saturday, they went to Haulover Beach in Sunny Isles north of Miami Beach on Route A1A at 158th Street. It was more than a half-hour ride south from Fort Lauderdale, but it was worth it. The closest nude beach, Haulover, was public run by Dade County and it had a gay section.

Haulover Beach was about a half mile long; part of the beautiful, wide, beach that began down in South Beach just after the Government Cut, whence the cruise ships depart. Like South Beach there was a footpath of pounded sand up at the land-side of the beach where people ran or walked naked.

Haulover had its *habitués*: A sweet looking curly locked, flitty Italian, who looked like Sophia Loren, did about five laps a day on the footpath at Haulover with a different exotic partner each time—sometimes another Italian, thin and almost skeleton-like, then a German professor with a paunch wearing rimless glasses and a long hayseed beard neatly cut straight across about a foot from his chin. The beard waved in the wind like a windsock. Once a day, "Sophia"s' companion was a fat, bald, hairless Cuban man, who wore big white jewelry, white sunglasses, yellow espadrilles and sometimes a towel as a turban, other times as a skirt. Although naked, "Sophia" walked like he was wearing a tight skirt and he gesticulated wildly while conversing, as if he were throwing rose petals. According to Rico, a young Genoese they met on the beach, "Sophia"s' spoken Italian was sissy as well. He used his hands a lot, but like an American teenage girl.

After the path there was brush and grass separating the beach from a hard-top road, off of which there was a filthy toilet building containing smelly urinals and hoppers. Sometimes there was some action in there, usually late in the day.

Beyond was the highway, A1A, aka Collins Avenue, and then the parking lot for Haulover. There was a tunnel under the highway from the parking lot to the beach.

People clustered on the beach in all kinds of groupings---ethnicity, age, geographical or racial origin, sexual fetish, tattoos or piercing. Some older Provincetowners and Bostonians hung out up next to the lifeguard station. Next to them were five lanky, lightly tattooed Alabama "'boys" in their forties talking about drag shows in Montgomery which were inspired by the movies. *Sordid Lives* or *Gone with the Wind* seemed to be the favorites. Twelve French Canadians in their fifties and sixties speaking French and eating homemade lunches and fresh fruit always lined up on a strip perpendicular to the water line. The New Yorkers, ever independent, tended to hang out in couples, dotting the beach with chic towels, lotions and bestsellers and the *New York Times*.

Joe's favorites were the five very tanned, blue-eyed, thin, wrinkled, retired or ex-priests, some wearing old turned-down sailor caps and big miraculous medals depicting the Virgin as the Immaculate Conception. They talked softly and looked very ascetic, like blue-eyed Gandhis. Joe once overheard one say to the other, "Father Tim wasn't a pedophile. He never looked at a boy under fifteen." Later the same man was exchanging a recipe which began, "First you crumble the Ritz Crackers…" His brother fathers were rapt with attention. It was like he was explaining the Council of Trent to a class of seminarians.

There were four lifeguard stands and the lifeguards, who were usually good-looking but straight Latinos, wore red Speedo bathing suits. Gay men settled at the top, the north end of the beach, clustered around the northernmost elevated lifeguard station, from whence they drifted down to just before the next lifeguard stand opposite the main footpath entrance to the beach. South from the entrance path past the two volleyball courts the beach was officially straight, although there was always a lot of same sex inspecting going on as men walked the footpath.

At Haulover it was legal to be naked and almost everyone was. Joe complied with the law, exposing his milky white bum and hairy torso. Joe liked sitting back on the beach away from the shore under an umbrella. He was too white to sit in the sun and he enjoyed being able to watch a wide swath of the men before him on the way to the water. It reminded Joe of being a judge, sitting up behind a raised bench in a courtroom where he could see everything. It was even better because not everyone was looking at him, nor could they see him, under the umbrella.

That Saturday it didn't look like Joe was going to find romance at the beach. That was alright. Joe had Angelo Bruno back in Boston.

Just then Tom's cellphone rang. "It's Angelo Bruno for you, Joe," Tom said. Joe felt not so alone. Tom was already chatting up a young, short Argentine with a hard, tight body, who spoke little English. Tom looked smitten as he tried pidgin Spanish, hand gestures and loud English to talk to the young Argentine.

Angelo said, "I'm just calling because I miss you. Where are you? It's hard to hear you."

"We're at the beach."

"Haulover?" Angelo asked.

Joe couldn't lie. "Yes," he said sheepishly.

"Are there some hot daddies there today? I love that place—all those geezers. Are there any fuzzies? I get a hardon just thinking about that beach. Are there any cute muscle twinks for you?

"Oh no, it's very dull here—just a lot of South American hotties. You have nothing to worry about. Nobody is looking at me. I can't wait to get home to see you. What are you doing right now?"

"Me? I'm sitting at the kitchen table in a jockstrap polishing my football helmet. Have you got any suggestions?"

"Yeah, take off the jockstrap."

"Okay Daddy coach. Now what?"

Joe left Tom and Cesar and walked back towards the path for more privacy. "Have you got a hardon yet?" he asked.

"Yes, Daddy."

"Whack it off onto the phone. I want to hear it splat."

"Oh, tell me how much you like my dick, Daddy. Tell me where you want me to put it! Tell me quick!" Then there was "Splat!" and "Was that okay, Daddy? What are you going to do for me?"

Joe had to sit down on the sand and hope that his stomach and his knees concealed his erection. "Oh, you'll have to wait for that. I had to sit down. My dick is so hard. They'll arrest me on this beach if I stand up. I may have to lie on my stomach."

"I like you on your stomach, Daddy."

"We'll talk later tonight, honey. I love you.

* * *

Joe didn't mind his solitude on the beach, and it wasn't always solitude. On the next day, Sunday, again at Haulover when Tom was off
on a walk, Jason, an old trick of Joe's from twenty-five years before,
spotted him. Jason now had a colossus of a boyfriend, like a polar
bear, fatter and whiter than Joe. Joe was willing to accept that he
needed to lose 20 pounds or so, but the evolution of Jason's tastes
into a full-blown "chubby chaser" made Joe worry whenever Jason
told him how good he looked.

Jason could talk and, although not Catholic or Irish, through his
romantic interests he was privy to Boston clerical and political gossip. So, Joe found out that the President of the Senate (whose duty
it would have been to call the Constitutional Convention of all Massachusetts legislators and preside over them while the Anti-Same-
Sex Marriage Constitutional Amendment was being considered for
the second time) had resigned to make more money as a lobbyist.
A few months before, that Senate President, with support from the
Globe and other straight liberals, had allowed an "up and down
vote" on the Anti-Same-Sex Marriage Amendment. Worse yet, the
Senate President, who used to be counted as a supporter of Gay
Rights, had voted with the "Antis," and they had won.

Jason reported that the new Senate President, the turncoat's
successor, the first woman ever to have the job, was more con-
genial to same-sex marriage. However, within hours of her taking
office, the newspapers quoted her as saying that she would not
propose a "procedural motion" (something less than an up and
down vote on the merits of the amendment) for a vote to recess
the proceedings when she decided to call the Constitutional Convention for its second vote on the subject. Such a "procedural motion," which would kill the amendment if passed, only required the
vote of a majority of the 200 legislators to pass.

Her statement, Joe noted to himself, did not mean that other legislators could not make such a motion. Joe did not tell Jason this because he was not sure of the intricacies of legislative procedure and because he did not want Jason to quote him, as he certainly would, complete with Joe's judicial title. Jason did not protect his sources.

If the "Antis" won again at the second Constitutional Convention, the proposed Anti-Same-Sex Marriage Constitutional Amendment would go to the voters. It was feared by Joe, and a lot of other people, that gay marriage would be killed by the general electorate. If that fear was true, a vote against the Anti-Same-Sex Marriage Amendment at the Constitutional Convention would require legislators to be ahead of their constituents, to be statesmen. That was not always an easy thing for politicians.

Jason, of course, had his own ideas about all this maneuvering; he so rarely stopped talking himself that Joe was not given the opportunity to respond. Finally Joe said, "I'm very warm. I have to go in the water. Would you like to go in the water, Jason?" Joe expected Jason to decline, but he followed Joe right down to the water's edge, still talking, now about the purge of gay priests in a Western Massachusetts Diocese. Fortunately, for Joe, a short chubby, as wide as he was tall, passed in front of them, walking in a few feet of water. Jason was gone like a shot, without even a goodbye to Joe.

Joe dove in the water and swam out to the sandbar.

The Florida clouds above Joe were magnificent, big puff balls floating across the sky and moving fast onshore in the direction opposite to Joe's swim. At first they were white with lavender bottoms, and they were pretty—sporadic interruptions in the beautiful blue sky: but in the distance, near the horizon, they became thicker and threateningly gray. There were about a dozen people on the sandbar. A couple of small boats had dropped anchor for the occupants to join in the frolicking, or perhaps just to look at the naked men gamboling in the surf.

The clouds moved faster towards the beach and soon covered the midafternoon sun. People on the beach felt a few raindrops, began to put their clothes on and hurriedly left. Most of the sandbarites swam back to shore, except for Joe and a few others, one of whom was a tall, handsome, light-skinned, Latino man about 35. He did not seem to be with any of the other people at the sandbar. As the others were moving away he appeared panicked. He was walking through the water towards shore, apparently unaware of the deep hollow between the sandbar and the beach.

He must have walked out here when he could, when the tide was lower, Joe thought. *I'll keep an eye on him.*

Of course, the man walked over his head into the water. And he screamed. Joe swam towards him. He grabbed him from the back around the chest and told him softly, "Don't worry! I have you. I know what I'm doing." Joe wasn't so sure. Fifty years before he had been certified as a lifeguard, but he had not updated any of the training since. Joe hoped he was remembering correctly and that he wouldn't kill the man. With his left arm around the man's chest Joe paddled with his right arm and hand.

As Joe pulled the man into shore the man looked back at Joe with fright, but he seemed to be mollified by Joe's soft cooings. He became more confident than Joe was.

Where the hell is the lifeguard? Joe thought. *Is he as big a sissy as these "silly billies" on the beach? I thought all these lifeguards were straight, tough guys. Did he run home when the rain came?*

Someone on the beach, it looked like Tom Murphy, was yelling and pointing to Joe and his charge, and then waving up to the lifeguard station, as if trying to direct the lifeguard to Joe in the water. Soon the lifeguard came into the water with his float. By the time he arrived Joe and the Latino man were about twenty feet from shore and able to touch the ground with their feet.

Still behind the Latino man, Joe moved his right hand down the man's body not wanting to make him panic by letting him go too quickly. The man's chest was smooth, as was his hard stomach. For no particular reason Joe's hand was drawn lower. The Latino man had a hardon, a big hardon!

And here is the lifeguard just when he's no longer needed, Joe thought. Perhaps he would rescue Joe, who was now very excited himself by the whole event.

"Are you guys alright? Take it easy! Walk slowly up to shore," the lifeguard said. The Latino man said nothing. Joe moved his right hand back up around the man's waist and put his left hand on his shoulder. As they moved forward there was a little bank, about three feet high, which had to be ascended before the shore could be reached. The three of them paused before it. The lifeguard was in front on the bank facing Joe and the Latino man, holding the man's extended left hand. Joe worried about what was going to happen once the Latino man pulled himself straight up and showed his glory to the lifeguard and the few people now remaining on the beach, one of whom he could now clearly see was Tom.

The stiffie had deflated however. Once on land both Joe and the Latino man lay flat on their backs on the sand. Smart Tom had come down to the shore with towels and he threw them over both Joe and the Latino man. The lifeguard knelt down and began talking to the man in English. The man just looked at the lifeguard blankly.

Tom Murphy knelt down and talked to the man in Spanish. *"Como esta? Esta seguro? Puede respirar?* How are you? Are you sure? Can you breathe?"

The man replied. *"Gracias a Dios y a este maduro que guardo mi vida!* Thanks be to God and to this old man who saved my life!" and he looked over at Joe lovingly. *"No se nadar. Gracias a Dios! Usted es un santo!* I don't know how to swim. Thanks be to God! You are a saint!" Again he looked at Joe. Then he rolled over and embraced Joe, kissing Joe all over his face.

"Alright guys, enough of that gay stuff. I just have to make sure that you're okay. Stop fooling around! I have to get back to work. There are other people here who need help," the lifeguard said as he got up, and walked away to climb back up onto his stand.

Joe, who was too exhausted to think in Spanish, said to Tom, who continued to kneel down next to the man, "Ask him where his towel is. Does he have any friends here? Ask him what his name is?"

Tom talked to the man, then looked up at Joe and said, "His name is Carlos. He's alone. He came off one of the speedboats that was docked on the sandbar. They left him here."

"They left him here naked? With no money, and no identification and no clothes? What is he going to do? Does he know anyone on the beach?"

Tom dutifully inquired some more, then looked up at Joe and said, "He sailed from Cuba six days ago in a boat with some other people, his brother and his brother's wife and four people from his town. They were met in the middle of last night by two speedboats. Carlos doesn't know where—somewhere out there," and Tom gestured to the sea. "Carlos got on one of the speedboats with his brother and his brother's wife. The men on the speedboat were kind. They fed them. They told the three of them to get off at the sandbar, but Carlos' sister-in-law refused to take off her clothes. She had a dress on. His brother refused as well.

"The men in the boat said they would take them somewhere else, but it would be more dangerous. They might get caught. He said this was the best place to jump. It was very unexpected. Carlos decided to leave right here. He took off his shorts and jumped in at the sandbar. He thought that naked he could blend in. He really hadn't thought much further than that. He asked if we could help him."

Joe said, "Well, he's touched ground. They have to let him stay, if he's really Cuban. That's the law!" Joe added, "Does he have any relatives here, in Miami, in Florida, in the States? How can he prove anything about himself? How can he even prove that he's Cuban? They might decide he's from the Dominican Republic, or that he's a Haitian who can speak Spanish. Those poor bastards get sent back."

"Slow down, Joe. Let's decide what we can do right now. This poor bastard is naked. Have we got any clothes to give him? He'd fall out of our shorts. We're too, uh…husky, but there must be an extra tee shirt in the beach bag. We could always wrap him in a towel but he'd look pretty funny walking down A1A in a towel. Do we have some extra flip-flops? Maybe one of those fleeing fairies left some clothes behind. We could ask the lifeguards, but they'd call the police, those bastards." Tom stood up and looked around the beach for clothes.

He didn't see any, but he did see Jean Louis, the well-tanned, hairy French-Canadian, who came to Haulover every day in his RMV with a handicapped placard, which let him avoid the parking fee. Despite whatever merited the placard, Jean Louis was in better shape than most of the men on the beach. Jean Louis was a great scavenger; he walked up and down the beach four or five times a day, checking the trash bins for refundable cans, beach chairs, and whatever else might be useful.

Tom, who was more gregarious than Joe, had chatted Jean Louis up on occasion. Tom stood up and approached Jean Louis next to a trash barrel up at the edge of the path. Joe could see them talking and then Jean Louis walked away. Tom remained by the barrel. Joe tried to talk to the still prostrate Carlos on the sand but his Spanish failed him. All he could say that was understood was, "*Calmate, Calmate!* Relax! Relax."

Carlos looked up at Joe with a wan smile, knowing that his fate was, at least for the time being, in Tom and Joe's hands. Joe wanted to pat Carlos on the forehead paternally but Joe was reluctant thinking such a public display of affection would bring the lifeguard's wrath down on them again.

Jean Louis soon returned to Tom with a Publix supermarket plastic bag that appeared pretty full. Tom smiled, shook Jean Louis' hand and returned to Joe and Tom's towel and umbrella, which was about twenty feet away from Carlos and Joe, who were still down by the water.

Joe realized that Tom knew that it would look peculiar for anyone to put on clothes at the edge of the shore. Joe stood up and gestured to Carlos to do the same. Carlos wrapped his midsection in the beach towel. Joe carried his towel. Carlos let the towel fall to his waist, to below his waist actually, so it hung sexily on his narrow hips, just below his hard, smooth stomach, as if the towel were being held up by the bulge in front and the rise of his round butt in back.

Joe followed Carlos up to their umbrella on the beach, marveling at the beauty of the movement of Carlos' ass, almost half of which showed above the tightly wrapped towel. *He's wearing the towel at "the pubic symphasis,"* Joe remembered bizarrely from a figure drawing class he had taken in Provincetown years before. Joe also admired Carlos' muscular back, which he'd already felt against his own chest as he brought Carlos in from the seductive, false security of the sandbar to the safety of the beach.

Tom laid out the booty from Jean Louis on a beach blanket. There were a pair of faded red gym shorts, a white sleeveless undershirt, flip-flops, clean, and almost new Calvin Klein briefs, and even a pair of old jeans, but who could tell their age, so myriad and diverse were blue jeans these days. The new ones are sold more tattered than the old ones.

Carlos dressed in the shorts and the sleeveless tee shirt. He did not put on the underwear, Joe noted. He put the other clothes in the bag and held it. He put on the flip-flops, which were just large enough for his big feet. He smiled at Tom and Joe.

"What do we do now? Where are we going to take him?" Joe asked. "There must be a refugee center on *Calle Ocho* in little Havana in Miami. Do we just drop him off there and hope for the best?"

"What do you want to do with him, Joe?" Tom said with just the hint of a lascivious smile. "We could bring him back to the Fig Leaf. They let you have tricks overnight just so long as they don't stay for days. I have a date, so I can sleep over in Miami. Are you sure that you'll feel safe alone with Carlos? How's your Spanish? How will you communicate?"

Then Tom laughed bawdily, "Ha, ha, ha, ha! Or do you need me to translate the international language of love for you. It's mostly sign language, done with your hands, anyway. I'm sure you can do it, your Honor. We didn't bring our passports and I can take your ATM card, so there'll be little to steal except your baggy Brooks Brothers boxer bloomers and a couple of shirts. I think you ought to go for it. He certainly looks like he could give you a good time. Ha,ha,ha,ha!"

"Stop fucking around, Tom, and let me think. I'm not comfortable leaving him here, and we ought to check on what's happening for refugees in Miami. We could call Maria. She knows everything Cuban, or knows people who do. Doesn't she throw that Catholic Charities party for Cuban relief in Cambridge every year with those other high powered Cubanas?"

Joe added, "It's the best party in town in the summer. I know she's mad at me but I still have her cell phone number. Perhaps you can talk to her. She's always liked you, Tom. And you're on the Board of Boston's Catholic Charities. You raise more money than anyone for them, and most of it from your Jewish clients. Her husband likes you even more than she does. You've stood up for him in the press a few times. Surely she'd want to help. In spite of her present fame and fortune, she used to be an old leftie."

Tom said, "That's a good idea, Joe, and our trying to do this right will let you get to know Carlos better. Ha, ha, ha, ha! I'll call Maria from the room at the Fig Leaf. I'll also have Cuban Sammy, the manager of the Fig Leaf, check on you hourly tonight. He owes me too. I've sent him four separate reservations for December already." Tom added, "Let's go then."

"Perhaps we ought to tell Carlos what we're doing, what our plan is. He's apt to think we're white slave traders."

"He's a little tawny for the white slave trade, Joe. But I'll tell him what our plan is." Tom talked in Spanish to Carlos, who now looked like a gym rat in the red shorts and white muscle undershirt.

Carlos looked serious as Tom spoke and said, "*Es rasonable*. It's reasonable," every once in a while in his deep voice. He smiled at Joe whenever Joe's name came up. It seemed that Carlos thought it was a good idea to spend the night with Joe as well. That made Joe happy, albeit nervous.

Of course, Joe could not remain content. It was not his nature. He had to think of all possible, future problems. When he began to say, "But, Tom, what if...."

Tom said, "With all due respect to your somewhat lofty position, Joe, shut the fuck up. Stop looking a gift horse, and horse this man is if you saw his cock, in the mouth. Unless of course, you're planning to put something precious, like your pink and white Irish dick, in it."

That stopped Joe for a while. This experience could satisfy many things besides his lust, like his deep-rooted Catholic sense of charity. Doing good things for mixed motives was not theologically unsound, Thomas Aquinas, or was it Saint Jerome, was supposed to have written. This could be a test.

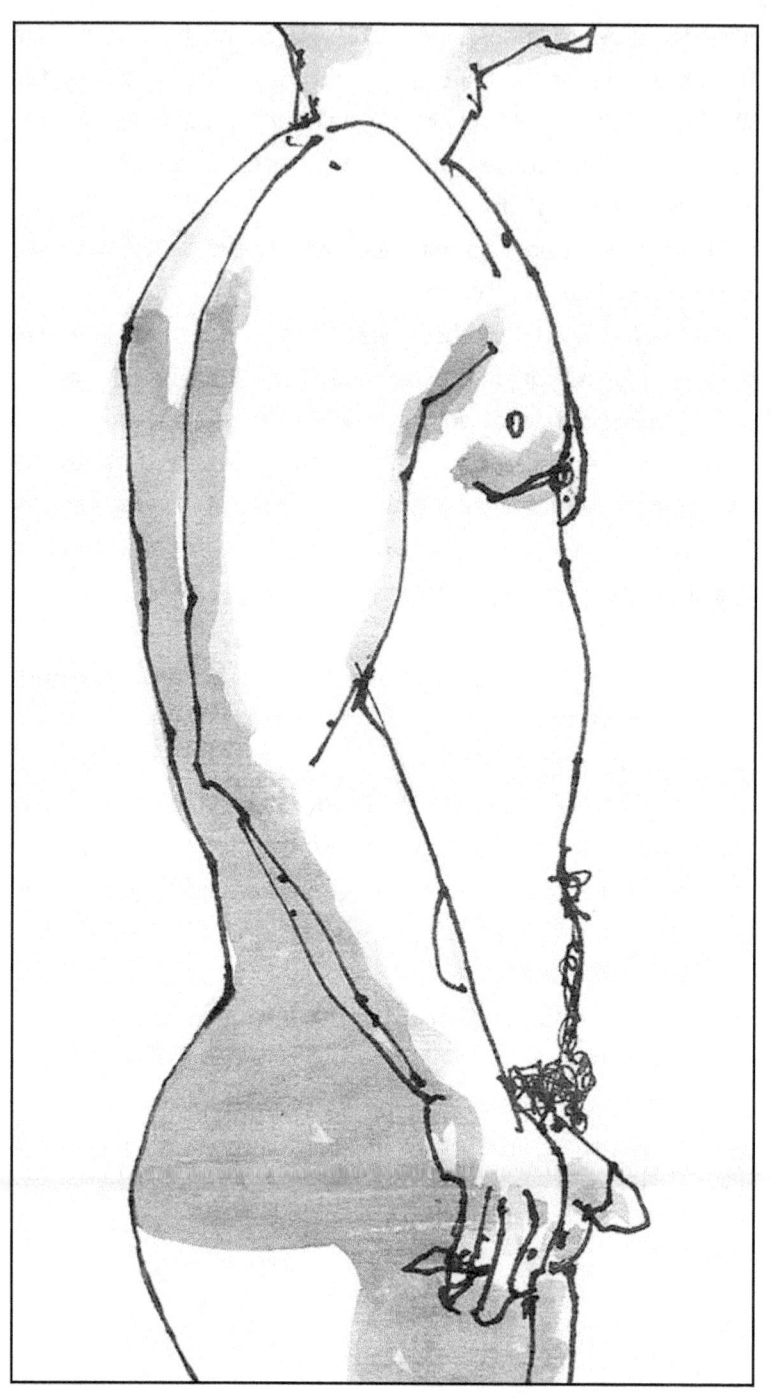

It's Not So Safe Here Either

The three of them, Tom, Carlos and Joe, walked back through the tunnel under A1A to the car. Carlos stared in wonder at the new models of cars in the parking lot. He lit up when they climbed into the silver gray Chrysler Sebring convertible that Joe and Tom had rented. Carlos couldn't decide whether to sit in front or back. Finally Tom directed him to the back seat after Tom put the top down. Joe gave Carlos his Red Sox hat to wear against the sun. Carlos really looked assimilated now. It was that easy.

Mucha ropa! Joe remembered that years before, at the same *Quince de Septiembre* event in Mexico City where he saw Dolores del Rio, some of the beautifully dressed young women had wandered out onto the balconies overlooking the Zocalo, the main square of Mexico City. The people below, the *campesinos*, the *hoi polloi*, had shouted up at them, "*Mucha ropa! Mucha ropa!* Lots of clothes! Lots of clothes!" They meant that there was little difference between those rich people up on the balconies and them, the poor people below except lots of clothes. At the time it both frightened and pleased Joe. It was so true and so revolutionary, but if the people below really revolted, Joe realized that he was in the National Palace with the rich people and wouldn't have a chance.

In less than one hour Carlos had been transformed from a naked Cuban washashore to a gay hottie. All it took was clothes—*mucha ropa.*

Carlos, however, was not content alone in the back seat. He asked Joe to join him. Tom said, "And what does that make me, the chauffeur? Oh well, always a bridesmaid, never a bride. Joe, go in the back seat. Carlos wants you."

Joe obliged after fishing out another Red Sox hat, this one pink. Joe had bought it in Boston as a joke. They drove up A1A until Wolfie's Rascal House when Tom turned around and said, "I'm starved and I bet Carlos, the poor bastard, hasn't had anything to eat. Let's go to Wolfie's," and with that declaration Tom swerved left into the Rascal House lot.

Inside the restaurant, Carlos was all eyes. It was still early enough for the early bird specials and all the old birds were there—the halt and the lame, the rich and the poor, the old and the older.

There were shades of blonde that God had never contemplated and more than a few redheads—Titian to Lucille Ball. Every third woman had a smile fixed in place by a facelift and most of them wore their jewels. There were lots of small bald old men in white shoes and white belts trying to keep their wives under control. Many old women came with other women, sometimes with their Haitian nursemaids. Some were with grandchildren, who they proudly showed off to their neighbors while the kids, much too cosmopolitan for grandma, buried their heads in the menu.

There were some booths off to the left, but most people sat at the counter that wove in and out and all around like a small intestine.

They were seated within minutes by a giant black woman, who had modeled her couture on the customers. She had a blonde bouffant too, and she was wearing hot pink Capri pants, and a red scooped neck top, all of which was balanced on very high stiletto heels. It was only 4:30 in the afternoon, mind you.

Carlos was agog, especially at the hostess, who was returning the favor. She spoke a little Spanish and gave Carlos a Spanish menu, with a big smile and a lingering pat on his sinewy shoulder. Tom soon had to go to the men's room. Joe was left alone and silent with Carlos, who looked at the food with lust—like the hostess had looked at him in fact.

When Tom returned, Carlos asked him, "*Donde fuiste?* Where did you go?"

"*Yo fui al bano. Esta atras y a la izquierda. Quieres que te muestre donde esta?* I went to the bathroom. It's in back and then to the left. Do you want me to show you where it is."

"*Si, por favor.* Yes, please."

"Joe, show Carlos where the men's room is. He's got to go."

"*Antes de ir que quieres comer, Carlos?* Before you go what do you want to eat, Carlos?" Joe said.

"*El bistec, por favor.* The steak, please."

Tom said, "A good choice. If I'd been on a boat in the open sea for six days, I'd want a steak too. This is probably not the best place for a steak, but it'll probably beat whatever they're serving to the homefolks in Havana."

Joe walked to the men's room and decided that he'd look foolish standing outside the door like a pervert, so he went in and stood at the urinal next to Carlos. Joe didn't dare look at Carlos although he really wanted too, but he thought that he could feel Carlos looking at him. So he tried to stand up straighter and thrust his pelvis forward in the hopes that his endowment would appear larger—the standard male response.

After he had done all that, yet still unable to pee, Joe felt a hand on his bum. Joe looked to his left but there was nobody there. He looked to his right and Carlos was smiling as he played with his own big appendage. Joe worried that someone might come in, but he also was gratified that he now knew with some certainty that he wouldn't get a fist in his face if he laid a hand on Carlos later in the room in Fort Lauderdale. Joe smiled too, zipped up his pants and they both returned to the counter and Tom.

Tom explained that he had ordered Carlos a steak, a salad and a baked potato with sour cream and butter, all in all a very American meal. He also told Carlos that he would call their friend, Maria in Boston, to find out how to get him to Cuban Refugee Assistance. Tom added that Carlos couldn't be the first Cuban refugee to arrive on shore without any documents. He then asked Carlos if he had any relatives in Miami or anywhere else in the United States.

Carlos replied that he thought he had cousins in Miami, but that he had two sisters in Union, New Jersey.

"Could you give their names and addresses to the social worker who interviewed you?" Tom asked.

Carlos thought he remembered their addresses, but it was usually his mother who wrote to them. She died last year, he added as he lowered his eyes sadly. Joe put his hand on Carlos' knee in consolation.

The brassy waitress, well into her fifties with a long, stringy, half-dyed blonde pony tail, and a name tag that read "Rita" in script that was supposed to look like handwriting, said in her Seagrams and Chesterfields voice, "Okay boys, keep it straight in here. You don't want to give these *alterkackers* a heart attack. One of my husbands was gay, but not everybody understands you boys like I do. Half the men in this place, customers and help, are *fagelas* too, but they're very nervous. No P.D.O.A.s, public displays of affection.

"What're you having, Whitey?" she asked nodding to Joe. "I got the other two orders." She had her pad and pencil at the ready.

Joe was a little taken aback, partly at being caught showing his affection to Carlos, and partly because he was called "Whitey," the name of Boston's most famous gangster, James "Whitey" Bulger, who had been on the lam for a while and was on the FBI's most wanted list along with Osama Bin Laden. *Of course, it could have been just because I have white hair,* Joe then thought, as his embarrassment diminished.

"I'll have the #10, the Nova Scotia Smoked Salmon special with lettuce, tomato and onion, and a toasted raisin bagel with chive cream cheese, please."

"A raisin bagel with Lox? You're a strange one, Whitey! Where're you guys from? Tipperary?" Rita said.

"Boston," said Tom with a laugh. "It's the next parish over."

"Why aren't you at Cape Cod, then? With Patti Page, 'The sand dunes and salty air,' cranberry juice and vodka?" Rita added as she walked away.

"*No me es simpatica la camarera.* I don't like the waitress," Carlos said. "*Que dijo ella?* What did she say?" asked Carlos.

Tom told Carlos that the waitress was making a joke about how white he and Joe looked and Joe's choice of food, which was a mixture of Jewish, Irish and God knows what.

As the food arrived Joe looked up. To his surprise and to his right, he saw Maureen Randozza and JoJo marching right at them. Joe said to Tom *sotto voce,* in an Irish whisper, "Carlos is yours, if anyone asks."

Carlos looked up from his steak and baked potato at the mention of his name. Tom looked at Joe and then where Joe was looking. Maureen had a big smile on her face. JoJo was her usual hip-hop dour self—showing no emotion, unless boredom is an emotion. Maureen was wearing a very femmy, dotted Swiss matching pants and blouse set and flip-flops with gold bindings. JoJo was in a warm weather version of her usual outfit—a two-toned grey man's seersucker suit, white shirt—no tie this time, it must be a concession to the heat—a straw porkpie hat and black and white saddle shoes with no socks.

"Well, what do we have here?" Rita said. "I can understand you guys. I like men too. But these lezzies I don't get." The waitress paused, and then added, "There's nothing there for me."

Maureen plunked down right next to Tom. "Howyadoin? Fancy meeting you here. What's up?'

"What are you doing here?" Joe asked. "Isn't it a women's weekend in Provincetown?"

"Yeah, but they're baby dykes, we're grown women, in case you haven't noticed. We're down to play golf. There's kind of a mini Dinah Shore Classic up in Lauderdale. JoJo's got a chance to win it," Maureen said. JoJo as usual said nothing but she stood up in the aisle and simulated her putting stroke. And she did smile, just a bit, which was a first in Joe and Tom's experience.

"What'll you girls have?" the waitress asked.

"Oh, give us a minute, darlin'. We haven't even had a chance to look at the menu. I have to kiss my almost uncle first." With that Maureen got up and passed behind Tom and Carlos to kiss Joe.

"Who's your Latino pal?" Maureen said to Joe nodding at Carlos.

"Oh, he's Tom's pal, Carlos," Joe said.

Tom jumped in and in Spanish and English, quite a feat, introduced Maureen and JoJo to Carlos.

"Maureen and JoJo, this is my friend Carlos. *Carlos, quiero presentarle a mis amigas, Maureen and JoJo.* Carlos, I want to introduce you to my friends, Maureen and JoJo."

"Hey Tom, I didn't know you were bilingual," Maureen said. "You could live in East Boston these days. Is Carlos your boyfriend? He's kind of cute in a rough, primitive way. I thought you liked them little and soft, like girly boys."

"There's a lot of misinformation out there, Maureen. Speaking of which, is there anything new on the Same-Sex Marriage front?" Tom asked.

"Well, it's very slow. The two Democratic candidates for the old Senate President's seat are with us, one more than the other. The Republican is an unknown, but she's also Norwegian, so what are her chances for an ethnic vote, huh? If we win that seat, there's only seven more to go. And the Speaker and the new Senate President, who's a woman, you know, ought to be able to put some pressure on those seven. We have an all points search on 'Queen Control' and 'Dyke Dish' for anything gay about any of them. So far we've only come up with a couple of cousins. We do have some solidifying info about some of the legislators who are already with us, however. You'd be surprised what gay skeletons hide in people's closets. If we can keep the *Globe* liberals from turning on us again, from demanding an up and down vote, we'll probably make it," Maureen said.

By this time JoJo had ordered Roumanian Pastrami sandwiches on rye and cream sodas for both Maureen and herself. Rita, the waitress, brought them quickly. Joe caught JoJo giving a little wink to Rita, the waitress, while Maureen engaged in *repartee* with Tom. Rita, for all her heterosexual protestations, even smiled back. Maybe she spotted JoJo as a big tipper.

Maureen asked, "Do you think I ought to invite my grandmother to our wedding, Joe? You know her. She'll probably bring your Aunt Josie. They've become quite the pair. They'll fit in nicely. My grandmother will probably want me to wear a white mantilla. She's been saving one for me since I was born."

Joe said, "Well, Josie is very good on this subject. There are gay men and lesbians in our family too, besides me. Josie's favorite niece, also my favorite cousin, Lizzie, has had a partner for years. Josie would be all for the wedding. Ever since she met your grandmother, Josie has been up for a party of any kind. It all began with your Uncle Rocco's consecration as a bishop in Rome last Spring. I'm very grateful to your grandmother for including Josie," Joe added. "It's too bad that we couldn't get Bishop Rocco to cool down the Cardinal Archbishop of Boston and his Massachusetts cronies."

"Maybe we could get Uncle Dino to…how do you say, exert his influence with the clergy. He's got a few persuaders. Isn't that right, Joe?" Maureen laughed. JoJo even cracked a smile. Tom laughed too. During all this banter Carlos finished off his baked potato and Joe's French fries too. He had his fork aimed at Tom's salad until Tom moved it.

"Let the poor man eat," Maureen said. "He probably just got off the boat and hasn't had a decent meal in years. Where did you meet him anyway? Down at that nude beach where all the old farts and their gerontophile admirers go? My Uncle Dino told me about that place. We all like rice and beans, but not every day. Have some decency, Tom. Think of your starving ancestors back in Mayo, or wherever the poor things came from."

Jojo had finished more than half of her sandwich. Maybe she was afraid Carlos would steal it.

"We also got a little more info on that pretty boy legislator, Billy Meadows," Maureen added. "He used to go to Jim's Gym in the South End. Do you remember that place? It closed a couple of years ago. All the hottest men, gay or straight, worked out there. Uncle Dino went there for a bit. Even JoJo worked out there."

JoJo stopped chewing long enough to flex her left bicep for their approval.

Maureen continued, "Anyway, Billy Meadows used to parade around the locker room in his towel. He brought his own towel, powder blue from Bloomingdale's. He stood out because most of the paraders walked around without a towel. Billy never took the towel off, not even when he took the steam. There was no hanky panky at the gym, but he was seen making a few hook ups," Maureen added.

"Were they with anyone we know?" Tom Murphy asked as JoJo

finished her sandwich and started in on Maureen's. *Perhaps she and Carlos would eat their way to the middle of the counter*, Joe thought.

"Most of them were with other closet cases, but there was one guy he was seen giving his card to who we all know," Maureen said.

"And who might that be?" Tom asked.

"Angelo Bruno," Maureen said after a studied pause.

"Angelo?" Joe said. "My Angelo? He never told me about Billy Meadows. Besides, Angelo only likes older guys."

"Well, Billy is a little older. Angelo had to start somewhere. And I don't think that you were the first man Angelo had ever…met," Maureen said. "Did you tell Angelo about all your previous conquests—like—my Uncle Dino?"

Joe was silent. He didn't know what to say.

Sensing Joe's discomfort on this subject and to test the credibility of Maureen's news Tom Murphy asked, "Who gave you all this information?"

"Jim, the owner of Jim's gym; he's a good guy. We worked on some AIDS charities together. He's very generous. Not only did he give a lot of money, but also he gave free memberships to people with AIDS sent to him by the AIDS Action Committee. Billy Meadows tried to beat him on a membership special Jim was running for students. Billy was in law school but already had a great business developing land in East Bumfuck or wherever he came from. Jim let him have it after calling him a 'cheap bastard.'"

Maureen added, "Worse than that, Billy tried to keep up the student rate after he graduated. Jim blasted him in no uncertain terms. Jim threatened to bar Billy from membership, but he wasn't sure that he could do that legally and he didn't want to be tied up in the courts by some pain in the ass new lawyer like Billy. So, he let it go. Once Billy was in the Legislature Jim approached him about the Gay Rights Bill—you know, the one that would prohibit discrimination based on sexual orientation, the one Mike Dukakis signed.

Billy didn't want to touch it. He wouldn't commit. He was the same about AIDS funding. Jim hates hypocrites; he doesn't miss a trick, if you'll pardon the expression, and he doesn't forget.

"I talked to Jim on the phone just before we came down. It turns out that he and his partner, Alfredo, have a place in Fort Lauderdale. They go to that nude beach too. You've probably seen them. Jim is about 5'9", short hair, beautiful face, and a body of death. Alfredo is taller, Latin, thick black hair, big shoulders and an ass you could balance a martini on. He's a sweetheart."

"You could drop a quarter on Alfredo's ass and get two dimes and a nickel back," JoJo added between bites of Maureen's Pastrami sandwich. These were almost the first words Joe or Tom had ever heard JoJo speak.

"We're going to have dinner with Jim and Alfredo tonight," Maureen said. "Do you want to come and talk to Jim? I'm sure he'd do whatever he could. He's a great guy, and he's tough. He doesn't like bullshit and he's been very brave about Gay Rights for years. They like the sushi at some Asian restaurant in Fort Lauderdale. We're going to meet them there."

Tom said, "Well, obviously because of his position and the politics involved, Joe can't have any part in all this. What time are you meeting them?"

"Sushi at seven," said JoJo, who was now free again to speak having devoured her own Pastrami sandwich, half of Maureen's and most of the pickles on the counter.

* * *

Joe, Tom and Carlos went to the room at the Fig Leaf. Both Joe and Tom had forgotten that it was Carmen Miranda Night at the pool. There was a lot of "boom chicka, boom chicka, boom" music going on, and it was so loud that a nap was out of the question. Tom showered.

Joe and Carlos looked at each other sheepishly. Joe finally

wrapped himself in a towel and indicated to Carlos that he should do the same. They went outside to the pool, which was empty, although the bar at the end of it was filling up with men in variations of Carmen Miranda drag and the music was playing her greatest hits, as well as Celia Cruz and a few old Desi Arnaz tunes.

Tom came out of the room fully dressed, on his cellphone and said goodbye to Carlos and Joe. "I'll be back in the morning."

Joe dropped his towel on a *chaise longue* at the end of the pool furthest from the bar. He signaled to Carlos to do the same. Carlos seemed shy, which struck Joe as peculiar since Carlos had only a few hours before jumped naked from a speedboat at the Haulover Beach sandbar. Two of the Carmen Mirandas, as they sipped their fruit filled drinks, watched Joe and Carlos. Actually they were a September to May white couple from the South, Daughters of the Confederacy, who looked at every man darker than weak tea with lust and longing. *I wonder how William Faulkner would write about this*, Joe thought. *Leslie Fiedler couldn't even imagine this scenario.*

Finally, with his back to "Scarlett and Melanie", Carlos dropped the towel and climbed down into the water. The two admirers looked at each other, then took off their fruity headdresses and ruffled dresses, and slithered in at the other, the deeper end of the pool.

When Joe saw them paddling down the pool towards them he grabbed Carlos by the hand and led him again back to safety, up to the pool deck. Joe wrapped Carlos in the towel and pushed him back towards the room. Carlos kept looking back at the pool with what Joe thought was more than curiosity.

This doesn't look like it's going to be a good night, Joe thought. *I've rescued a sea monster.*

Once inside the room Joe didn't know what to do. He was stuck with Carlos for the night and Carlos was clearly frisky, to say the least. Joe decided that the next right thing would be to take a shower and he invited Carlos to go first. Carlos, once he understood Joe, declined, so Joe dropped his towel while under Carlos' burning gaze. Carlos dropped his towel as well and Joe got a good look at that which he had only felt before. Carlos was hung, uncut and hung. The chest, which was not defined in the way American gym bunnies are defined, was not hairy, but sinewy and sexy nevertheless.

Carlos smiled seductively. Joe hesitated, then said he had to go in the shower. Carlos lay down on his back on one of the two queen size beds. "*Yo te esperare*. I will wait for you," he said.

Joe was torn. Although there was no compact of fidelity between Joe and Angelo, Joe had been with nobody else since he and Angelo met. What Angelo did was Angelo's business, Joe said, but Joe didn't want to hear about it. Even the information that Angelo might have hooked up with Billy Meadows long before Joe and Angelo met was enough to make Joe jealous. Joe knew that he could turn this jealousy into a jump with Carlos. *Which led the other, the jealousy or the lust?* Joe pondered this as he washed himself down, not knowing what he'd do once out of the shower. He stayed in the shower a long time.

When he returned to the bedroom the problem was solved. Carlos was on the bed, surrounded on either side by the two guys from the pool. The younger looked up at Joe and said with a smile and a drawl, "We just came over to borrow a cup of sugar."

Carlos was leaning over, hugging the older guy, a man about Joe's age. The younger man got up from the bed and approached Joe. He looked much better out of his ruffled dress and Styrofoam fruit Carmen Miranda headdress, Joe decided. Although he was blond, not Joe's usual type, he was hairy across the chest and had a treasure trail of hair straight down to his fat cock. Before Joe could say, "Aye, yes or no," Blondie was on his knees in front of Joe sucking him off as he gripped Joe's ample ass. Joe had no choice, he told himself; his cock got hard involuntarily. Soon Joe was pumping his hard cock into Blondie's mouth while watching Carlos expertly turn over the older gent on the bed.

Joe said in English, and as best he could in Spanish, "The condoms are in the table drawer between the beds." The older guy, no novice he, still on his stomach, without even moving his head, reached over, opened the drawer with his left hand and pulled out a plastic baggie containing condoms and lube.

Carlos looked quizzical as he reared his upper body up off the old guy's back, but the older guy turned around under Carlos and pulled a condom and some lube out of the zip lock bag. Carlos leaned back and up on his knees. The older guy spit in his hand, rubbed it on Carlos' cock, squeezed a drop of lube out of the tube, put it on the head of Carlos' cock, opened the rubber packet with his teeth and then put that on Carlos, who marveled at the technique, as did Joe from the other side of the bed, still getting sucked off by the younger blond, who Joe had now decided was a cowboy, or at least a Wyoming sheepherder, Ennis Delmar perhaps.

The older guy squeezed some more lube onto his right index finger, arched his back and applied the lube "where the sun didn't shine." He slipped his legs out from under Carlos and rested them on Carlos' shoulders.

Carlos didn't need any more coaching. He was unusually affectionate, frequently leaning down to kiss the older man as he pumped. He also worked the old guy's cock. Soon the moans increased. "You got me! You got me, you bastard! Oh Jesus! Don't stop!" the old guy shouted.

Carlos didn't stop and soon he too began to moan, "*Ay, Yi Yi!*" then a long "*Ayyyyyyy,*" and Carlos collapsed onto the old man's chest. Joe began to moan as well. Ennis Delmar took his mouth off Joe's cock and Joe splat all over the sheepherder's hairy chest.

You Never Know Who You'll Run Into

On Monday morning while Carlos, the fame of whose endowment and sexual talents spread fast, cavorted in the pool with two husky white-haired farmers from South Dakota, Joe, from his room at the Fig Leaf, said into the telephone, "Angelo, I know that we have a kind of 'Don't ask. Don't tell' agreement not to talk about our other...our other romances, but I have a very important question to ask you. It's bigger than both of us. It's really important. Don't answer if you don't want to. I wouldn't ask if it weren't important. It just came up that you may have the key to the whole thing. But don't feel pressured to answer me," Joe added.

"Do you want to know if I fucked Billy Meadows?" Angelo said. "I just got off the phone with your pal Tom Murphy, who wasn't quite so delicate with my sensibilities, by the way. I'll tell you what I told Tom. Billy Meadows gave me his card at Jim's Gym about five years ago, and somehow he got my telephone number. I'm still listed in the phone book—even though I've been getting hangup calls recently, probably from some of the little darlings I teach. A couple of the girls have a crush. They mature faster than the boys, you know.

"Billy never laid a hand on me, nor I on him. You know me Joe—nobody under sixty, and always pink and white. That's what I like, Joe, not some Ken doll with a nose job. You're my ideal, Joe. Don't change a thing."

Joe was both relieved and disappointed with this news. He was relieved because he wanted to continue to think that he was the only one Angelo had ever made love to. Those others he didn't specifically know about didn't exist. And he was disappointed because the hard evidence, as it were, against Billy Meadows' gayness was weaker. Underneath the black robe and his proscribed detachment from political life Joe was still a campaigner and part of him wanted to be in the campaign for Gay Marriage and gather some more evidence that would influence Billy Meadows. Joe had turned over what he already knew about Billy—the shirtless clinch with Guido in the "Staff Only" room of Guido's Back Bay Grille—to Tom Murphy. Joe could not, and had not made any attempt to, control what Tom did with this information. Frankly, he suspected and hoped that somehow Tom had confronted Billy with it. But, he wasn't going to ask. It is with such Jesuitical distinctions that Joe felt he had to conduct his various lives—professional and gay.

Joe was also disappointed because if Angelo had had sex with Billy Meadows, even before Angelo had met Joe, in some distorted way that would justify Joe's most recent, still fresh blow job from Blondie, who he'd fantasized was Ennis Delmar, the shepherd from Wyoming, from *Brokeback Mountain*. That was how justification for adultery goes. That "A stiff prick has no conscience" is an astute observation, but it was not a satisfactory justification, as Bill Clinton and Eliot Spitzer had discovered. And Joe was looking for some justification for his not-so-minor part in the scene that had recently happened.

Joe told Angelo, "I'm glad to hear that. I care for you a lot. I'm happy that you won't have to be brought into this battle."

"Well, Tom still intends to confront Billy Meadows with the card he gave me. Billy wrote his personal cell number on the back. And Tom is going to tell Billy where he got it. So, I am in the battle, a bit," Angelo said.

"Oh, that's too bad."

"Look, don't you worry about this. Tom is right. You have to stay out of it. I understand," Angelo said. "You're a judge and can't do anything political. Now tell me about your day. Did you go to Haulover again? What happened? Who was there?"

Joe was caught completely off guard. How could he tell Angelo about the beach? He had never lied to Angelo. He may not have always told him everything, but he never lied. More important, what had Tom Murphy told Angelo already? The only way to avoid the truth would be to get off the phone.

Propitiously, just then there was a knock on the door.

Carrying the phone with him, Joe opened the door. It was Cuban Sammy, the manager.

Before Joe could say anything, and even though Joe was holding the phone in his hand, Cuban Sammy started, "Look! I got two things to tell you." Joe covered the speaker of the phone just in time. "Your Cuban pal is out in the pool causing a commotion. He's fucking everything in sight. I've got long-term lovers here and they're complaining. He's broken up three marriages already. He's like Spanish fly, for Christ's sake. We run a loose ship here, but he'll sink it. You gotta do something."

The manager shut up long enough for Joe to say to Angelo, "Honey, there's a crisis here and I have to deal with it. I'll call you back. Bye."

Cuban Sammy added, "The second thing is some guy named Harry Jones has been calling here looking for you. He won't leave a number. Do you know this guy? He sounds like a big fruit to me.

He makes me check the room to make sure you're not here. Why don't you have a cell phone like every other queen in this country?"

*   *   *

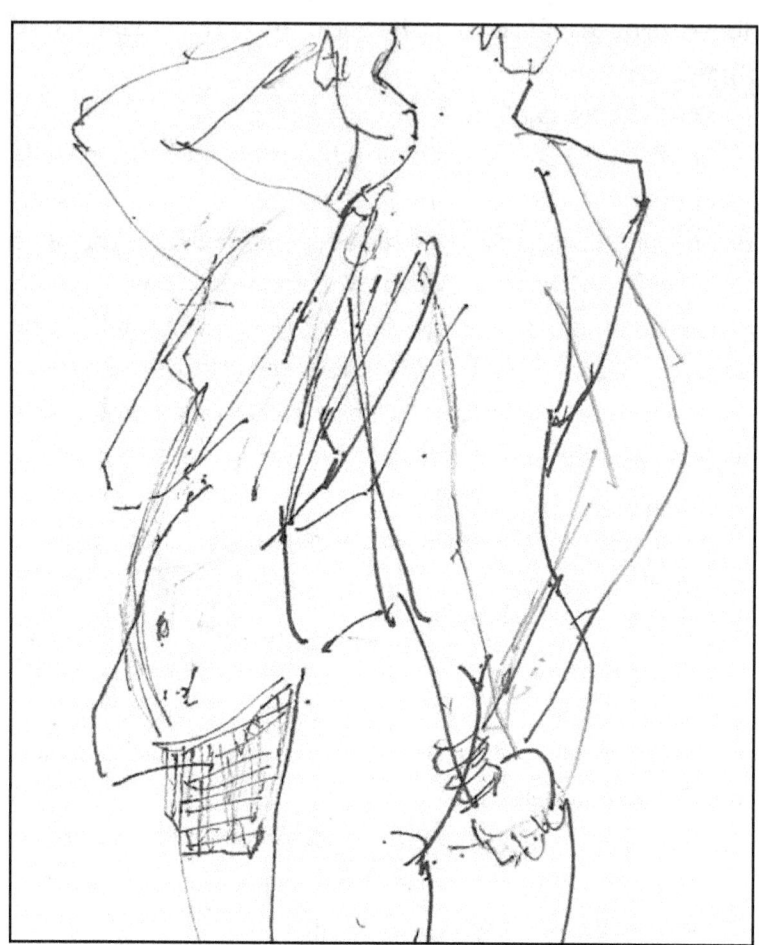

Cuban Sammy, the manager of the Fig Leaf, himself a first generation Cuban-American delivered the spent Carlos to the Cuban Refugee Assistance Center on *Calle Ocho* in Miami, after getting Carlos drunk and locking him in the pool house once Carlos passed out.

Joe and Tom passed their last day in Florida, on Sebastian Beach, the local clothed gay beach in Fort Lauderdale. They each realized that there had been too much excitement at Haulover the day before. Besides, they had to catch a 6:45 P.M. flight and sometimes there could be heavy traffic coming back from Haulover on Route 95. Sebastian Beach was three blocks up and four blocks south, a fifteen minute walk at most, from the Fig Leaf. Tom and Joe walked there carrying their umbrella and chairs.

"I really like Cesar," Tom said as they walked. Cesar was the young Argentine Tom had met on Haulover. "Do you think Guido would hire him at the Back Bay Grille? Would the other Argentine waiters get jealous? Is that place a closed shop—Argentines only? Cesar could begin as a busboy."

"I don't know, Tom," Joe said wearily. He really didn't want to participate in Tom's romantic manipulations. Maybe Joe was jealous. He didn't feel the need to manage Angelo's life like Tom was trying to manage Cesar's—and Angelo didn't need him to.

In spite of the 25 year age difference there was equality between Joe and Angelo. Part of it was money; Joe didn't have to provide for Angelo financially, either directly by giving him money, or indirectly by getting him work. Angelo had been very clever, and between investments and inheritances Angelo probably was worth more money than Joe, Beacon Street condominium and all.

Angelo's financial independence was a great relief. Joe knew that. Joe had gone out with men, beautiful men, who had no work or low paying jobs, and it was awkward for Joe—probably for them as well, but certainly for Joe. So, he really didn't want to revisit that awkwardness by getting involved in Tom's plans for Cesar. He didn't trust Tom's concern because he had heard it from Tom before about other young men with low paying or no jobs. Also Joe had had the same concern about some of his own relationships. The concern never balanced the inequality in his relationships. Joe believed that economic inequality in a relationship wasn't healthy for him. Maybe he was just cheap, or maybe he just wasn't rich enough so that the inequality wouldn't matter.

Tom was different. Tom certainly had enough money to keep a partner while Joe, realistically or not, had always thought that poverty was lurking just around the corner. In his head Joe couldn't overcome the financial gap between himself and those who would be supported by him. Maybe Tom could. After all, Tom earned three times as much as Joe. Millions of straight men supported a wife. Why was it wrong for a gay man, to wit, Tom, to support a spouse?

With Angelo, Joe followed his friend Arianna's advice. He was generous; Angelo was equally, if not more, generous. Their mutual generosity did not only concern itself with money. Joe, being in his mid-sixties, was not as horny as Angelo, but he usually said, "Yes," when he would rather have gone to sleep. Fortunately, once started, Joe could still deliver. He worried how many more years that would last, however. Joe did not decline sex often, but Angelo took it graciously when Joe did.

Angelo must have kept a running inventory of Joe's household supplies as well. He loved to shop—COSTCO was his favorite store--- and he often returned from his shopping excursions with bales of paper towels, dozens of sponges, computer paper, a new shirt, the latest squeegee mop, and most recently with a new Hewlett/Packard printer for Joe's computer.

Angelo's virtues and Joe's good fortune ran through Joe's mind as they approached the Sebastian Street Beach. Joe thought silence was the best response to Tom's manipulations, unless Tom asked him directly what he thought.

As soon as they sat down and after Tom set up the umbrella, Tom said, "Don't be such a sphinx. What do you think the chances are for Cesar and me?"

Joe paused and then said, "You can probably do it, Tom. I couldn't, but we're different people. I'm not a very good 'Sugar Daddy,' even though, like you, I look like one—the white hair, the husky build, the paternal demeanor. All that has nothing to do with the way I am. I want to be taken care of myself. I'm 66 years old and I'm looking for a 'daddy' myself—but he has to be younger. I don't go for these old farts. If I did, I'd have been in your pants years ago," Joe added, laughing gruffly, hoping that would stop Tom's further inquiry.

As Joe sat down in the beach chair he added, "That's why Angelo and I will work out. He's got the maturity and good sense. I'm too emotional and sensitive. Without being patronizing to me, he takes care of me. I'm not so good away from him—not so self reliant. I've learned a lot from him about how to live, more than I learned in any school. He's very practical. He doesn't always have to make a point. Life is to be lived, not won. And he works to live, not the opposite. It's an Italian thing, I'm convinced. That culture is about enjoying life, not enduring it. Look at the Italian attitude about food, for Christ's sake. Look at the food itself! It's delicious no matter where you go in Italy. And it's healthy besides! Can you beat that?!"

Tom hadn't expected all this, this discourse. Tom didn't know that it was prompted not only by his direct question, but also by Joe's *peccadillo* with the "sheepherder" of the previous night, *the details of which were not known to Tom—thank God!* thought Joe. Even though Tom would have been an understanding confessor concerning this subject, as he so often had been on other matters, Joe wasn't feeling like being confessional with Tom today.

Joe was grateful that he did not project his doubts about himself, his ideas about his ability to deal with someone like Cesar, onto Tom. It had taken Joe a long time to realize that he could not assume that everybody else was like him, and that his nature and experience were not universal. And Tom, without saying so, was grateful that Joe didn't throw cold water on his nascent romance. A man smitten by a handsome Argentine does not want to be diverted, even when he asks to be.

After the two of them had plopped into their high beach chairs (because they couldn't get out of the lower ones), while they each began to ponder what had been said and not said, just after this little dialogue, they heard a shout behind them.

"Go Red Sox!!!! Hey Tommy boy! Howya doin? Joeeeeeeey?" Who would it be but JoJo Danieli accompanied by the ever smiling Maureen Randozza!

"Those girls are like bad consciences, appearing every time we might stray," Tom said.

Maureen was almost in a little yellow polka-dotted bikini—just like the song. The dots were pink and so was her white skin going to be if she didn't get out of the sun soon, Joe thought. JoJo was wearing red, below-the-knee nylon boys' athletic shorts with a white stripe down the side, and a light blue tee shirt that said "Dykes on Bikes" on the back, and "Softballs" on the front. JoJo was holding a Frisbee, as well as two beach chairs and an umbrella which matched Maureen's bathing suit in contrasting pattern— yellow polka dots on a pink background. They were just about the only women on this section of the beach.

"Hey guys, can we sit with you?" JoJo asked, as she speared the polka-dotted umbrella into the sand next to them.

Joe knew that the women's presence would diminish the possibility of sex, the unspoken reason that brought Joe and Tom to Sebastian, the gay beach rather than Windamar or some other beach closer to their guest house but he was frankly weary of the sexual pursuit. Without even asking Tom, Joe said, "Sure, there's plenty of room."

JoJo already had the chairs set up to the side of Joe. Tom was making a face at Joe, but Joe was not paying him any attention. Tom turned his scowl into his book, a new biography of Robert Kennedy, one of his heroes.

Joe said, "How are you doing? How was dinner last night with your muscle pals?"

Maureen replied, "It was good. They're fun. The food was good. JoJo and Jim talk weight lifting together. Alfredo and I speak Spanish to each other and that pisses JoJo and Jim off. It's fun."

Tom looked up from his book and said to Maureen, "I'm sorry that I couldn't meet you last night. I had to go to Miami. It was important." It was Cesar. He then asked, "How about the vote? Can those guys do anything? Do you have any news from Boston?"

Tom's political itch needed scratching. He was feeling a little guilty about not joining the women the night before to plot with Jim and Alfredo. As soon as the political talk came up he overcame his pique at the two women destroying his cruisability on the beach, like that was really going to happen anyway.

Maureen said, "Jim knows some of the state reps including two who are on the other side. He went to Malden Catholic with them. He's going to call them. Both of the guys who want to win in the old Senate President's district are with us, for sure. So, that election is a wash. I talked to Boston this morning and we still need seven votes. They're saying that although the Constitutional Convention was scheduled for the end of May, they're going to adjourn until mid-June. We have some more time." Maureen paused and then said, "The rumor is that if we don't have the votes, there'll be a 'procedural vote' to kill the amendment. Some of the righteous lefties, the 'process liberals,' like the *Globe* columnists, have shut up about the necessity of an 'up and down' vote. I think they were shocked that at the first vote the bad guys won. The reality that this bit of bigotry might pass and that the liberals and their doctrinal purity would be responsible was too much even for them. I hope that the 'procedural' business doesn't have to happen but if that's the only way to beat these bastards, so be it," Maureen added.

"An interesting development is that some English guy has been financing Marriage Equality and donating to state rep candidates who are on the line. He seems very well informed. Nobody I know knows who he is. He's got a lot of dough and he's some kind of duke or something. They call him 'The Discount.' They keep him well under wraps. You can't blame him. If he was to become known, every *mickola* in the State House would be up his ass. He's given a ton of money and he keeps on giving. Somebody who knows what goes on in Massachusetts at the grass roots, from Pittsfield to Provincetown, is advising him, but nobody knows who that is either."

Tom smiled behind his fan.

"Why is that twink staring at us?" JoJo interjected.

"Where?" Tom asked.

"Down in front, near the water. The very white Irish looking kid in the blue Speedo with the straight dark hair next to the big black muscleman in white sunglasses—and not much else," JoJo said.

"He could be a cousin of mine on my mother's side," Maureen said.

"Or mine," said Tom.

"Me too," Joe said.

"Well, I don't know the little prick. What's he staring at us for? Hasn't he ever seen a dyke before? If he keeps it up, I'll go deck him," JoJo said.

Maureen said, "Now, Jo, don't be so sensitive. We aren't in Maverick Square surrounded by straight boys. Did you guys ever hear what JoJo did to some loudmouths in Maverick Square? They're cool on this beach, JoJo. I think that he's looking at Joe. Maybe he was one of his defendants—or one of his tricks. We'll soon know who he is. He just got up. He's walking up here. Now behave, JoJo."

The starer approached and, as Maureen predicted, he went straight for Joe. "Excuse me. I didn't mean to stare. Are you Judge Joseph Lyons?" the starer said, leaning down to get a better look at Joe.

"Who are you?" asked Maureen, the Amazon warrior at the ready to protect her charge.

"I'm Patrick Foley. I recognize the judge from his pictures," the young man said.

Then directing his remarks to Joe he added, "I sent you some correspondence a little while ago. I haven't had a reply. I don't mean to be impatient. I know you're very busy. However, seeing you here I thought I'd take the opportunity to introduce myself. It's not every day that you meet a hero on Sebastian beach. Forgive my intrusion."

"No, no. You're not an intrusion," Joe said. "These women, my friends, are very protective of me. I didn't expect to be recognized here. I do remember your package. It was quite…unique and… very beautifully presented, the red envelope, beautiful script, and the photo—which is unusual."

Tom and JoJo and Maureen were making faces at each other at this point, like *what brought on this bullshit? The kid is cute, but this is going too far. No fool like an old fool.*

"Well, I studied design when I lived in New York and I used to model, still do a little, and I was educated by the Benedictines, who are famous for their script. I hope you didn't think it was too much. I can get carried away sometimes," Patrick said, lowering his eyes.

Joe replied, "I came to Florida rather suddenly—almost on a whim—and I intended to offer you the internship when I returned to Boston. However, there's no reason I can't offer it to you here, on this lovely beach, right now. When would you like to start?"

"We're returning on Wednesday. I could start the next Monday. I think that'll be June 4th.

"Very good, I'll see you on Monday, June 4th ."

"I'm here with my partner, Rodney. He had a couple of days off from the State Police and I flew down with him." Patrick Foley looked back to the black colossus. "I just wanted to say 'hello,' but to be given the internship…Wow! Thank you, Judge Lyons. I look forward to working for you. I'd better get back to Rod." And then he ran off, without another salaam or bow.

Patrick Foley was smart to return to Rodney. As soon as Patrick had gone five steps away the neighboring queens had moved in. Rodney was entertaining quite a buzzing bevy. Patrick had something to break up indeed.

"Nice kid, that Patrick Foley," Joe said. "He sent me a very imaginative job application—albeit for a nonpaying internship. It had the lobby talking. Gigi Boland was dying to open the red envelope he sent it in, but Patrick had closed it with sealing wax and even she didn't know how to get around that. He'll add to the beauty of the lobby. I think he's smart too. He wrote a good memo about the demise of the 'gay assault' defense in homicide cases. I think he'll work out. I was about to hire him before we came down here. It's good that we saw him."

Tom said, "He certainly looks hotter than your usual law clerk geek. What's really hot is the trooper he's with. I saw him full frontal when they came on the beach. He's out of Tom of Finland. I'm surprised that Foley kid can still walk."

"Whaddaya mean?" JoJo said.

"Let's just say the Trooper is carrying a big gun," Tom answered back.

"How do you know who's doing what to whom?" JoJo piped in with an emphasis on the 'whom.'"The sweet little Irish boy may be bopping the big black man. Looks are deceiving, Tom. You'd never know I was the *femme*, would you?" She paused, laughed, and then added, "Well you never will know. We ain't talking. Girls like to fool you guys. And sex isn't everything. Maybe they have a spiritual relationship."

Tom was taken aback by JoJo's candor, and a little embarrassed to have brought the subject up at all. He was of an age where men didn't talk about sex in front of women. Part of that was because

Tom had always been a good little boy; another part was that the idea of having sex with a woman was just not in his realm of consciousness; and a third part was that he didn't want women, most particularly his mother or the nuns who taught him in grade school, to know that sex was on his mind most of the time.

Joe felt similarly, but his work sometimes forced him to talk and even write graphically about sex. How far in the orifice constituted "penetration" in the legal sense, for example? He too was surprised by the unusually loquacious JoJo.

The girls got up to get some drinks and to visit the ladies' room in the highrise behind them. "Do you want anything, anything we can bring back?" Maureen said. "We'll leave you to the studfest in front for a while. Don't embarrass yourselves. Put on the sunglasses and if it gets too exciting, jump in the cold water." She left laughing.

As soon as JoJo and Maureen were out of earshot, Tom said, "I'm glad to see that the law enforcement establishment has been successfully infiltrated by our team. That trooper is so hot. He must be six foot three, 215 pounds, a 30 inch waist, and he's hung like a stallion. I'd love to be fly on the wall when they're doing it. Do you think he wears his harness and jodhpurs and boots when they have sex? All that and probably no shirt! I'll bet Mr. Foley wears a pin stripe suit and a rep tie and the trooper takes it off him piece by piece with his teeth for a strip search. Wouldn't they like a daddy to supervise the arrest? Oh, could I direct that scene! That billy club would be everywhere!"

"Tom, get a hold of yourself! JoJo is probably right about men thinking with their dicks…although I hope not. The strange thing is that the memo Patrick Foley sent me about the demise of the 'Gay Assault Defense' is a big help to me in a case I just heard. I'm having a hard time persuading my colleagues to see it my way. Can I tell you the facts? They're all in the record and there's little dispute about them. It's the interpretation that's creating the problem."

"Sure, tell me the case," Tom rushed to say, trying to sound casual, even though he knew he was being let into the mysterious workings of appellate judicial decision making. It was a rare peek most lawyers never get.

Joe began, "After a night of drinking some guy wakes up in a strange bedroom with his pants down by his knees and his dick wet. He decides that the poor slob in the other bed must have given him a blow job against his will ("Against your will?" "No, against the refrigerator") and he starts beating the guy up. He hurt him badly, blinded him in one eye. He was arrested for assault and battery, mayhem in fact, and then claims he was raped. In spite of his defense, he was convicted and appealed.

"Would you believe it!?! A couple of my colleagues wanted to acquit him."

"Who were they?" Tom asked.

"You know I can't tell you that. I probably shouldn't be telling you anything. But you can keep a secret. I'm sure you've heard worse scandal than I'll tell you. They were the usual suspects. You figure it out. I really had to get graphic with these guys. 'First of all,' I said, 'We don't even know if he got a blow job. He may have whacked himself off, spilled something, or peed his pants. Then we have the whole issue of consent. The defendant was in a blackout. He didn't remember leaving the gay bar. He doesn't know what he agreed to. It's unlikely that he was dragged to the victim's apartment. The defendant is much bigger than the victim.' The victim was a tiny little thing, a bit of a Nell, if you want the truth. I said to them, to my brothers on the bench, 'The two of them weren't even on the same bed. There's more than enough reasonable doubt about his defense, if you can even deign to call it that. The jury didn't believe the defendant, who was pretty repulsive, even cleaned up and dressed up. That was that. The jury may have thought he had some kind of 'buyers regret' when he woke up wet, but that doesn't permit him to beat the bajeezus out of the victim. Get a grip, guys, and guys they were on my Court who believed the bullying bastard. The women judges saw right through the defense, thank God."

"I painfully explained to them, what should have been obvious, that 'wetness on a penis' could be a lot of things other than saliva or sperm. The defendant could have peed his pants and forgotten to zip up. He could have spilled his beer. Just because the victim was known to be gay didn't mean that he was after every man who crossed his path. Some straight men, particularly the unattractive ones, like these two, my brothers on the bench, think that every gay man is after them. You know that type. Remember that pious fraud, the professional Catholic who used to be a judge, the altar boy at the Latin mass in the South End, the one who talked about 'fairies' in his moonlighting class at Norfolk Law School, the jerk who stopped talking to you when he found out you're gay. Billy Volponi, the Hedda Hopper of the Courthouse says he's obsessed with the ever increasing number of gay judges. He goes apoplectic when a new one is appointed and talks about them all the time when Billy and his butchy boys have lunch with him in the State Office Building cafeteria. Get a grip!"

Tom nodded assent. He was in his professional listening mode now. Obviously Joe had wanted to spill this story for a while.

"The victim may not have testified as well as he could have because he was being abused all over again by the defendant's attorney. He was being asked about his sexuality, his sex life, what kind of men turned him on. The women judges on the panel knew that no judge today would let a female victim be cross examined that brutally. And my two male colleagues were going to let this bastard go. Thank God for the women!" Joe added a little louder.

"Right on, brother! Thank God for the women!" JoJo said, returning with her arms full of sodas and hot dogs. "I thought this one would be good for you, Tom," she said as she handed Tom an obscenely giant hot dog overflowing with everything on it, mustard, relish, onions and sauerkraut.

"You're a doll, JoJo, and reading my dirty mind. What did you bring for Joe?" Tom asked.

"Grilled ham and cheese on whole wheat with tomato and onion. He's not as frisky as you."

"I have tuna fish on rye, and a big pickle, of course. Miss Maureen Randozza is dieting. She bought a chef's salad, oil and vinegar, hold the ham. She'll be here in a minute. She's talking on the cell to her uncle—Dino, I think."

Maureen came rushing back, kicking sand on any number of muscle boys, leaving them to ponder their misogyny.

"Hey! Guess what! I just got off the phone with Boston. We're down to four votes that have to be changed! And it may be only three. One Boston state rep wants to go on some Commission and supposedly he'll be appointed before the next Constitutional Convention in June. His successor won't be elected until after. There are another three legislators who are waffling. They're all getting a lot of pressure from the party, the Democratic Party, both in Massachusetts and in Washington. Nancy Pelosi is even calling, they say. The reps don't have to vote against the amendment. All they have to do is not be at the State House that day."

"Me and my girls on bikes could think of some ways to accomplish that," JoJo said with a malicious grin. "We could slice some tires, for starters."

*　*　*

All of a sudden Joe wanted to be home, back in Boston. It had nothing to do with the Constitutional Amendment. He just wanted to be home. He was tired of this frivolity, this imitation of a life—of being on a gay beach surrounded by all the trivialities of gay life—cruising, desire, controlled lust, little bathing suits, shaved chests, big baskets. It really didn't interest him anymore. It hadn't interested him in a long time, he realized. This was not a way of life; it was a distraction. That's why he and Tom had come down in the first place—to be distracted—but it was time. It was over for Joe.

Joe wanted to be lying in bed with Angelo Bruno, running his fingers through Angelo's perfect chest hair, pinching his nipples, watching Angelo smile beatifically as he rapidly got a hardon. Angelo would smile as if the hardon were a gift from the universe, and as if Joe was its uniformed delivery man. Joe wanted Angelo to rub his head and call him "a nice Irish boy." And he wanted to feel Angelo on top of him, still smiling as if he were saying, "Isn't this the best fun anybody could ever have!?!"

Joe didn't want to have to worry about the Anti-Gay Marriage Amendment or any of the weighty legal issues that cropped up in his work—like why it wasn't mayhem if someone bit off your nose, but it was if he pulled out your eye. He didn't want to think about the human constructions, like the Law, that made life work in a reasonably civilized way.

Nor did Joe want to think about the silliness that "gay life" could be sometimes, like a couple of sixty somethings sitting on a beach looking over their bifocals at the young pumped-up studs passing and posing before them in their tiny, expensive bathing suits. He had no humor or patience right then for what had become the conventions of gay life for men. He just wanted what his father always said he wanted when Joe would ask him what he could give him for his birthday. "Love and affection," his father would say. Ironi-

cally these were two things that his father had a hard time giving—
or receiving.

Granted, some of this feeling was a function of Joe's age. Except
for a specialized few gerontophiles, more likely found at Haulover
than here on Sebastian Beach, he and Tom were out of the gay
game that was being played in front of them. Joe, at one time in his
life, had been very much in it. Back in his day, in his salad days, Joe
was the "Star of the Bars" for a bit—two weeks maybe. "You were
the "Numero of 1965," one wag had told him—in 1967.

Joe knew the power of being desired in gay life—he had been
a hottie for a brief while—but, of course, he had minimized it because he himself was usually desiring someone who wasn't interested in him. Occasionally, and even for periods of time, he connected, but there wasn't staying power to the romances. Most of
his old beaux remained his friends, even good friends, but until
now, until Angelo, none had stayed long as lovers.

Joe became very involved in promoting his career for a while
and he'd been successful. He was the first openly gay judge in Massachusetts—no mean feat. And once he was a judge, gay life in the
bars, on the beaches, in the dance clubs, at the Gay March in Boston
or Washington, was not open to him. That was O.K. for Joe most of
the time. Joe was in his late forties when he was made a judge and
at that time he was getting too old for most of that stuff anyway.
But every once in a while, he would get a glimpse of that life and for
a moment he wanted to be part of the carefree existence that gay
life seemed to be. Of course, it wasn't carefree. The cares were just
different from those he as an older man who was a judge had. They
were sillier—like "Am I too fat?" or "Will these jeans get me laid?" or
"How do I look dancing?" or "What is the latest song?" It was vapid
and Joe could smile at it, but at times he wanted to be silly like that.

Right then, right there, on the Sebastian Beach in Fort Lauderdale, sitting in the sun with his old friend Tom Murphy, in their high

chairs, listening to the latest Massachusetts gay political gossip, surrounded by some of the most beautiful gay men in America, maybe in the world, Joe wanted nothing but to be home in the arms of Angelo Bruno thinking only of what would be his next move, a hand to Angelo's crotch or lips to his left nipple. That desire hit him so hard he could taste it.

He'd stopped listening to the conversation beside him a while ago, so when Tom said, "What do you think, Joe?" Joe had no idea what Tom was talking about. The three of them, Tom, Maureen and JoJo, were staring at him, but he had no idea why.

Joe's Return:
The Hazards of Public Office

Joe and Tom arrived in Boston very late on Monday evening. Joe called his courthouse phone as soon as he got home. There was another call from Harry Jones but again no return telephone number. *If Harry really wants to talk to me, he should at least leave a number*, Joe thought. *This is just another silly call. The last time he wanted me to hire his partner's daughter as a law clerk.*

At home there was a lot of mail for such a short period of being away. One envelope was addressed in the same Palmer Method, Catholic School hand as the earlier "Somdomite" letter. This letter said, "Repent!! The time is nigh!" in red cutout letters pasted on a white 8 1/2″ x 11″ sheet of paper. The type of the cutout letters was Germanic Gothic, like motorcycle clubs use for the back of their leather jackets, and the letters were shiny, as if they had come from a magazine. This letter didn't alarm him like the first one had and neither bothered him like the letters from Dino of the previous year. *Who says 'nigh' these days?* was Joe's first thought.

The most recent of the piled-up newspapers reported that the vote on the Anti-Same-Sex Marriage amendment was down to three or four votes. The gay newspapers along with Marriage Equality were urging everyone to show up at the Statehouse for the vote. Although they didn't put it this way, their thought was that presumption (one of the cardinal sins; the other being despair) was responsible for the previous vote in January that resulted in 61 votes for the Anti-Gay Marriage Amendment, 11 more than needed.

Tales about legislators being bought out by the new Governor were rampant. There was even talk, from people who had no concept of the Constitutional Separation of Powers, that the Governor would postpone the vote. Constitutionally, and politically in Massachusetts at that time, the Governor had no say in this legislative prerogative. As is often the case, the people who might have known what was happening were not talking.

Joe was glad that he was not involved in gay politics any more; the tension among the players was nuts. But Joe did have to walk past the State House every morning on his way to work and his mind could not help but wander to the Anti-Same-Sex marriage Amendment vote, now scheduled for Thursday, June 14, 2007.

Angelo came over the night after Joe returned. They played another game of "football." Angelo seemed fond of being slapped on the bum by Joe the Coach as he was sent out to play. And Joe liked it when Angelo fell on the Bokhara while feigning being tackled. Angelo called for his coach to come help him up to his feet. Of course, Angelo did not get up on his feet even when pulled. He pulled the coach down on top of him and kissed him madly while pulling off the coach's hat, shirt and pants. Then he rolled Joe the coach over onto the rug, reached up to the sofa and grabbed some pillows, which he placed under Joe strategically, and gave Joe the touchdown he was really looking for.

This game went on for a while. They almost skipped dinner, but finally Angelo was spent after he took care of Joe a second time and they showered together.

"Where should we eat?" Joe said.

"I don't care—anything but Italian." Angelo said. "I visited my family a lot while you were away and I couldn't eat any more pasta."

"Let's go to Legal Seafood. The fish in Florida was terrible. They gloop everything up with a sauce. I just want to get schrod," Joe said.

"You just did, Mabel," Angelo said, referring to the old joke about the Ohio spinster who came to Boston and on her return to Akron told her friend that "in Boston I got schrod." Her friend said, "Oh Mabel, you and your Harvard accent!"

They decided to walk to the Legal Seafood Restaurant in Park Square. It was a nice night and the walk through the Public Garden would be idyllic, albeit a bit sticky in this humid heat. The flowers on the trees had gone by, but the trees were lush which combined with the ponds made the park smell like the countryside.

Outside of the clearly gay neighborhoods like the South End or Jamaica Plain it still was not common for same-sex couples to hold hands in Boston but Joe wanted to anyway. As they walked through the Public Garden Joe reached for Angelo's hand. Angelo held Joe's hand until they were approached by another couple coming the other way, a man and a woman, who were themselves holding hands. The straight couple felt no need to let loose their grip upon seeing Joe and Angelo but Angelo dropped Joe's hand as soon as the straight couple was in eye's view.

Joe then realized how important Thursday's vote would be. There it was in graphic display—the whole Equal Protection argument! He and Angelo did not feel entitled to show even the most innocent sign of affection, the holding of hands, which their straight peers did not think twice about. "Separate but Equal" was not good enough for gay people either, Joe realized once again.

He wanted to slap those liberals who said, "Why do you have to have marriage? Haven't we given you enough? Aren't civil unions enough? You're ruining the Democratic Party. You're the reason John Kerry lost in 2004."

Joe completely lost objectivity on this subject. He feared his own rage. He knew that and wanted to hide somewhere until the marriage question was all decided. Fortunately, his workplace, the third floor of the John Adams' Courthouse, could be a hiding place of sorts. No politics were allowed there, and for judges, according to the Supreme Judicial Court's Ethics Advisory Committee, civil rights for gay people was still to be treated as a political rather than a moral issue. If only he didn't have to walk in front of or behind the State House in order to get to work, Joe would feel safer.

* * *

When Joe returned to his office the next day, the Wednesday after Memorial Day, there was a pink telephone slip on his desk that listed Harry Jones as the caller. Again there was no return number on the message. Joe still did not recall any of Harry's phone numbers. *Sic transit memoria amoris*. It had been at least ten years since their romance after all. Nevertheless Joe looked in his Rolodex, which he'd had for years and which was busting out of its roller, and found an old number on a card marked simply "Harry." Joe tried it and Mary Alice Finnigan Jones, now simply Alice Jones, answered. She recognized Joe's voice and when he asked for Harry without acknowledging her she coldly said, "Sure, Joe. I'll go get him."

"Joe, you're in trouble, Joe," Harry said. "I probably shouldn't be calling you, but I had to let you know. That nutty right winger Nemesis, the guy who used to own all those local papers, is on your case big time. He's been keeping a dossier on you ever since you were appointed and now he thinks he has you. Last year you sat on a case involving the Randozza family and he knows that you were, uh…involved…with one of them. Half the city knew that before it ended, but nobody was going to fault you for having a little fun.

And, if you ask me," Harry added *sotto voce*, "he's one of the most beautiful men I have ever seen, even if he's not my type. But Nemesis has proof, the advance sheet, the slip opinion and the report of the case, that show you were on the panel in the Randozza case. It doesn't matter that you decided against the Randozzas, so don't tell me that. It doesn't make anything better. Nemesis has been following you for years and he has spies on the court, your court, who tell him everything. He has spies everywhere. It's like some religious conspiracy, like *Opus Dei* or something. You know how zealous they can get and how sneaky they are. It's not only that you're gay it's also the partners you pick. It was bad enough when you were going with me—a swamp Yankee, but then you pick a gangster. You know you can't deviate too far from the norm with those guys. It's like you're a disgrace to the race, some of them think."

All this was before Joe could say anything. Joe knew that he had not sat on the Randozza case. He remembered all the shenanigans he had to go through to get out of sitting on that case, calling the old, now dead, Chief Justice while the Chief was on his fishing trip vacation. The Chief had Miss Mary Margaret Managhan line up Mildred Bailey as a substitute, so Joe could be off the case. Joe left the conference room when the other judges were talking about the case. This wasn't New Hampshire, where the judges recused themselves in court and then participated in the discussion about the case in conference.

Joe was smarter than that. He always erred on the side of caution. He knew from the day he was sworn in that he was vulnerable because he was the first gay judge. *The report of the case was wrong. What was that Reporter of Decisions doing? Didn't he even know who was sitting on the cases? Didn't the presiding judge, Mildred Bailey, announce the switch of presiding judges before the case was called— from Lyons to Bailey?* Joe was back in his chambers before the Randozzas' lawyer even opened his mouth. *Why didn't the clerk make an announcement? Don't they know they are supposed to be making a record and getting it right?*

Slowly Joe realized what the problem was. He, Joe, was listed on all the papers in advance as the presiding judge for the day and had been the presiding judge for the first three cases. For all the theatricality of appellate proceedings—the judges dressed up, their honorifics, the coming out from behind a curtain in order of seniority—there was no stage manager or producer to come forward at the beginning and announce changes in the cast. Nobody came to the front and said, "The Honorable Justice Mildred Bailey will be sitting in for Justice Joseph Lyons in the fourth case." Joe did not announce his recusal and departure before he left the bench, and, obviously Mildred Bailey did not announce her arrival when she sat in his chair after the break.

I can probably straighten this out, but the harm may be done already, Joe thought. Just mentioning that Joe was involved romantically with Dino Randozza would be very embarrassing. The *Herald* would have a field day. They had been gunning for a judge to bring down ever since they lost three plus million dollars to Judge Ernest Murphy after a jury found that the *Boston Herald* had libeled him, *Sullivan v. New York Times* be damned.

And what was this stuff about Joe betraying the race? What race were they talking about? Sam Nemesis wasn't Irish. The white race? The Irish race? What about Roger Casement? Oscar Wilde? Wasn't there a skip to the hip of Brendan Behan? Closer to home, David I. Walsh was both the first Irish Catholic Governor and Senator in Massachusetts. He was busted in a male brothel in Brooklyn. Joe's uncle Jim liked to tell the story of coming into a christening party with his father, Joe's grandfather, when he, Jim, was a very handsome fifteen. "David I.," as they called him, who was regaling the ladies in the back parlor, took one look at young Jim and said, "Come over here and sit on my knee, young man."

Joe's grandfather told young Jim, "Don't you move." Everybody knew about David I..

All this went through Joe's head as Harry talked. He had a defense to everything, but he also knew none of the defenses were going to do him any good if "they" really ganged up on him. Sure, he had always known of his vulnerability, and he had been careful. But he wasn't going to take saltpeter and a vow of celibacy in light of it. The bastards were not going to grind him down. Now it looked like they could and maybe they already had—all those pursed thin-lipped pious bastards, like Sam Nemesis and his ilk.

"I did not sit on the Randozza case, as you call it, Harry. The case was *Williamson v. Randozza Enterprises, Inc.*, by the way. Some people call it the *Williamson* case. Williamson won after all. I'm not stupid. Who thinks I did sit on it?"

Harry replied, "Well, Sam Nemesis does, and whoever on your court put together the report of the case, the Reporter of Decisions, I think that's the archaic title you give him up there, thinks you did, and Nemesis called the District Attorney and he's investigating the matter. The D.A. has been wanting to bring down the Randozzas for a long time and he thinks this may be his opportunity—'Obstruction of Justice' is what the D.A. is thinking of indicting one or more Randozzas with. You saw me with him a week or so ago. That's what we were talking about. Wolfie called me to verify the facts and then asked me to sit in. However, the D.A. may even call in the United States Attorney. And the Commission on Judicial Conduct was sent a copy of Nemesis' letter to the District Attorney. That's never good," Harry Jones added. "And it goes on. That's why we were all at Guido's when you saw me last. The District Attorney likes you, but he has to do something. That you might suffer too is a problem for him. Perhaps you can stop him with the truth, but the papers will soon have it, I'm afraid. You know this town. Nothing is confidential. If Nemesis doesn't get the D.A. or the Judicial Conduct

Commission to knock you out, he may leak the story—or the romance part of it—to the *Herald*. Wolfy is trying to keep them quiet. You know his connections."

"No, I don't know his connections, and I don't want to know them. That old closet case! He just wants to be part of the action. He can't stand to be out to pasture. Besides I'm too 'out' for him. Who called him into this bullshit?" Joe asked.

"The District Attorney," Harry Jones said. "He and his assistant, you know that good-looking guy we were with, the one who wins all the murder cases, they rely on Wolfy for a lot of things. Wolfy has known me for years, and he knows about you and me in the olden days, so he called me. I think that he has your interests at heart, Joe. Trust him. I'm glad I called you. You ought to get a lawyer. Dewey Battle is great on things like this and he used to be a judge. I can call him if you want," Harry said.

"No, no. I'll call him," Joe said. "That's a good idea, Harry. I'll call right now." The reality of the mess had hit him. He had often thought, *What will I do if I get into a jam?* He was prepared in a way for this day and this news. He was more than happy to turn it over to someone, especially Dewey Battle, Esquire, the leading lawyer in Boston for getting judges, lawyers, doctors and other professionals out of messes, usually of their own creation.

And Joe did call Dewey Battle's office. Joe tried not to sound as worried as he was feeling.

Joe also called Tom Murphy but Tom was "tied up in a meeting in Los Angeles."

"More likely Las Vegas," Joe muttered. Joe couldn't wait for the call back from Tom Murphy before calling Dewey Battle, Esq., again.

Dewey Battle scheduled an appointment for Joe for the very next morning. On the phone, because he didn't know who might be listening in, Joe simply said that he may be in trouble regarding a case he had sat on. Dewey Battle asked Joe to fax the report, the decision, of the case to him. *Williamson v. Randozza Enterprises, Inc.*, which had still not been bound in a book, had been widely distributed as a slip opinion, an advance sheet, but Joe did not want to name it over the phone. Faxing the report was something to do, something that Joe could do to begin to defend himself. He walked down to the fax room and waited in the queue behind two law clerks and one secretary. The law clerks said, "Go ahead, Judge," but the secretary was not so inclined and glared at Joe. It was good for his humility to wait, Joe decided. So, he did.

Mostly Joe was dispirited, defeated, brought down. This craziness made him question his whole judicial career. He forgot all the good he had done—his breaking of the unwritten prohibition against gay judges. There were now more than a dozen gay judges—mostly lesbians. He forgot that he had stood up and forced the Supreme Judicial Court to say "orientation" rather than "preference" when they finally passed a rule banning discrimination against gay people in the courts. He forgot that he had been out there for a long time as "The Gay Judge" for people to make jokes about. He even forgot all his well-reasoned decisions.

Joe was over it—the judging business. He didn't want to be the judge whose sex life made the newspapers and killed the judges' pay raise, and he didn't want the world, at least metropolitan Boston, to know all about his romances. He knew that in these "enlightened" times it was okay to be gay—just so long as you didn't talk about the details. This craziness was going to get into the details.

Joe also wanted to call Dino Randozza to tell him stuff was coming down and to be prepared, but he knew he should talk to Tom Murphy or Dewey Battle before doing that. Dino Randozza could handle it. He had been called a lot worse than a judge's boyfriend in his day. All the people Dino cared about probably knew already but the same rules probably applied in Dino's world as well. *Don't talk about it! Don't flaunt it!* As one straight lawyer friend of Joe's said, "I don't care what you people do, just don't rub my nose in it."

*　*　*

At 9:00 A.M. on Thursday Joe left his building, went up Beacon Hill past the State House and then down the other side to Dewey Battle's office on State Street. It was unassuming as law offices go, but professional. A prospective client would not think that his fees were going to opulent furniture and bad paintings picked by some "interior decorator/art consultant'" who was probably the spouse of one of the partners. The waiting room was small and the furniture comfortable. Joe did not wait long. He'd just sat down when the receptionist led him into Dewey Battle's office. Dewey Battle came around the desk to greet him and sat opposite him in one of the client chairs, equalizing the situation. Dewey Battle asked if Joe would like some coffee or tea or ice water. Joe declined. He really wanted to get to the point.

"Tell me the story, Judge," Dewey said.

Joe did, leaving out nothing. "I met Dino Randozza on the Internet. I didn't know who he was. As a matter of fact, he gave me a false name at first. It was a rough beginning but we had a romance for a while. It didn't last long but it was intense. I met his mother. She became friendly with my aunt. I met his brother, now a bishop. I met his nephew Lorenzo and his niece Maureen. I came to know more about their reputation. I read the papers in the *Williamson v. Randozza Enterprises, Inc.* case. However, I left the bench quite publicly before it was called for hearing.

" I did not sit on the case, and I talked to no one about it. Judge Mildred Bailey filled in. She was designated by the old Chief Justice when I called him on vacation and told him that I had a conflict. I didn't tell him the nature of the conflict and he didn't ask. On our court it is not necessary to reveal any more than that you think that you ought to be out of the case," Joe added. "I can't believe that the record of the case doesn't show that this substitution was made. It was the fourth of six cases and I sat, presided even, on all the other cases. I would hope that my absence would be on the record somewhere but, if necessary, I can get affidavits from the other judges that I never touched that case. I'd rather not draw their attention to this…situation, which is delicate to say the least."

Nothing seemed to shock Dewey Battle. "Let me walk up to the Commission and talk to the Director. I suspect that they've not even listened to the tapes yet. That's usually the way they operate. It's a little like *Alice in Wonderland* up there. They send out the complaint and then check to see if it has any merit. They're short staffed; some of the people up there have never been in a courtroom. They're also very righteous. You're guilty until proven innocent. Maybe that's the way they should be, but it's not the best way to proceed in my book."

Dewey Battle added, "I'll also call the District Attorney. He won't want to make a gaffe on this one. He's a pro. He may already know that you're clear. Now this Harry Jones, why would the District Attorney have called him?"

"Because he called the Honorable J.J. Wolf first and Wolfy knew that Harry and I had been 'an item,' a couple, years ago." Joe hated having to reveal so much of himself. *Is that internalized homophobia?* he wondered. In for a dime, in for a dollar, so he added, "And I think that Wolfy and Harry and Harry's wife play bridge together with Monsignor Owen every Wednesday night. Harry says that he and Wolfy have never talked about our relationship, but Wolfy knows everything, as you may know," Joe said.

Dewey Battle said, "Oh yes, I know Wolfy. He called me to congratulate me on my appointment to the bench 15 minutes before the Governor called to offer it to me. And he called me to congratulate me on my retirement two days before I submitted it. I know Wolfy. He lied about his age so that the Constitutional Amendment stopping judges from serving after age 70 didn't knock him out.

Eventually somebody found his birth certificate and he resigned at 75. Did you know that? He likes to be in on everything, especially since he had to retire and has little to do except go to breakfast at that joint in the Back Bay, Guido's something or other, or the Ritz, or the Four Seasons. It's a good thing he can walk to all of his hangouts. That's how he stays healthy. He stays at the Ritz Café until two or three o'clock in the afternoon and there's always someone sitting with him. I see him strutting along Commonwealth Avenue on my way to the office. He gives me a courtly bow and addresses me as 'Judge.' I do the same with him. We get along, I think. I can call him too, and find out what he knows and what he's doing. He might tell me. He likes people to know his influence. I'll get back to you tomorrow after lunch. I don't think that you're in any serious trouble, except for the publicity, if this gets around. I understand your concern on that point. We'll try to nip it in the bud."

Dewey Battle leaned back in his chair and added, "I look at it this way. A judge is entitled to have a little romance. The work is hard enough. There's no rule that the other party in the romance has to be respectable. Try not to worry. As Saint Teresa of Avila said, 'Everything passes. Nothing stays the same.' That's particularly true for scandal. There's always something new. Think about taking a vacation. I can keep in touch with you by email if I need to. You don't have to be in town to read the tabloids, if they dare print anything. We've trimmed their claws recently with the Ernie Murphy case and they're running a little shy when it comes to judges. You seem to be fond of Italians. Go to Italy! Go to Sicily! Get out of town! I'll call you tomorrow."

Dewey Battle then got up and extended his hand. The meeting was over.

Ego te absolvo in nomen de patris, et filii, et spiritui sancti.

Joe felt like he had just been to confession to and received absolution from Dewey Battle. Here was one of the leading lawyers in

Boston, and he didn't blink an eye at Joe's reckless romancing. Joe was relieved—for the time being. *The shame and guilt would return, he just knew it. In the meantime, why not plan a trip? Angelo Bruno would be out of school soon. The fourth grade did not go on forever.*

* * *

Joe returned to his office at the Adams Courthouse. There were three calls from Tom Murphy. Joe took back every terrible thing he had ever said or thought about Tom.

Joe called Tom Murphy's cell phone. Surprisingly Joe reached Tom. Joe was right, by the way. Tom Murphy was in Las Vegas. He was at the blackjack table at the Bellagio when he took Joe's call. Joe told him the whole sorry story.

Tom responded to Joe's narration with the usual Irish response, "That bastard, Nemesis! That bastard! I've got something on him, something the Cardinal won't like either. I can't tell you now, but I'll be home tomorrow and I'll tell you then. I may just call his office now. He knows I know. He'll sweat a little. But he's a crazy bastard, Joe. So you may not be out of the woods yet. He's not a rational man. Didn't Machiavelli say, 'You've got to kill the enemy?' My information may do that to Nemesis—not literally, but you know what I mean. It should shut him up. It would give a normal man pause, but we're not dealing with a normal man here, Joe. We'll know more tomorrow."

A Weekend in Provincetown

That night Angelo tackled Joe as soon as he came through the door and pulled him to the floor. Joe lay there passively as Angelo took off Joe's clothes, leaving only the red and blue striped tie. Joe went through the motions of lovemaking, but he couldn't shake his troubles. He had a sudden jolt of reality—well, if not reality, at least fears that he perceived to be reality; *post coitum omni animales tristi sunt* in one of its myriad forms. Lying naked on the rug, on the floor, looking up at the ceiling, he could feel Angelo's right shoulder, arm and hip touch his left side.

"You're somewhere else, Joe. Is everything alright?" Angelo asked.

Joe told Angelo about Harry Jones' phone call, explaining in tedious detail, as is the wont of lawyers and judges, the possible, even most remotely possible, legal and other ramifications of the whole business, as well as his even more frightening fears about the publicity that he was convinced would occur even if he were to escape the legal lashes of the District Attorney, the United States Attorney and the Commission on Judicial Conduct. He told him Dewey Battle's more optimistic assessment, even though he now did not believe it. Finally he told Angelo that he was scared, really scared. Then he leaned over to cry in the comfort of the nook between Angelo's hairy chest and his strong right shoulder.

All his life Joe had worked hard to look good, to maintain *la bella figura*, to appear respectable, to pass in spite of his differences. He took to heart Flaubert's advice, to be respectable and *bourgeois* in your outer life so that you can be crazy and wild in your inner one. This veneer helped make him a judge—that and the fact that in 1989 in Massachusetts it was time for a gay judge. In those days if there had to be one, Joe was it.

Joe was a known quantity to the legal establishment. He had done all the good things a lawyer does. He joined Bar Association committees and the boards of worthy charities. He did *pro bono* work representing indigent defendants in civil cases brought by their greedy creditors. He served on a hearing committee for the Board of Bar Overseers. He was known by the leaders of the Bar, that interchangeable committee of legal elders, as a smart, trustworthy man with good judgment. "As for the 'gay thing,'" as one of them said to him when he was seeking the judgeship, "Let's just say it's something you do on Saturday nights—like bowling."

When Joe was a kid this veneer, this *gravitas*, was a way to cover up being different, being gay. When puberty hit it was a way to pass even though he knew his own desires. Then when he was older and "out" it was a way for him to be a "regular guy," albeit gay—as opposed to the Radical Faeries or the Act Uppers, for example. He was a gay they could trust. He had established his credentials in the profession. He was not "outside of the box" or "off the reservation."

Joe stood up for gay issues whenever they arose, but in a non-confrontational way. He ran a Bar Association symposium on legal issues regarding people with AIDS and found two gay lawyers with AIDS to speak at it. For the hierarchy of the Bar he was a connection to Gaiety rather than a threat from it. He did not demand; he persuaded. And he was persuasive because, except for his sex life, the particulars of which they did not want to know, or him to talk about, Joe was just like them—or so they perceived.

Now they were going to know differently. To lose all his credibility by having the world, well, his world, the legal world in Boston at least, and the readers of the tabloids, which never liked him anyway, know that he had been so indiscriminate as to have been the paramour of Dino Randozza, a gangster, was too much for Joe. He wondered if there were any pictures. *Oh my God! Dino wouldn't have done that!*

Joe was about to crack. The image that he had built for and of himself since childhood was about to crumble, and that was almost worse than being pursued by the Judicial Conduct Commission for something he did not do. He could handle the charges against him because they were not true, but he thought that the knowledge of his indiscretion would ruin him. He would probably not lose his job, but he would be like Clarence Thomas on the United States Supreme Court. He'd be tainted, marginalized, without prestige or respect. Worst of all, people would laugh at him.

Angelo, who dealt with ten-year-olds all day long, who was Italian and who well knew about keeping and saving face, understood all this. Apart from hugging Joe, Angelo did not know how to let Joe know that everything was going to be alright. Angelo was not sure that everything would be alright. However, he was sure that Joe was not going to be dead from his humiliation, even if it occurred as Joe so dreadfully predicted. And Angelo was sure that he loved Joe, whether or not Joe was a judge, a gay hero, or a paragon in "The Community," whatever the hell that was.

"Joe, let's get out of here this weekend. Let's go to the Cape, to Provincetown. It's beautiful there this time of year before the tourists come, before the season starts. I'm sure that we could stay at Franny Flynn's. He likes us both and he's always asking us down. I'll call him right now. It's only 7:00 P.M. Come on, we'll have a good time."

* * *

The weather was beautiful and more beautiful was Franny Flynn's house on the bay in Provincetown. Joe and Angelo were given the yellow bedroom with the canopy bed, usually reserved for Franny's older sister and her husband, newlyweds of whatever sexual combination, or beautiful men who Franny was trying to woo. The room had a view out to Long Point and its lighthouse and beyond that to Truro, Wellfleet and down the inside of Cape Cod.

Franny was a very generous host and uncle. The house was usually filled with lots of guests as well as nephews, nieces, their spouses and the resultant grand nephews and grandnieces. This weekend, however, there were just Franny and Angelo and Joe. Franny had known Joe for years, but they had become more friendly about twenty-five years before when Joe helped a friend of Franny's get into McLean Hospital after a crackup, a nervous breakdown combined with cocaine, the drug *du jour* of the eighties, and booze. Not many people knew that Joe himself had been at McLean in the early seventies for a "nervous breakdown" but Franny did and he'd stored that information away.

Up to that time Franny knew Joe only slightly. Franny was embarrassed that he knew Joe's mental health history, but he didn't know where else to turn and he was desperate to help his friend. Franny called Joe. Joe did not fail him.

Therefore, Franny, Irish and loyal ever since, had no qualms about entertaining Joe and Angelo for the weekend when Angelo called to ask if they might come down. Besides remembering Joe's kindness to his sick friend, like a lot of other gents of Joe's vintage, Franny had a not-so-secret crush on Angelo. Franny, like other old-timers, told himself, *If there is an Angelo for Joe Lyons, maybe there is one for me too.* Joe knew this, but was secure in Angelo's affection.

The first night of their visit, Friday night, Franny took Joe and Angelo to the Mews, a good restaurant run by a former Boston radio host, now Provincetown community benefactor. The Mews stayed open all year. Before the season started and before other restaurants opened it was just about the only place to go. Joe almost always saw someone he knew there, often someone he had slept with in the Sixties or Seventies and whose name he could not remember if he ever knew it to begin with. Such were the Sixties and Seventies. Although Joe might not remember the names of all his bedmates from the olden days and they might not remember his, they were happy to see each other alive.

This night they were seated at a table right in the middle of the main dining room. At one table in front of them and to Joe's left sat a man Joe thought he recognized. "I think I know that blond man at that table up there. Do you remember him, Franny?" Joe asked.

"Do you mean the old guy with the comb-over, his hair a blond color God never imagined, the fat guy wearing eyeliner?" Franny said looking the other way because he thought it was impolite to stare at the person you were talking about.

"I guess you could describe him that way," Joe said.

"No! No, I don't know him. How old do you think I am?"

"If he is who I think he is, he's almost my age, only a few years older than you, Franny," Joe said.

"Well, she's had a hard life then," Franny said. "Who do you think it is, Joe?"

"I think he's Donny Gaetano from East Boston. He used to be a fixture at Sporters in the old days, in the sixties. He always had those big Gina Lollobrigida eyes and batted them around all night. "

"We all have our virtues and talents, Joe," Franny added before sipping his Pink Cosmo still looking in the other direction.

Joe said, "I never talked to him in those days, but it's nice to see that he's still alive. We had mutual friends.

" Angelo, I know I told you I was a virgin when we met, but there were a few other men before you. Donny Gaetano's best friend was Paolo, a big, dirty blond Sicilian from Revere. He took me up to that giant Shrine to the Madonna in East Boston on our first date. We had to light a candle for our romance. And he had a wife and two kids! I haven't seen Donny since Paolo's funeral in 1985. Do you think I should say hello? Am I just being nostalgic? He probably doesn't even remember me."

Angelo, who was generous in spirit and who knew Joe had a busy history with a lot of men who were no longer alive and, thus, no longer a threat, said, "Joe, you should talk to him. He'll probably be happy to see you."

Joe walked over to the table where Donny Gaetano sat with two other men of the same age, also carefully coiffed blonds of varying hues.

"Excuse me. Aren't you Donny Gaetano?" Joe said. "I remember you from Sporters—in the Sixties," he added. Joe thought it better to leave Paolo's name out of the reunion. All of a sudden he remembered that Donny was jealous of Paolo's romances.

"I am and who might you be?" Donny Gaetano said.

"I'm Joe Lyons."

"Oh, my God!" Donny said. He paused, looked at the other seated blonds, and then added, "You used to be so thin!"

The other men at the table laughed. After a second Joe laughed too and then said, "So did you, Donny!"

"Thanks for coming over, Joe."

Joe returned to his table. He couldn't wait to tell Angelo and Franny what had just happened. Franny roared, but Angelo said, jokingly, "I'll kill the fat bastard!"

Franny said to Joe, "That'll teach you to look back. Now what do you want to eat? The cod here is very good. So are the scallops. Hurry up and decide. The waiter has already been over once. He's very cute and I don't want to upset him. I told him you were in the loo."

"You also asked him when he got out of work," Angelo said. "You're very forward, Franny."

"Well, if I can't have you, I have to amuse myself somehow. Besides he told me that he's usually done by midnight. I told him that I can't stay up that late. He'll have to come over and sit in the sun on my deck tomorrow."

Angelo said, "You've already asked five other young men to come over and sit on the deck. These young guys don't want to sit on the deck, Franny. They want to ride their bikes shirtless down Commercial Street, park them on the fence up at the edge of the National Seashore and walk the Bataan Death March to the deserted part of Herring Cove where they can strut around naked, get bitten by horse flies and have sex in the dunes. You know that Franny." Angelo said. "I'd be with them if the old guys were out there, but I know they're all at your house. There's great eye candy for me on your deck. Next to Joe, and you, of course, I love that married guy with the furry chest who sells insurance in town."

"And you are eye candy for them, my darling, or for most of them. The married insurance man only likes women, especially his wife. Why do you think I invited you down, Angelo? Because I love Joe?" Franny said lovingly.

Joe, who had been a bystander in this repartee, said, "Do they still have sex in the dunes?"

"Of course they do. What do you think the dunes are for?" said Franny. "Nature walks?"

The waiter, who was handsome and flirty, returned and took their order, cod for Joe, scallops for Franny, and a steak for Angelo, who didn't have to worry about cholesterol yet.

Just before the dinners arrived Joe looked behind him and to the left. There was Eleanore Emmet, the Somerville and Ross scholar from Harvard, sitting next to Tom Murphy. Across from them were Hasan and Maureen Randozza. *How did this happen*, Joe wondered? *Where is JoJo Danieli? That Hasan certainly is resourceful! Whatever country he works for—Egypt, Ireland or the U.S.—will be lucky to get him.*

Eleanore saw Joe and smiled. Hasan turned around and waved. Maureen blew Joe a kiss with a big smile on her face. Franny Flynn turned to see what all the fuss was about. Hasan waved to Franny as well.

"Oh, my God! That beautiful man is here. He's supposed to be straight! I met him at Kitty Boudreaux's house on Beacon Hill. She's two blocks away from you, Joe. You must know her. Her husband is with Swords, Healy and Fiske, just like that Tom Murphy, your political friend who is always upsetting the Cardinal. That dusky lad studies with Kitty's son at Harvard. Oh, my God! Nobody told me he's gay too."

"Maybe he isn't, Franny," Joe said. "A lot of people who aren't gay come to Provincetown these days. We've made it attractive for them—just like the South End. You don't have to go through *gaydar* to cross the town line. Maybe he's staying in Truro or Wellfleet."

"You're right, Joe. I know," said Franny, "As for the South End, you can't walk down the street there without being hit by a stroller."

Joe said, "I told one young Talbot's pink and green matron on

Clarendon Street, 'Is that a baby carriage or a dangerous weapon you're pushing? Just because you were fertile doesn't give you the right to mow people down on the sidewalk.' When she started to talk back I said, 'Listen, lady, the gays were here first, before you were born. We made this place. Why don't you go back to suburbia, where that outfit passes, and drive your brat around the mall!'"

"It's a good thing you don't live down there anymore, or do business there," Franny added, as an afterthought.

Franny then rushed over to Hasan's table. There was much animated conversation and when Franny returned with a big smile on his face he announced, "We are going to have a party tomorrow night."

"Why?" Said Joe.

"For the Europeans!"

"All of them?" Joe said.

"No, silly!" Franny said. "It'll be for those people at that table, and the Dutch Ambassador to Poland is here visiting Bunny Liddy, who is his best friend. It'll be fun. I can get Café Cielo to do the catering and that humpy bartender from the Macho Bar at the Atlantic House to bartend. Do you know any Jamaicans who can serve?"

"No, but I heard that there are some Bulgarians here this year, and a few Ukrainians," Joe said, as if they were talking about turnips.

"Can they speak English? I want them to be able to explain the *hors d'oeuvres*. Oh, I'll let Catherine at Café Cielo take care of that. There really is nothing to worry about. Sweep and Dust are coming tomorrow to clean anyway. Be sure to make your beds." Franny added. "That's it then. We're all set," he added with a self-satisfied smile as he began to write out the guest list on the napkin. "Joe, do you know if that sculptor, Simon Schuyler, still goes with the TV actor and, if so, what's his name?"

"I don't know, Fran," Joe said. "But we can find out tomorrow. Maybe you should just ask Simon to bring his boyfriend."

"He has a new boyfriend every other day. It's his lover I want to see. I suppose you're right, however."

Angelo piped in uncharacteristically cynically, "Tell him to bring his trick from last night. That should narrow the field."

Franny went back over to Hasan's table to extend the invitation. He then went outside to call the caterer and the rest of the "Europeans," at least those who he was going to invite for tomorrow night.

When Franny returned, just as they were finishing their meal, David Brennen, a respectable gay lawyer and activist, who also went to church with Franny every week at Saint Cecilia's in the Back Bay, stopped by and sat down next to Franny.

Joe couldn't resist. He knew that he was supposed to be politically inactive and that he shouldn't be indiscreet in front of a lawyer who knew the rules, but David was just the man to ask. "What's the latest on the Anti-Same-Sex Marriage Amendment? The vote's in less than two weeks. How does it look?"

David replied, "It's very strange. People 'in the know', or who should be 'in the know', just aren't talking. I know that both Marriage Equality and the MLGPC[1] are flooding the legislators with gay married couples, or couples who have been together a thousand years and want to get married. They're coming in with their kids, their dogs, their cats, their relatives. Who knew there were so many gay couples and how many relatives who vote they have? They're very earnest and can't help but tug on your heart strings. One State Rep I know, who is for us, by the way, said, 'I can't take it anymore. I want to put a sign on my office door that says 'Don't worry. I'm voting NO. Leave me alone.' As astonishing as it may seem that three quarters of the Massachusetts Legislature, usually a pretty cautious bunch, will vote for gay marriage, I think we're going to win, but nobody official, either in the Legislature or from the gay groups working on the vote, has told me that. Others think we're going to

---

[1] Massachusetts Lesbian and Gay Political Caucus

lose by two or three votes. The rumor is that the Cardinal himself will start making house calls on the legislators."

Joe nodded sagely and smiled at David's positive report. He thought it better that he say nothing in reply. He'd already gone too far by asking the question, he thought.

Angelo said, "That's great. I hope that you're right. My Rep is for us, but my Senator, the troglodyte, is opposed. He won't take any more of my calls."

David Brennen just rolled his eyes.

Franny said, "I can't wait for the next round of weddings. What fun! We'd better go now. It's wonderful to see you, David. Keep up the good work! By the way, I'm having a party tomorrow evening for the Europeans. Come by around six." That was Franny's way of responding to the good news. Invite the messenger to a party.

And the three of them got up to leave as David walked back to his own table. They were stopped by Maureen Randozza, who said, "Can I bring JoJo Danieli to your party, Franny?"

"Of course, you may," Franny said.

Just outside the door Franny said to Joe and Angelo, "Who is Jojo Danieli?"

"She's very important in the North End," Joe said.

"Oh, okay then. Do you want to experience my sex life?"

"What?" Joe and Angelo said together.

"Come on. I'll show you my sex life," and Franny led them to his car which was parked just up Commercial Street. Franny took a right on Washington Avenue and then headed East, back out of town, away from his house to the junction of Bradford and Commercial Streets.

"What we do now is ride all the way down Commercial Street, from East to West, look at all the houses with 'For Sale' signs and guess the price they'll go for. That's my sex life these days."

A Very Eventful Party

The next evening, a half hour before the guests were to arrive, at Franny's direction, Joe and Angelo were on the terrace rearranging the patio furniture into conversational groups. They had already clipped the privet, weeded the gardens, mowed the lawn and folded Irish linen tea napkins. Franny called the liquor store; soon after gallons of booze arrived and were set up on a faded pink and moss green Pierre Deux fabric draped bridge table on the terrace just where the stairs went down to the beach. This placement of the bar not only barricaded the entrance to the deck to strangers from the beach but also prevented guests from falling down the stairs onto the beach. It did not leave much elbow room for the bartender, however, but it wasn't going to be a long party.

Although there were four bathrooms in the house, the ancient water heater only allowed two showers to run with hot water at the same time. Joe said that he and Angelo would shower together.

"Can I watch?" Franny said.

They all laughed and went upstairs. Franny showered first in the bathroom off his bedroom, then dressed in yellow linen slacks and a lighter yellow linen shirt and went downstairs. He wanted to be there to greet the guests himself.

The first arrivals were a surgeon and his wife, Dr. and Mrs. Oscar Wilson, who were staying nearby at the Red Inn. "Call me Prissy," she told Franny after Franny greeted her as "Mrs. Wilson" when he opened the screen door to let her in. Her husband, on the other hand, liked to be called "Doctor" at all times. As a matter of fact, that is the way he introduced himself, "I'm Doctor Wilson."

Are you a doctor a doctor, or a doctor a dentist? Franny wanted to ask.

The Wilsons had never been to Provincetown before. They usually went to Nantucket, occasionally to the Vineyard. She, Prissy, the wife, had recently read about Provincetown in *Boston Magazine*. The article said it was the place to go for straight people now. She checked with her husband, the doctor, and he said that it was safe, that the AIDS virus was not airborne. So she booked a room at the Red Inn. Franny and Prissy had a mutual friend, the Cardinal/Archbishop of Boston.

Thus far, after only a day and a half, Prissy just loved Provincetown; she thought it was beautiful, and that the people were clever and creative. The Doctor found a golf course in Truro, so he liked it too. He wasn't sure about all the shirtless men and the low slung tight jeans on them, but it made life easier with Prissy for him to turn a blind eye to the male sexuality and the glamour. Besides, the food at the Red Inn was very good, and there were always gin and tonics to make any place palatable.

"Oh, what a beautiful house!" Prissy said as she entered the front hall with its handsome paintings.

"You've never been here before?" Franny said, well knowing that they hadn't ever been invited. "Let me give you a tour." He started on the first floor, vaguely mindful that Joe and Angelo were still showering or dressing upstairs. But so involved was he in the tour that he soon forgot Joe and Angelo and brought the Wilsons up-stairs.

On these tours it was Franny's custom to show his magnificent bedroom with its big canopy bed, papal balcony, French doors and full harbor view last. The streetside bedrooms were first. Joe and Angelo were in the Yellow Room, the other bedroom on the water side, so theirs would be the next to last bedroom on the upstairs tour. While Franny was ciceroning the Wilsons, Joe and Angelo were in the bathroom between the Yellow Room and one of the streetside bedrooms. They had finished showering together and the water was turned off. Franny believed they were no longer showering because he couldn't hear the running water.

All of a sudden Franny, now in the second streetside bedroom, chatting away about the bedspreads, hand crocheted by blind Belgian nuns, followed by Prissy and the Doctor, pushed through the bathroom door. Imagine the surprise when they saw the naked and magnificent, hirsute and wet Angelo standing in the tub with his arms up rubbing a towel over his head.

Surprise quickly turned into action as Franny pushed poor Prissy back out the bathroom door. Of course, she saw the naked Angelo. She made a mental note to ask the Doctor about foreskins, unless she had one drink too many, in which case she might ask the beautiful Angelo himself. Franny did not seem to be the person to ask tonight.

Franny said, "He seems to be busy in there. We'll just go around the other way. They walked back into the central hall and entered the yellow bedroom just as the naked Joe, backside facing them, bent over to run the towel, like floss, between his legs.

"Oh Jesus," Franny said, "Will you guys get a room! Come on, Prissy! Let me get you a drink. You too, Doctor. These guys have had an energetic day."

By the time they returned downstairs ten other guests had arrived. After a brief introduction Franny left the Wilsons with a re-tired drag queen, also a carpenter, who was dressed as a gondolier tonight. Franny rushed to greet the very handsome and talented young sculptor, Simon Schuyler, who had arrived with his retinue of poets, writers, artists, poseurs and pretty boys, and perhaps his lover.

The bartender, Antonio, a tall dark triathlete with a big nose and thick black hair like an Indian, also a landscaper and an artist's mod-el in his daily life, was flirting with Brendan, a handsome, young, gray-haired, freckled, blue-eyed cop from Cambridge at the bar table out on the deck. Dressed in a white shirt, black tie and cum-merbund—Franny wanted you to be able to distinguish the ser-vants from the guests—Antonio was whispering sweet nothings in Brendan's right ear while the Darceys, Kitty and Harry, a straight couple from Wellesley and Oyster Harbors, the Irish Riviera further down the Cape, waited impatiently for their drinks. Kitty was in a little white cocktail dress, a lavender, as a nod to Provincetown, pashmina shawl over her shoulder and Harry was wearing a blue blazer, emblazoned with the Wianno Golf Club crest, white linen pants and black Gucci loafers with no socks, as if he'd just docked the yacht out front.

"We just drove fifty goddamn miles in heavy traffic to get up here and it's seven o'clock, for Christ's sake. I want a drink," Harry Darcey said. "Why did I let you persuade me to come to this fairy-land anyway? We could've had a good steak and martinis at the club, and walked there. Just because you serve on charity com-mittees with Franny Flynn is no longer a good reason to wait for a vodka martini while that Spanish dancer romances the little lepre-chaun at the head of the line. I hope Franny has some edible food at this party. I'm not going to a restaurant in this town. They give you a lettuce leaf, a forkful of fish, and lots of queenly attitude, all for two hundred bucks. Get me out of here!"

Just then Franny walked by the bar. Antonio jumped to attention and Brendan wandered off. "We'll talk later," Antonio said to the departing Brendan with a big smile. "And what can I get you this beautiful night?" he said to the yachtsman *et ux*.

"Two Stoli martinis, one ice cube in each, and a Chardonnay for the lady," Harry Darcey said. When the first martini was prepared he drank it down and waited more patiently for the remainder of the order.

Franny looked at Kitty Darcey. She looked blank, then lifted both eyebrows and said, "Harry's tamed the savage beast. Now we can relax. How are you, darling Franny? What a beautiful linen outfit! Did you get that on your last Mediterranean trip?"

"I did. How did you know?"

"Because my Aunt Clara has one just like it, which she bought in Portofino *last* year. Great minds must think alike. Who is the beautiful bartender? Does he bowl in my alley too?" Kitty Darcey asked.

"Only when the price is right, Kitty m'dear. It depends. S'cuse me I have to go say 'hello' to someone important."

With that and a toss of his hair Franny strutted off to the other side of the terrace. Hasan, Eleanore and Tom Murphy had just arrived, each of them in navy blue curiously, like they were a song and dance trio. Hasan wore navy linen trousers, Eleanore a navy and light blue striped cotton shirtwaist dress with a wide navy belt around her tiny waist and Tom Murphy wore the always safe blue blazer *sans* medallion and buttons of any club or cause. No telltale social appurtenances for him. He had always been a Democrat after all, even if he was a rich Democrat now.

As Franny was approaching Hasan from the right, Joe was heading to Tom Murphy from the left. That left Eleanore alone in her glory, radiating goodness and light in the middle of the terrace. This social vacuum was quickly filled by Alice Allen, the butch lesbian auto-parts heiress from Indiana, who had been writing a novel, that nobody had ever seen, for the past twenty years. Alice always dressed down, and today was wearing a World War II Army Air Corps jumpsuit, which she had bought at the Provincetown Marine Supply store some fifteen years earlier, when she was thinner, as well as brand new unlaced Timberland workboots.

"I'm Alice Allen. I haven't seen you down here before," Alice said to Eleanore. "Are you visiting Franny? You should come over and see my house. It's bigger than this one and I have better art. Do you have dinner plans? I'm having some of the girls over after this party. Do you like clams?"

Eleanore, who was sophisticated and polite—she had been raised in Manhattan after all—was charming. This was not her first lesbian. Besides her worldly upbringing, she had graduated from an all girl prep school where she played field hockey and rowed on the crew.

"How very kind of you to ask me! I'm here with my friend Hasan," she added, nodding in his direction. Franny Flynn was all over Hasan like sauce attempting to get him to stay for dinner with a special few group of men. They were not going to be eating clams. Hasan was dodging the net with a *finesse* similar to Eleanore's. He was using her as his excuse.

Off in a corner Tom Murphy gave Joe his latest assessment of Joe's disciplinary case. He was a little jealous that Joe had sought the services of Dewey Battle. Tom Murphy was trying to direct the matter indirectly although he was not a trial lawyer, and had no experience of such matters.

Tom added, "I got a call from Abel Jonas, the columnist at the *Globe*. He was sniffing, but he's heard something. He said that his 'gal at the *Herald*' was working on a story about you. Did I know anything about it? Like most things with Abel, he's playing both sides. Anything I tell him he'll report to his 'gal at the *Herald*' and what the Herald tells him, he'll report to me. All I said was, 'They better be sure of what they write because they'll have another Ernie Murphy libel case on their hands, and I don't think their insurer is going to cover their sloppy research this time.' I don't think it's anything to worry about, but I thought I ought to tell you. I suspect that right-winger Nemesis has been dropping leaks. He's a no good bastard. If you see anyone following you, let me know. We'll put a tail on him, or her, right away. Be discreet, Joe."

Such advice was not comforting to Joe. Joe had no patience for it right then. He did not want to have to think of his ethical crisis today. He had come here to escape his professional life. He wanted to tell Tom to mind his own business. Joe trusted Dewey Battle to take care of the mess. However, Joe and Tom had been friends for years and Joe understood where Tom was coming from. Tom always wanted to be a player, even now in Joe's troubles, even when he had no experience.

But Joe had just had great sex with Angelo. He was on this beautiful terrace in Provincetown Harbor where everyone and everything was beautiful. Franny was a perfect host, delighting in the diversity of his guests. He threw them together like he was making a salad and hoped that it would come out tasty. It usually did. The affairs of the world, even his professional world, were the last thing Joe wanted to think about even though every once in a while his mind involuntarily wandered back to his current crisis.

Where was Angelo anyway? Joe wondered. Joe couldn't see him on the terrace. *Maybe he'd gone inside to the canapé table.* One of Angelo's gym friends had come in with Simon Schuyler's retinue, and the last Joe had seen of Angelo was the two of them talking together. In the face of Tom Murphy and his intrusion Joe forgot about Angelo for the moment.

"How did you come to be with Hasan and Eleanore? Where are you staying? Wasn't Maureen Randozza with you last night? Where's JoJo?" Joe asked Tom, all in a rush.

"Oh, Maureen and JoJo will be along. Hasan and Eleanore and I are staying at the same guesthouse. They're in separate rooms, by the way. Hasan heard that Maureen was coming down this weekend and he called me to ask where he should stay. I invited myself along. Hasan is still hopeful about Maureen, although I told him she's 'problematic.' That was discreet of me. No?" Tom added. "I didn't say she was the lesbian niece in a gangster family with very tough uncles. By the bye, our host, your pal Franny, is certainly losing no time with Hasan."

With that Tom and Joe looked over at Franny and Hasan. Franny was now holding Hasan's hand, introducing him to the Doctor Wilsons and the Darceys, the visiting straight couple from Oyster Harbors. The Wilsons and Darceys had been drawn together like magnets by their heterosexuality; they must have had "straidar." At the moment Franny arrived to present Hasan, who for some unknown reason he was calling "Abdul," Kitty Darcey, the blond-streaked wife, whose back was turned, was beginning to dish Franny and his yellow linen outfit.

At the sight of Franny approaching, Harry Darcey gave Kitty a kick to Kitty's shin with his soft left Gucci. She looked at him in surprise. Harry nodded towards the approaching Franny and Hasan. She turned, shut up and smiled gamely. They all perked up, even the men. Franny was their host, after all. Besides they did not know what an important personage Hasan might be. At his parties Franny often pulled a surprise dignitary out of his hat and they wanted to be able to say they had met him. Kitty Darcey, already preparing her reportage for the other ladies on her committees, noted that Hasan wore beautiful clothes well—and that said something about a person in her book. Coincidentally Hasan's clothes were from Montefiore, the best tailor in Portofino, the same shop where Franny and Kitty's rich old aunt Clara cum yacht had bought their *jaune* ensembles.

Franny also often had a priest or two at his parties. They never were in clericals, but usually wore black shoes. This party was no different. In fact there were three visiting Jesuits amongst the crowd. One of them, the oldest, a little, bald guy about Joe's age, was talking to Angelo in Franny's dining room, over the big bowl of chilled jumbo shrimp, which the good father was dipping into as if he had a tip on the Famine. Angelo tried to get away as the eleventh shrimp reached Father's mouth, but the priest had just one more thing to say.

The conversation had started with Angelo revealing that he taught the fourth grade. Somehow it had progressed to, "How do you keep in such good shape?" and the brushing away of a nonexistent mosquito from Angelo's chest. By this time Angelo was getting the picture and hoping that someone else would find her or his way to the spread in the dining room so that he could leave politely.

Angelo's prayers were answered when JoJo Danieli came in the back door with Maureen Randozza and what looked to be a bishop in full regalia, miter, crook, green cope, white alb and magenta cassock underneath. "Make way for the Bishop! Make way for the Bishop!" JoJo shouted until she saw the shrimp bowl. Then she shut up and let the Bishop find his own way into the living room.

Franny must have heard the first announcement. Of course, he knew the Bishop was coming. Hasan was not going to be the prize at this party, not unless Franny captured him. On the Eastern edge of the terrace Franny excused himself to Alice Allen, Tom Murphy, Kitty Darcey and Prissy Wilson, all of whom had been laughing it up with Franny, as he lasciviously praised the obvious virtues of the priapic bartender.

"Excuse me. Oh dear, I have to get the Bishop. Excuse me," Franny continued to say as he looked up into the living room where the Bishop was standing, leaning on his crozier, as if to give a blessing, like a vision behind the softly lit living room picture window looking out at Franny's assembled crowd on the terrace and the harbor behind them.

In spite of his asserted haste to get to the Bishop, Franny kept talking. He wanted to set the stage. "I saw the Bishop at the Blessing of the Fleet today and invited him over. We were on the Catholic Charities Board together. You remember that, Tommy Murphy." Franny always used the Irish diminutive of men's names. "You were on that board then too. That was before he was consecrated in Rome. Today he's filling in for the Bishop of Fall River, who had a heart attack last week. Bishop Randozza was going to be with his mother, the Countess of Trapani and her husband, the Count, in Chatham this week. Isn't it good of him to come here for us?!" Franny exclaimed.

"He didn't come for me," Alice Allen said. "I wouldn't be caught dead in that outfit. That Blessing of the Fleet thing is primitive and superstitious."

Prissy Wilson, who had been busy sipping her drink and thus hitherto silent, now became the Defender of the Faith. She said, "You'd probably go for it if there were women involved, if they had the women drummers bare breasted, and if a couple of lady preachers in gauze from the Unitarian Church were sprinkling the holy water."

Prissy's spunk surprised everyone. It silenced Alice Allen, and everyone else, for a minute.

"Well you know what they used to say in the fifties, Franny," Tom Murphy said, picking up the slack.

"No! what?" Franny said, like he never knew the fifties, as he was trying to rush off.

"The Irish Catholic dream was a house in Scituate with a Monsignor on the porch. You've done them one better. You have a Bishop in full regalia at your house in Provincetown! Did his mother, the Countess from Revere, by way of Dorchester, come too?"

"Oh Tommy, you're terrible! Let me go get the Bishop. I'm sure he'll want to change his clothes. He just left a reception at Saint Peter's rectory."

"I'll hold his hat," Kitty Darcey said.

"I could use that shepherds' crook out on the dunes walking my dogs," Alice Allen said.

"Tommy, do you want the dress?" Kitty Darcey said, before she went off in search of her husband, Harry, who had had a few more vodka martinis and was last seen talking up LaLa, a cute little blonde cosmetician with big boobs from Neiman Marcus, who was really still a man, but Harry had not found that out yet.

Kitty didn't have to look too far. Harry and LaLa had slipped behind Antonio and found their way down to the beach; they were sitting on the sand smoking a joint when Kitty found them.

Kitty shouted, "Harry, get up here!" Harry crawled his way from the beach up the stairs behind Antonio, the bartender, who had sold Harry the joint for twenty bucks. Harry was hastily rearranging his clothes. Once back on the terrace Harry looked up at the picture window and exclaimed, "Jesus Christ, I knew Franny was important, but how the hell did he get St. Patrick to this party!"

Indeed Rocco Randozza did look like Saint Patrick in his green cope holding the crozier with the mitre on his head. All that was needed to complete the picture were swirling banished snakes at his feet. Soon Bishop Rocco moved from the picture window to Franny's bedroom upstairs so he could change into civilian clothes. A few years before, after a trip to the Castel Gandolfo, the Pope's summer residence, Franny had built the balcony, a very papal balcony, off his bedroom. Franny and the Bishop, still in his vestments, appeared on the balcony. Franny, who himself had had a few drinks, gave the swirling papal wave, although it also looked like Queen Elizabeth's salute.

"If he thinks I'm dropping to my knees for his blessing in this dress, he's nuts," Kitty Darcey said. "There are very few men I get on my knees for these days, and the Bishop, handsome as he is, is not one of them, nor is Franny Flynn. Who's that handsome boy who just joined them? I'd lie down and roll over for him!"

Joe also saw the handsome boy. He looked almost exactly like Patrick Foley, his new legal intern, except plainer and wearing glasses. *What was he doing here? Was he with the Bishop or Franny?* It looked like he was part of the Bishop's entourage. *What is Patrick doing with the Bishop, Joe wondered? Where is his State Trooper boyfriend, the black colossus?*

Shortly thereafter, the Bishop, now in dark slacks, an open-necked gray and blue shirt showing the famous Randozza hairy chest, in this case mostly gray and white, and a dark jacket came on to the terrace with Franny, still a buttercup, and the handsome boy with glasses. Franny had a ball introducing the Bishop around. He started with the Darceys. Harry Darcey was leaning against a pillar, barely able to stand up. Kitty Darcey ogled the bishop's chest and quickly knelt to kiss his Episcopal ring, in spite of her previous declaration and tight skirt.

The handsome boy with glasses, who was dressed very plainly in a dark suit and striped tie, like a Mormon Missionary, went directly to the bar where Antonio, the bartender, became very attentive. Antonio had no apparent success. The handsome boy was given a ginger ale and quickly retired to the far wall where he stood alone and looked out over the water. Joe, who was standing in the middle of the large terrace talking to Tom Murphy, decided that he would not approach the boy, but wait to see if the boy approached him. A couple of times Joe thought the boy was looking right at him but there was no spark of recognition. *This is strange,* Joe thought. *Is he on drugs or something? Is his secret life being an aide to the Bishop? Is he the Bishop's boyfriend? Does he have to deny me, open and notorious queer that I am? I just gave him a job. What is this about?*

Finally Franny arrived at Joe with the Bishop. Tom Murphy was standing to Joe's left. "And your Excellency, these are two of my dearest friends, Judge Joseph Lyons and Attorney Thomas Murphy," Franny said with his most ingratiating smile. Actually, Franny didn't like Tom Murphy very much and would have liked to have passed him by but Tom was standing right next to Joe Lyons and couldn't be avoided. Tom was always trying to knock Franny off the tightrope Franny walked between the gay community and the Catholic Church. Franny was a little worried about what Tom might say to the Bishop. Tom did not disappoint.

"I've met Judge Lyons before. Mr. Murphy and I served on the Catholic Charities board together. How are you, gentlemen?" the Bishop said cordially.

Tom replied, "I'm fine, your Excellency. What a surprise to see you down here in Babylon!"

"Oh, Mr. Murphy, the Church is everywhere. God's work needs to be done in Provincetown as well as other places. We can never give up on anybody."

"Well, you should tell that to the Cardinal Archbishop of Boston. He just shut down the one parish in the city that was serving gay, lesbian, bisexual and transgendered people," Tom said. "Why, even Judge Lyons went to Mass there."

"I've heard about that closing. It's too bad. You could come to my diocese. We still have a church with…urban concerns."

"Is that the Church's euphemism for us these days, 'urban concerns?'" Tom said.

The Bishop smiled patiently at Tom, as if to say, *there's no pleasing you, and there never will be.* He then turned to Joe and said, "And Judge Lyons, did you find what you were looking for when we last met? I'm sorry I wasn't more help. Rome beckoned and I had to direct my energies there."

Joe replied, "It worked out. I have a question, however. Is that young man with you named Foley?"

"No. No, he's a seminarian. His name is Michael Nemesis. He's the son of the prominent layman, Sam Nemesis. Perhaps you've heard of him? Sam has a peculiar and persistent interest in judges," the Bishop smiled at Joe. "Michael wants to be a monk, a Trappist in fact. His father wants me to persuade him otherwise, to get him to study in Rome and work there a while before committing to anything contemplative. Frankly, I think the father wants young Michael to become a Cardinal, another Ratzinger or Ottavianni, and he thinks I know how that can be accomplished," Bishop Randozza said with false humility. "It's a vicarious vocation for Sam, one might say. He really thinks that he's the *Defensor fidei*, that we ecclesiastics are too accommodating. Sam forgets that Jesus forgave sinners. The son is very holy and shuns the more political side of being a priest. He's not interested in the Church Militant. I'm on the son's side. His father is not going to be too happy with me."

Joe looked at Tom and Tom at Joe. Tom, who never gave up the fight, said, "Maybe someone should tell Sam that the only people Jesus threw out were the moneychangers in the temple. I don't think Jesus would go for some of Sam's enterprises or those of his right-wing friends."

The Bishop wisely did not respond. He knew that you don't have to go to every fight you're invited to. Franny moved him on to Alice Allen, who was now talking to JoJo, Maureen and LaLa. *This'll be a tough bunch,* Franny thought. *But I think he's up to it.* JoJo had just asked Alice Allen if she was the plumber. Alice, who thought dressing like the proletariat was as fashionable today as it had been in the late Sixties, was horrified and told JoJo that she was a writer. Jojo told Alice that she was a mess and was giving dykes a bad name with her outfit, whatever she did for a living. Of course, Alice did nothing for a living, unless cashing checks counted. JoJo knew LaLa from the olden days at Sporters Café, when both men and women went there. JoJo, along with the most of the rest of the world, had never known whether LaLa was a boy or a girl and was about to ask as the Bishop and Franny approached.

"Good evening, Ladies," the Bishop said, not quite certain if he was correct. JoJo, who incongruously had a great deal of respect for the hierarchy, did a little curtsy and kissed the giant aquamarine on the Bishops right hand.

Maureen said, "Are you enjoying yourself, Uncle Rocco?"

LaLa looked lustfully at the ring and the chest hair alternately, unable to decide which he/she wanted more.

Alice, so recently chastised by JoJo, had no idea what to say or do. There was nothing in her background or ideology that prepared her for dealing with a Roman Catholic bishop. She was uncharacteristically silent until the Bishop addressed her directly and said, "Francis [meaning Franny Flynn] tells me that you're a writer. What are you writing now?"

Alice, who, of course, hadn't written anything in years, replied, "I'm writing a novel about the plight of poor women in this patriarchal society."

"Very interesting," said the Bishop.

"Yes," Alice said, now becoming bolder. "The heroine eventually takes a machine gun to all the men in her life."

"Oh, a cheery book," said Maureen. "What would you know about poor women, Alice?"

Franny Flynn said, "Alice lives in a mansion up the street. She has the best Art collection in town. Perhaps she'll invite you girls over."

"My grandfather was an Episcopal bishop," Alice said helplessly In an attempt to regain some dignity.

"That's redundant," Franny said.

"Oh, really! Where did he serve?" Bishop Rocco inquired kindly, ignoring Franny's appropriation of one of Evelyn Waugh's better ripostes, and thinking that too much sport had been made of poor

Alice.

"He was the Episcopal Bishop of Connecticut," Alice said. "The Cathedral was in Hartford. He was my mother's father."

"How interesting! I'd like to know more about him," Bishop Randozza said.

"I have a scrapbook about my grandfather at home. I could send it to you…if…if you'll return it," Alice said, grateful to have been restored some dignity, even if it was for that which she pretended to deplore, her WASPy past.

"Of course, I will. Francis has my address. Thank you very much."

Franny and the Bishop moved on. Joe looked over to the spot near the wall where Michael Nemesis had been standing. He was no longer there. Joe looked around the terrace.

Michael Nemesis had bolted.

Extra Ecclesiam Nulla Salus

When Joe arrived at the Courthouse on Monday morning there was Patrick Foley, bright and shiny, waiting for him on a chair right outside the door to Joe's office. This was the chair that a court officer usually sat on after notifying the judge that his session was ready. Because some judges did not respond promptly to such a summons the ever considerate-to-staff Miss Managhan had put chairs outside each judge's office so the court officers could at least sit while waiting.

From the distance down the long corridor of judges' offices Joe looked at Patrick Foley closely to see if perhaps he had been mistaken yesterday in thinking that Patrick Foley was also Michael Nemesis, the son of Sam Nemesis. Two days later, Joe did not think so. *Does this kid have amnesia on weekends when he assumes another identity?* Joe asked himself. *How does he do it? Does he have two lives? Is he a spy in my office? Does the Church really care what I do? Am I that big a threat? Are they following me like the* Herald *does some judges?*

As Joe approached, Patrick saw him, stood up and looked at Joe eagerly. *He's like a kid on the first day of school,* Joe thought. *What can I get him to do? Maybe I'll give him that zoning case from Newton. The town won't let a self proclaimed psychic read tea leaves out of her house for money even though two dentists and a physical therapist have their offices out of their houses on the same street.*

"Good morning, your honor," Patrick said cheerily. "How was your weekend?"

Well, that breaks the ice, Joe thought. "Come into the office, Patrick. I have a case for you. How was *your* weekend? Did you go away?"

"Yes, Rodney and I went to Provincetown. It was beautiful there. Did I see you on Commercial Street on Saturday afternoon?"

"You could have. Did I see you at a party in the West End on Saturday night?"

"No, I had dinner with my brother at the Lobster Pot on Saturday night. It has the best fish in town."

"I didn't know you had a gay brother."

"I don't. At least I think I don't. I do have six sisters and one or two of them may be lesbians, but they are so in the closet I don't think they will ever come out."

Before Joe could inquire further Court Officer O'Brien came to the door and announced, "The Chief Justice wants to see you. He's in his conference room. Her Imperial Majesty, the Chief Justice of the Supreme Judicial Court, is in there with him. I think it's about the *Herald* this morning."

"What's in the *Herald*?" Joe asked.

"You didn't see it?"

"I have it, Judge," said Patrick Foley as he pulled the newspaper out of his shiny new attaché case. It was opened to the gossip page, called the *Eye* column. There was Joe's picture in color walking up Commercial Street arm in arm with Tom Murphy. Joe was wearing pink pants and a navy blue linen shirt. Tom was in black leather chaps, a matching codpiece, and a harness over his shirtless torso.

"Oh shit!" Joe said.

"What's the matter, Judge?" Patrick Foley said. "You're not allowed to walk arm in arm with another man these days? Would it be better if you were married to him?"

The Court Officer, who had very distinct beliefs about how everybody else should behave, gave Patrick a look, as if to say, *What are you, an idiot, kid? This is the Courthouse! We can't have judges wearing pink pants, walking with people dressed in harnesses and codpieces!*

The story was complete with a quote from a retired judge, the self-appointed guardian of judicial conduct, who the *Herald* and Fox News pulled out every time they wanted to get righteous about the Judiciary. "Maybe I'm old fashioned," the pompous old sage said, "but I don't think it looks very judicious for a judge to be wearing pink pants and to walk arm in arm with a man in leather chaps, a codpiece and a halter. Judges cannot do what other people can do. They give up certain rights when they take the robe. If you want to be a judge, you're going to have to live a very clean, dedicated life. If you can't, don't be a judge. That's a very strict code, and I tried very hard to abide by it," said the *Herald*'s judicial conduct expert.

"Are you ready, Judge?" Court Officer O'Brien asked.

"I might as well have an empty bladder and look good for this," he said to Patrick Foley. "You wait here. I should be back. I hope." Joe went into the lavatory to pee and comb his hair.

Joe felt like he was in a bad movie, like a prisoner being taken to the electric chair as he followed Court Officer O'Brien to the Chief Justice's conference room.

Court Officer O'Brien knocked three times. The door was opened by Joe's Chief Justice.

"Come in, Joe," he said. "Sit down," as he nodded to a chair. "You know the Chief Justice, I assume?"

"I do, Chief," Joe replied.

During this exchange the Chief Justice of the Supreme Judicial Court busily looked at the papers in front of her, avoiding Joe's gaze.

"You probably know why we're here, Joe," Joe's Chief Justice said.

"I just saw the *Herald*."

"Well, as you know, we're not prudes, like certain retired judges who can't let go. We don't care if you go to Provincetown, or even if you wear pink pants. We might suggest that you refrain from strolling arm in arm with a man in leather chaps and a harness, especially someone without a shirt, but we can't enforce that," the Chief Justice said as he smiled painfully.

"What does concern us is that which the *Herald* does not seem to know yet. The man in leather, Mr. X to the *Herald* and Thomas Aloysius Murphy, Esquire, to us, is a lawyer whose firm frequently appears in this court, and which firm has occasionally appeared in front of you, we are informed.

"As you probably know, we recently received a complaint which alleges that last year you sat on a case involving the business interests of a, uh… a…a romantic interest of yours. The panel in that case did not rule in his favor, but some people, including a very aggressive complainant, question the fact that you sat on the case at all and did not recuse yourself. We haven't investigated that case yet to our satisfaction and did not want to bother you about it until we were certain about the facts, but today's *Herald* photo and the implications of it, whether or not the *Herald* has caught onto them yet, raise similar concerns.

"Do you have any comments at this time?" Joe's Chief added.

The Chief Justice of all other Chief and associate justices—in Massachusetts, at least—continued to look down at the papers in front of her during this introduction.

Joe paused for a bit. He then said, "Chief, I hate this fucken job!"

That got the Chiefest of Massachusetts Justices to raise her head.

Joe continued, "I'm a good judge. As far as I know, there have been no complaints about me. Only twice in 16 plus years have I been overruled by a higher court, and if your Eminence from that higher court will forgive me, I was right. Those reversals were on minor issues. In one of those cases, the law later came around to my position," Joe added.

"In spite of the supposed liberalism of this state, a gay man's personal life, if examined, will not meet straight society's standards of decorum. Therefore, I have tried to keep my personal life under wraps, even in situations where my straight *confreres* would not think twice of exposing theirs. Unlike some of my colleagues, who I'm sure you are aware of, I have not brought my romances, extra-marital or otherwise, to court functions, nor do I entertain them in my chambers.

"I have not taken a bribe, favored a friend, or lost my temper or composure during a hearing. Tom Murphy is my oldest friend. We went to law school together. As you probably know, he is not a lawyer in the sense we know lawyers in this courthouse. I think he was in court once—for a speeding ticket, and he lost, as I remind him. He puts together deals and dabbles in politics, mainly for LGBT—lesbian, gay, bisexual and transgender—causes, but he also works for the homeless, to obtain health care for the poor, and for better treatment for addicts and alcoholics. He has his finger in a lot of pies.

"He also is one of the two lawyers representing me in the matter you referred to. Dewey Battle is the other. I have consulted them both and they are working together. I believe that I can prove that I did not sit on the *Williamson v. Randozza Enterprises, Inc.* I recused myself. Although the record of the case does not indicate that, I believe I can prove it. The Reporter of Decisions, who, as you both know, is never present at arguments and who relies on schedules and records for his notations, made a mistake in publishing the report of the decision in the case with my name on it as the presiding justice.

Joe continued, his voice rising, "In fact, on that day I had retired to my lobby during the break of that sitting after hearing three cases. I did not return until the fourth case, the *Williamson v. Randozza Enterprises, Inc.* argument, was concluded. I did not participate in the discussion of the case after argument either. My sister, Justice Mildred Bailey, presided at the hearing of that argument pursuant to the assignment of our now deceased and beloved previous chief justice, after I told him that I had to recuse myself in the case. Miss Managhan facilitated the assignment. The old Chief was on vacation when I raised the issue. I called him at his cabin in the Berkshires and he told me to have Miss Managhan handle the matter. I did so instruct Miss Managhan.

The Chief Justice nodded and Joe went on, "I appreciate the delicacy with which you have proceeded, or rather not proceeded, with that investigation. I know that the subject of gay life in all its shiny facets is new for you and that although the concept of same-sex romance is not alien to you, the particulars of it are novel and unfamiliar.

By now the Chiefest of Justices was looking up with interest. Joe saw this and said, "As for my sitting on cases involving Tom Murphy's firm, I am not aware that I ever have done so. I've scrupulously avoided his firm's cases and have instructed Mr. Hawthorne, who schedules our sittings and prepares the assignments for you, Mister Chief Justice, not to assign me to such cases. In order for me to respond, I would appreciate it if you would tell me which cases they are, on what dates they were heard, and what lawyers argued them. As you know, Mr. Murphy's firm, which was big to begin with, and which has recently become larger, has been through a number of permutations and mergers over the past few years. I don't know, but perhaps that is the source of the confusion. Its name has changed twice and then reverted to the original, Healy, Swords and Fiske.

"Also, Mr. Murphy was away from his firm for two years while he was an undersecretary in the Department of Housing and Urban Development in the Clinton Administration. All these details are pertinent. I would appreciate your patience and assistance on this matter before a rush to judgment inflamed by this photo, which, by the way, is at least three years old. I threw those pants out long ago. My house cleaner now wears them in an entertainment, a drag show in fact, at a bar called *Jacques* in Bay Village."

Joe knew that the reference to "a rush to judgment inflamed by this photo" would get them.

He was right. The Chief Justices looked at each other. Eyebrows, plucked and bushy, rose. Then Joe's Chief Justice spoke, "Joseph, my friend, we are not accusing you of anything, but, as you can appreciate, this bizarre photo causes concern. We were informed by a member of the staff that on at least one occasion you sat on a case involving Mr. Murphy's firm. Perhaps she is mistaken. We certainly hope so."

Joe interrupted, "It would not be the first time the staff has been mistaken. They were mistaken regarding the *Williamson v. Randozza Enterprises, Inc.* case, to my discomfort, and expense, I might add. Dewey Battle does not come cheap. God only knows how many other mistakes have been made."

Joe's Chief Justice blinked a few times, and then continued, "Of course, we will inform you, and your lawyer, of the problematic situations as we see them. We are no more anxious to cause scandal than you are. The judiciary has had a tough enough time in recent years."

Madame, the Chiefest of Justices and Chief Justices (within the boundaries of the Commonwealth of Massachusetts) rose, nodded to Joe and departed. Somehow the door opened without her engaging it.

Joe returned to his office. Patrick Foley was reading at Joe's conference table. Joe had little patience for playing games now. He went right to it. "Patrick, were you with Bishop Rocco Randozza on Saturday night in Provincetown at a party given by Franny Flynn? Do you also go by the name 'Michael Nemesis'? Do you sometimes wear black rimmed glasses like Clark Kent?" All of this was said in a rush as Joe's face got redder.

Patrick looked stunned. He stared at Joe, looked away, stood up, sat down, then stood up again. He walked to the window, which was as far away as he could get from Joe but still be in the room. Finally he looked hard directly at Joe and said, "Michael Nemesis is my twin brother. And Sam Nemesis is my father. I've renounced everything my father stands for!" Then Patrick ran out of the room.

Joe did not go after him. For one thing Joe was not given to such dramatics. For another, Patrick left his attaché case and the jacket of his well-tailored suit in Joe's office. Third, Joe wanted to be alone while he digested what had just been said in the Conference room. *He'll be back*, Joe thought as he picked up the phone to call Tom Murphy.

After he recounted who said what to whom, Tom said, "I'll meet you for lunch at the Parker House, the big dining room. Jimmy will get us a table away from everybody."

* * *

Joe arrived first. Joe always arrived first. Tom was always late. If it wasn't a phone call as he was going out the door, he was bumping into somebody important during the three-block walk from his office at Healy, Swords and Fiske to the Parker House. Today it was the latter; the intrusive dignitary was none other than the Mayor of Boston, who was leading a delegation to the State House to seek home rule status to permit energy producing windmills in Roslindale. Tom had to explain all this to Joe and Jimmy, the solicitous *maitre d'*, who was seating him at Joe's table, far from the other diners, who included at one table the President of the Senate, the Speaker of the House, and the Editor in Chief of the Boston *Herald*.

At another table were two of the Cardinal Archbishop's lawyers, one for the defense of priests in sexual abuse cases and the other his real estate lawyer. They were sitting with the First Assistant Clerk of Courts for Middlesex County. On the other side of the room, also isolated from the crowd, were the Chief Justice of the Boston Municipal Court, the Chief Justice of the Superior Court, the Executive Secretary of the Supreme Judicial Court and an unknown very good-looking, young black woman, who Joe thought he had seen before. At the next table was Monsignor Owen, the Chancellor of the Archdiocese and Louise McGee, a very wealthy widow and donor to Catholic causes, also the mother of two lesbian daughters, one an ex-nun. Louise had been about to divorce her philandering husband, the source of their fortune, when he died of a heart attack in his girlfriend's bed. Louise inherited everything; the Church received some of it from her. They'd like to receive some more.

Along the side of the room were two pairs of badly dressed, overweight tourists and their slovenly children. The adults in one set were asking Raul, the Latino waiter, how to eat the lobster, which, to their surprise, had come to them in a shell.

Joe had a little shine for Raul and hoped that Raul's lobster eating instruction would be brief and that Raul would soon arrive at Joe's table so that Joe could try out his Spanish on Raul, who would praise Joe's efforts in Spanish, and then in English for the benefit of Joe's companions. Raul's very deep rolling voice always got Joe thinking impure thoughts.

After Tom had explained his delay he jumped right in and said to Joe, "You were great. It seems that Madame Chief Justice, came downstairs to land on you with all fours. However, you put the brakes to that. I'd like to have listened in on the call between the Chieftains that followed your interview. They don't have a case where my firm appeared in front of you. Do they? I think I would've known about that. We always knew that we had to be more careful than other people. There are always bastards out to get us in the private sector too."

Joe replied, "I don't think they do have a case, but if there is one, Sam Nemesis will let them know. By the way, do you know who his son is?"

"Yeah, that kid at Franny Flynn's party with Bishop Randozza."

"That's one of them, but didn't he look like somebody we met in Florida?"

"Who? Carlos Colorado, your Cuban refugee?"

"No, he was your Cuban refugee and don't forget that. Don't you remember the kid who approached us at Sebastian Beach, the one who wanted to be my intern?"

"I remember a tight little white body in a navy blue Speedo and his big black trooper boyfriend. Why?"

"Do you remember his face?"

"When I'm sitting at crotch level looking at a nice package in a Speedo, the face doesn't matter. I remember that he was not Jewish or Muslim."

"Well, I noticed right away that the kid at Franny's party, the Bishop's acolyte and my intern, who reported for work today, looked very much alike. At first I thought they were one and the same person. So after leaving the Chief Justices I couldn't tolerate any more bullshit intrigue and I confronted the poor kid who was in my office waiting to start work. He didn't know what hit him and burst into tears. He told me he is Sam Nemesis' son and the Bishop's minion is his brother."

"Jesus! Are they infiltrating your office?"

"More will be revealed. Patrick Foley, *ne* Nemesis, told me that he renounced everything his father stands for. Then he ran out of my office."

"Did he come back?"

"No, but he will. He left his briefcase and jacket behind."

"Well, can't he go in and get it?"

"No, I locked the office. Here's the key." Joe held it up. "He'll have to see me first. I think he'll want to explain himself more."

"What a crazy place that courthouse is! I thought working in Washington was bad. What do you think they are giving away here today? Look at the combos in this place! Who do you think is sleeping with whom?" Tom said, drawing out the "m" on the tyrannical "whom" for emphasis.

"I know I'm not supposed to ask, but what's the latest on the Anti-Same-Sex Marriage Amendment?" Joe asked.

Tom replied, "We're so close I can taste it, but something could screw it up. For instance, I wonder why the President of the Senate and the Speaker of the House are here with the *Herald*'s publisher. Is it to soften her up, to give her the bad news? Or are they trying to make nice for the next big issue? Do they want to give her a heads up? It's very mysterious. My source tells me that there is one possible unlikely switch for us."

"Is that Billy Meadows?" Joe asked, hoping that it was and that he, Joe, could know that he had made a contribution to this fight, even though he could never tell anyone about it.

"Billy Meadows cannot be found. I swear I saw him in Provincetown last weekend. I'm not telling you where but you can guess. Did I say the back room of the Vault? No, never, not me. We have the boys at Ganymede Farm looking for him in their area."

"Is the Ganymede Farm in his district?" Joe asked.

"It's next door, and over the years Billy's been known to visit, to ride his horse over," Tom said.

"We're supposed to go to a party there next week. Maybe Billy will be there. He'll be happy to see me I'm sure," Joe said.

"All we need is for him to stay home on June 14th, the day of the Anti-Same-Sex Marriage Amendment vote," Tom said.

"Maybe the Ganymede boys can tie him to a tree," Joe said.

"He might like that," Tom said.

After that they talked about everything but what had just gone on with Joe. Who knew if the place was bugged? Years before the FBI had bugged a diner in Dorchester in an attempt to get some Boston cops. The tapes were still popping up in one context or another. Most recently, a new trial judge, formerly an FBI agent, who made a dumb decision in a case involving Freedom of the Press was reviled by a columnist for her part in listening to those tapes and telling what she claimed to have heard.

Over their specially prepared, by Jimmy, the *maitre d'*, lobster salads with pine nuts, sun-dried tomatoes and balsamic vinaigrette, they talked about men. And, in spite of the possible tape listeners, they talked about sex. Tom's sex life was always to be admired. He flew to Paris, Amsterdam and Berlin in search of sexual freedom. "This town for all its lofty talk about Gay Rights is no better now than it was with the Puritans. This mayor is basically a prude at heart. In Berlin the bars are open almost all night and they love their daddies there. Punishment night in the Toilet in Paris is the best sex in the world. The more beautiful they are, the harder they want to be spanked. Here it's a twink contest. These Boston boys don't appreciate men. They don't understand real sex."

Joe said very little. He could not add to Tom's expertise, but he enjoyed Tom's company and Joe knew that when Tom was not on a rant he was full of wisdom.

After lunch Tom walked Joe to the steps leading up to the courthouse. Then Tom was going to walk down State Street to return to his office. Just as Joe shook Tom's hand in farewell, the Chiefest of All Justices (in Massachusetts) passed them and said, "Hello, Judge

Lyons. Good afternoon, Mister Murphy. I see you're dressed a little warmer than in the *Herald* this morning." She did not wait for a reply but kept on walking, away from the Courthouse.

It was no secret that Joe and Tom were friends, as the morning's conversation with the Chief Justices indicated—Joe never pretended otherwise—but it was perhaps a little too soon after that chat for them to be seen together. On the other hand this was no clandestine meeting and its openness could be interpreted as a sign of innocence, something like a blush on an innocent pretty girl. If the *Herald* was taking pictures, Joe was not in pink pants and the only leather Tom had on was his belt and shoes.

As Joe walked down the long corridor to his office he could see Patrick Foley in his shirtsleeves, again sitting on the court officer's chair just outside Joe's office.

Patrick stood up silently as Joe approached. He made no response to Joe's greeting but followed Joe inside the door with his head down like a boy who had just broken a window following his father to be spanked. Unlike Tom, Joe was not into corporal punishment.

"Are you better, Patrick? I shouldn't have jumped on you like that this morning. I'd had a difficult meeting and your brother had been on my mind. I don't mean to open painful family matters to you. They have nothing to do with you on this job, except, as you probably know, your father is not one of my biggest fans. The only judges he likes less are the four on the Supreme Judicial Court who voted in the affirmative in the *Goodridge* case, the gay marriage decision."

"I know. I know, and I am very sorry for that," Patrick said. "My father disowned me when I told him that I'm gay. I was seventeen, in high school. Thank God, I'd been accepted at Harvard. I later was given a Point Foundation scholarship, you know, the gay scholarship. When I told Harvard the story they arranged to get me another scholarship and some financial aid. I changed my name to my mother's maiden name, 'Foley,' my grandmother's married name. My grandmother was still alive and she supported me after I left my father's house.

Joe was agog. Patrick continued, "You may know things about my father, but you probably don't know that my mother died when I was ten and my father remarried. It's his second wife, the Polish reactionary, who changed my father and made him so hateful—she and Father Scyzwycz. She brought that priest into the house and soon we were moving to Lancaster. We went to school at Saint Philomena's until I got thrown out for drinking and smoking. Michael, my twin brother, who you saw on Sunday, stayed at Saint Philomena's and then went into the seminary.

"My father saw me as trouble. His wife thought I was Satan. I see my brother occasionally. He sneaks away. He tries to reconvert me. He's not a happy guy. That Bishop Randozza has taken him under his wing, which is a good thing because the Bishop is a pretty worldly guy. I met him once or twice. Michael is loosening up, but he still wants to be a monk," Patrick Foley added.

After some breaths he began again, "I really do admire you. I read about you in *Bay Windows*. They had a subscription for it at my high school library. As a matter of fact, that's how I came out to my father. I came home with a copy of *Bay Windows* and he started to question me. Finally, I just said, 'Look! I'm gay. I've always been gay, and I always will be gay. And that creep priest you have hanging around here is gayer than I am. And if you don't like what I am, I'm out of here.'

"Before he could answer I got in my car and drove to my grandmother Foley's house in Malden. She loved having me move in. We tried to persuade Michael to come too, but he wouldn't. He did visit, however. He told me that the priest was not around so much. But by then my father had gone around the bend on the Catholic stuff. I'm sure that he's *Opus Dei* and everything else by now. His wife did it to him. It's her fault."

"How did you know you were gay?" Joe asked.

"I kind of always knew. Didn't you, Judge?" Patrick said disarmingly.

Before Joe could answer, if he were so inclined, which he wasn't, at least not in his chambers, Patrick continued, "I had crushes on classmates and teachers. As a little kid my brother and I would look at *National Geographic* for the naked natives. When I got thrown out of Saint Philomena's my father gave me a car to go to the regional public high school. That was my 'last chance,' he said. Then when I moved into my grandmother's house I went to Saint Cosmas and Damien's High. My father agreed to pay for it because it was Catholic. Of course, I used to drive to Boston to go to Calamus, the gay bookstore. I had quite a library stashed in the trunk. As you know, I like African American guys. That's why I'm with Rodney, the guy you saw me with at Sebastian Beach, the State Trooper in the white bathing suit."

"Oh, I remember him," Joe said. "He's quite unforgettable."

Patrick nodded and continued, "I had black guy muscle magazines in the trunk, besides James Baldwin, Carl Van Vechten, Langston Hughes and some more modern black gay novelists. My high school was very progressive. Why wouldn't it be, only a few miles outside of Boston? They even bused in some kids from Boston. I had a big crush on Roberto Banks. He played football. I got to be manager of the football team just so I could take showers next to him. He didn't have a clue. I'd have to think of the worst things to keep my, uh…excitement down.

"I'm probably talking too much now, Judge," Patrick said with a small smile, knowing that Joe was eating up this tale of adolescent passion. Joe loved the euphemism—"excitement" indeed. Joe was getting an excitement of his own. Joe's story was like Patrick's. Except for Joe the crush was on a blond diver rather than a black football player. Another difference was that Joe's fondness for his crush was reciprocated. That was a good thing.

"Thanks for listening to me, Judge. I was lucky to have my grandmother and the guidance counselor at high school, Brother Sebastian. He was right out of the sixties—everything but the love beads…and maybe he had those on underneath his cassock. He really let me be myself, whatever that was…and is."

"Alright, Patrick, now I have to give you the standard judge-to-law clerk lecture. Don't take it personally even though you are a special case. We give it to everyone. You could do me and this court, a lot of harm, were you so inclined. You know of your father's obsession with judges—particularly those of a liberal bent, and those, like me, who are bent, period.

"Anything you hear or see here stays here. You should not talk about it to anyone, your husband or your wife, your lover or your friends. We've just been through seven years of controversy because of what a law clerk allegedly said to a scoundrel who set him up and offered him filthy lucre for his betrayal of a judge he served. Thank God the Supreme Judicial Court saw the light and disbarred that louse and the other louse, who was going to buy the first louse's information. I don't know what happened to the law clerk, but I'd suggest that just the whiff that he may have violated his judge's confidence has made him damaged goods around Massachusetts. Do you think that you can keep our confidences?"

To Patrick, this sounded like he had to renew his baptismal vows. *Do you renounce Satan and all his pomps?*

"Yes, I can keep your confidences and those of the Court," Patrick said. "I've kept my own secrets for a long time. I'm used to keeping secrets."

"Ah yes, but keeping your secrets was not a healthy thing. Keeping our secrets insures that we are able to function, to reach agreement and write decisions without fear of exposure. Bismarck's remark about the making of legislation being like the making of sausages sometimes applies to judicial decision making as well. And like legislation and sausage making, it should not be too closely examined. By and large we work things out up here. It's rare that we cannot do that. Part of our individual worth as judges comes from that ability to work things out. Of course, there are the *prima donnas*, even here, who don't care about consensus, and the stability that it creates. They go off halfcocked on ego trips in dissents, sometimes even in concurring opinions—perhaps just to read, see, or hear themselves talk. You'll soon know who they are. They aren't ever going to leave us, but, if you ask me, retirement day cannot come soon enough for them. Do you have any questions?"

"What about the other interns and clerks? Do they get this lecture?" Patrick asked.

"Yes, they do. Our Chief Justice insists on it. There are even forms that must be signed. The very able Miss Mary Margaret Managhan, who you will soon meet, will give them to you. One of my colleagues tells his law clerks and interns that they will be shot after their service—kind of like male praying mantises that must die after sex. We are aware that law clerks and interns gossip as well. That's why we keep you all together in those sorry cubicles out front. You can gossip, but you do so at your peril because there are always some clerks or interns who tell their judges who can and cannot be trusted. The walls have ears and eyes around here. It's crazy but you'll get used to it. Nevertheless, it is still a great place to work. Just be discreet," Joe cautioned.

"Now I have to decide whether to tell my Chief who you're related to. We each have a lot of latitude to bring in whomever we want as interns, but you, my lad, are a special case. You could harm all of us more easily than the others. I trust you but I'm not sure what the Chief Justice would say, particularly when your father is trying to bring me and us down. I have to think about that. I'm in enough hot water right now so I won't bring it up today.

Joe sat down and said, "Right now I have a job for you. A case has been assigned to me with the following facts, which I gleaned from the very well-written findings of the trial judge in the Boston Municipal Court as well as the transcript and papers in the case and the briefs of the parties."

Joe searched through the papers on his desk. Having found what he wanted he said, "On a summer's eve last year a state trooper, Massachusetts State Trooper Horace Mulligan, was driving through downtown Boston on his way from the barracks on Storrow Drive at Leverett Circle to the Massachusetts Turnpike at Copley Square. You don't know him, do you? He's not a friend of your boyfriend Rodney's is he?" Joe interjected.

Patrick nodded negatively.

Joe continued, "In Park Square, *en route*, Trooper Mulligan saw a ramshackle old, blue Toyota Corsica with four young African-American kids in it. He claims that when they were both stopped at a red light he, the trooper, who was stopped behind the Toyota with his window down, could smell marijuana coming from the Toyota. He also noted a broken taillight on the Toyota. So, Trooper Mulligan turned on all his bells, whistles and lights, including the wig wag lights, whatever those might be. The Trooper pulled up on the left into the oncoming traffic lane and signaled the driver of the Toyota to pull over to the right, which he did.

"As Trooper Mulligan approached the driver's side window he noticed much commotion in the car; the back seat passengers looked back, then ducked down, rose up and looked back again. One of them, the Trooper claims, was the defendant in this case, Thomas Jefferson Mobutu. Trooper Mulligan 'removed' the driver and front seat passenger and looked into the car. Trooper Mulligan's police report says that on the front console, that platform between the front seats, from outside of the Toyota, the Trooper saw 'in plain view,' magic words those, a 'blunt,' that is a cigar into which drug users stuff marijuana. The trooper seized the blunt, smelt it, noted in his mind that it smelt like marijuana, and put it in his left jodhpur pocket. Trooper Mulligan also wrote that he got a good front face view of the back seat passengers, and the one behind the driver's seat was the defendant.

"'In plain view' are magic words because they take the whole question of an unconstitutional search and seizure out of the discussion. A police officer can seize contraband that he sees 'in plain view.' There is no search if something is 'in plain view.' You understand that?"

Patrick said he did.

"By that time two other troopers arrived in a marked car and a Boston Police Officer also arrived on a bicycle. The driver and front seat passenger were both put under arrest for possession of marijuana, it being impossible to tell which of them actually possessed 'the blunt' that sat between them. They were handcuffed and 'placed' in the back of one of the other State Police cars. As that was occurring the back seat passenger on the left, behind the driver, jumped out of the Toyota and ran down the street towards the Public Garden. Trooper Mulligan claims that he saw him 'discard' certain small objects in the vicinity of the giant Chinese horses in front of P.F. Changs on Charles Street while running. A 'subsequent search' by the Boston Police officer revealed two small packets of 'crack' under the upraised hoof of one of the horses.

"Trooper Mulligan noted that the man fleeing was entirely dressed in black, including a hoodie, a hooded sweatshirt, unusual garb for a hot summer's night, in the trooper's opinion. Trooper Mulligan got in his cruiser and pursued the runner. He did not immediately find him, but fifteen minutes later, after the driver and front seat passenger were taken for booking, Trooper Mulligan drove down Tremont Street. Outside the Park Street Station, the

'Hub of the Universe' in Boston legend, there was the back seat passenger, leaning against the granite wall of the station, near the pay phones, 'engaging two young white girls in conversation.' Trooper Mulligan claimed that he recognized Thomas Jefferson Mobutu by the black hoodie at first, and then by face as the result of his original view of him in the back seat once he, the Trooper, pulled back Mr. Mobutu's hood at the Park Street Station. Trooper Mulligan arrested Thomas Jefferson Mobutu over the objections of the two teenaged girls he was talking to and others who had gathered.

"Thomas began shouting, 'It ain't me. It ain't me. I didn't do nothing.' Thomas was charged with Possession of Marijuana, to wit 'the blunt,' for which, by the way, if you've been following me, two other men had just been arrested and booked, as well as Disorderly Conduct for causing a crowd to gather at the Park Street Station.

"During the hearing on the Motion to Suppress the Evidence, 'the blunt,' as it applied to Thomas Jefferson Mobutu, Trooper Mulligan testified that he found 'the blunt' at the feet of Mr. Mobutu, on the floor of the back seat behind the driver. He was quite certain of that. His police report, again if you've been following me, Patrick, said that he saw 'the blunt' on the console between the two front seats and that he picked it up, smelt it and then put it in his pocket.

"In his findings of fact the judge who heard the Motion to Suppress noted that Trooper Mulligan's sworn testimony contradicts the police report written within hours after the incident by Trooper Mulligan. The trial judge allowed the Motion to Suppress 'the blunt.' It cannot be used against Thomas Jefferson Mobutu. Without 'the blunt' being introduced the Possession of Marijuana charge would fall and under the doctrine of 'The Fruit of the Poisoned Tree,' perhaps the Disorderly charge should go too. That is something you should look into as well."

"I will," said Patrick.

Joe continued, "The Commonwealth appealed and, among

other things, argues that because the police report was never introduced into evidence at the hearing the Judge's use of it to contradict Trooper Mulligan's testimony under oath at the hearing was improper. They claim that unless the report was properly introduced as a 'Prior Inconsistent Statement,' let's say, it is inadmissible Hearsay.

"In the words of the leading guru on Evidence, Professor Irving Younger, 'Hearsay is any out of court statement offered to prove the truth of the matter asserted.' And that includes written statements. A police report is not written under oath and its maker is not subject to cross examination at the time of its writing.

"The Commonwealth notes that the practice seems to be that the Police Department provides police reports to the Clerk's office when the police seek a complaint; that since 1995 it is the practice of the Clerk, if he decides a complaint should issue, to put the police report into the case file. Nobody seems to be too sure why that is done. In 1995 substantial changes were made to Massachusetts Criminal Law Practice and Procedure but there is no mention of what should be done with police reports."

Patrick interjected, "We were taught the most recent version of the Rules."

"That's good. Note as well that the case file also acts as a docket calendar because the clerk's notes about what occurred in court and when are written contemporaneously on the back of it. The case file is available to the judge in the courtroom. As a matter of fact, the judge needs to look at the file to examine the pleadings, the papers in the case, such as a Motion to Suppress. If one watches a trial, or a hearing such as this, one will see the file being passed back and forth frequently from the clerk to the judge during the proceeding. Keep your eyes on it."

"I will, sir." Patrick said.

"It would be a good thing for you, and within the purview of your work here, to go down to the Boston Municipal Court and watch what goes on there. It would be very enlightening. I should send some of my colleagues, who have rarely seen the inside of a trial courtroom, to go with you, but, of course, I do not have the authority to do that," Joe added with a smile.

Patrick smiled weakly as well, just to be agreeable.

"As a matter of fact, if you want to go tomorrow or Thursday, I'll call down to Mary Rose Quirk, who is the First Assistant Clerk. She's an old pal of mine from the time I sat there briefly as an experiment in Judicial democracy—or something. Mary Rose has been there since she was 19. What time do you want to go?" Joe asked.

Patrick, who thought he was getting the "bum's rush," and in fact, in part, he was, had no idea what to say. "I thought that I would hang around up here for a while," Patrick said. "Kind of meet the other interns and clerks, get to know the lay of the land. You know."

"Alright, hang around here tomorrow. You'll have time soon enough to learn all our bad habits. Go down to the Boston Municipal Court, the venerable B.M.C., the 'Old Bailey' of Massachusetts, on Thursday. You'll learn twice as much as any of these ivory tower and Ivy League types can teach you up here. Come back at the end of the day and we'll talk. Can I tell Mary Rose that you'll be down on Thursday?

"Oh, okay," Patrick Foley said weakly. He then gathered up his things and stuffed them into the black attaché case he had opened on Joe's conference table at his first entrance today.

"There's a desk for you in the corridor with the law clerks. Put your stuff there and meet your mates. Hang around here a couple of days. Go into the sessions whenever you can. There's nothing like observation. Note the names of who you see and hear—both the judges and the lawyers. The head law clerk, Ina Fernandes, will show you around up here. When you go to the B.M.C. leave all your equipment behind. Don't bring a briefcase. It'll make them nervous. You're just going down to see how the B.M.C. works. If they see you with all that gear, they'll get scared and nobody will tell you anything. Mary Rose is an old friend, but depending on the judge whose courtroom you're going into, she or he will probably be forewarned about who you are and that you come from 'upstairs,' which is what they call this court and the Supreme Judicial Court. The CIA could use the intelligence system that goes through the B.M.C. So just be charming and polite. You'll learn a lot. They'll tell it all to you if you treat them right. Remember the old adage, 'A judge can hurt you, but a clerk can kill you.'

"Don't, under any circumstances, tell them who you really are or where you come from. They'll do a 911 on you within minutes. Tell them you're from…Montana—part of the great migration of Irish copper miners who went to Butte at the end of the 19th century.

"Good luck!"

Ivory Boxes within Ivory Boxes

On Tuesday morning Joe called the Boston Municipal Court Clerk's office.

"Hello, Mary Rose. This is Joe Lyons...from 'upstairs.'"

"Oh hello, Judge Lyons, how are you? What can we do for you today? Will you be coming back down to work with us? We need someone speedy in the First Criminal Session. You're still fondly remembered there, particularly by the court officers. Unlike some of the slow pokes down here, you always got them out early—in time for their second jobs."

"Thank you very much Mary Rose. I learned a lot working at your court. All my colleagues ought to do it. But that's not why I'm calling. Mary Rose, I have a new intern. His name is Patrick Foley. He's a very nice young man, but he doesn't know how anything really works. Would you be able to take him under your wing for a few days and show him 'what's what'? He could come down on Thursday, the 7th of June.'"

"Of course, Judge. Is he as good-looking as you?"

"Better looking and twice as nice, Mary Rose,"

"Send him down. I'll be out from one to two P.M. I have to bring lunch to my mother in the North End. She's not well, Judge. Pray for her."

"I will, Mary Rose. I'm sorry to hear that. You've been a very good daughter, Mary Rose. I wish that I had a daughter like you."

"Well, first you have to have a wife and that doesn't appear to be in your cards, Judge, with all due respect," Mary Rose said.

"A husband would do, Mary Rose; this is Massachusetts after the Millennium."

"Well, just get one who can cook. That's too often overlooked these days, Judge. Send the Foley boy down. Is he related to James Foley from South Boston?"

"Not that I know of," Joe said, knowing that Mary Rose would find out within seconds. She was Italian from the North End and her husband was Irish from South Boston and that's where they lived, in a Victorian on East Broadway. Her husband was a legislative aide at the State House. Mary Rose and her husband had two branches of government, or as John Adams so beautifully put it in the Massachusetts Constitution, two of the "Great Departments of Government," represented. Joe's call only added to her sense of power. Joe wasn't calling the Clerk or the Chief Justice of the Boston Municipal Court. He was calling Mary Rose Quirk, the real power in the Boston Municipal Court. She could take care of those other figureheads.

The first thing on Thursday Patrick Foley was at the counter of the Clerk's office of the Boston Municipal Court. A lady of the night was standing next to him with a fistful of bills to put up as bail for her "sistah" who had been arrested the night before. About 12 feet behind her a man, who looked suspiciously like a pimp from the movies (Life follows Art once again) in a lime green suit with a matching big hat and red boots, slouched in the only chair in the waiting area glancing up from his cellphone every once in a while to see how the woman at the counter was doing. If asked, she would have said he was her "fiancé." He was impatient. Just like a lawyer, time was money in his business too. The girl behind bars charged $250 an hour on the street and she was usually done in less than thirty minutes.

On Patrick's other side was a guy in a bad and rumpled brown suit, who probably was a lawyer. He wanted to file papers "right now" that were due five days before. The gray-haired man in his shirtsleeves on the other side of the counter was patiently refusing to take them. "The case is on for trial tomorrow, Mr. Paintheass. The judge is not going to dismiss the plaintiff's claim because she did not answer interrogatories you just filed today. The judge 'was born at night, but not last night.' You've heard her say that, I'm sure. That's her family motto!"

Patrick was entranced by the stuff of life going on around him, so entranced that he failed to see or hear the gentle voice of the small woman before him. "Can I help you, dahlin'?"

After a second inquiry Patrick turned back from watching the circus around him and said, "Oh, excuse me! I'm looking for…"

Before he could finish the small, energetic, well-dressed, bright-eyed and dark-haired woman before him said, "You're looking for me. Come around the counter. Don't worry about them." She nodded towards the other people on both sides of the counter who were staring at them, wondering who is this kid with the pull to be escorted into the Clerk's office by Mary Rose Quirk herself? "They won't bite. I'll show you around. I'm Mary Rose," she added unnecessarily.

"Excuse us, Ma'm. Please let the young man through. Thank you very much, Ma'm, " Mary Rose said with a sharp smile to the miniskirted, platinum blonde wearing a snakeskin tanktop with deep décolletage, whom Patrick now walked in front of.

At the right end of the counter Patrick crossed through the swinging gate where Mary Rose grabbed his hand as if he was exiting a sinking boat. "Come on down here and meet the Clerk. Then I'll take you to the judges," she said, still holding his hand as they hustled down the hall while all the other employees stared at them wondering who his "daddy" was. Patrick and Mary Rose, still hand in hand, stopped outside an office. Patrick could see a beautiful old mahogany conference table squeezed into the center of the office and an almost life-sized oil portrait of Calvin Coolidge on the wall. At the head of the table was a matching antique banker's desk, and standing behind the desk was a white-haired slicked back old man dressed like a diplomat in a grey chalk stripe suit with a mother-of-pearl tie inside a vest and a white shirt with a gold pin pulling together the points of the collar.

Behind the desk were photographs of every Massachusetts Irish American politician beginning with Mayor Patrick Collins, including Alderman Patrick J. Kennedy and Mayor John F. "Honey Fitz" Fitzgerald (the grandfathers of the late President), Martin Lomasney, Senator David I. Walsh, Mayor and Governor James Michael Curley, Mayor John B. Hynes, Governor Paul A. Dever, President John F. Kennedy himself, Senator Edward M. "Teddy" Kennedy, Mayors Kevin White and Ray Flynn and Congressmen Joe Moakley, Congressman Joe Kennedy, Jr. as well as Michael Collins. Leverett Saltonstall, who passed for Irish even though he was a Yankee, also was in the pantheon.

The Clerk, Austin Ignatius Costello, bowed almost to the waist at Mary Rose's introduction of Patrick as Judge Lyons' intern.

"I have the greatest respect for Judge Lawlor. It's an honor to meet you," Mr. Costello, the Clerk said

Both the bow and the confusion about Judge Lawlor, whoever he might be, mystified Patrick, who had never before been received with such dignity, not even when his father had taken him to Rome to meet the Pope.

Mary Rose said, "It's Judge *Lyons*, Mr. Costello, Judge *Lyons* at the

Appeals Court."

"Let me tell you about Judge Lawlor. Judge Lawlor took the oath in August 1951 from Paul Dever who appointed me to this job. He was a great man, that Paul Dever. Let me show you his picture." Mr. Costello pointed up to the left, to Leverett Saltonstall, in fact.

"No, Mr. Costello, it's Judge *Lyons*," Mary Rose said again. "C'mon kid, let's go meet the judges. Bye, Mr. Costello."

Patrick extended his hand to Mr. Costello. Mr. Costello looked at it quizzically, then stuck out his own hand and said, "Say hello to Judge Lawlor for me. He's a great man and so was Paul A. Dever. They are both great men."

Within earshot, or so it seemed to Patrick, Mary Rose said, "He's getting up there. He'll be 93 in December. He remembers everybody, if you can get him to the right bus stop in the first place. Let's go into the 'Holy of Holies.'" They approached a door that said "Judges' Lobby" on one line and "Judges Only" on the next. It was locked. Mary Rose pressed the appropriate buttons on the lock, opened the door and walked in. She stopped after a few steps and looked back at Patrick standing in the doorway and waved him on. "Don't worry about that sign. They love me here. It's the spies they want to keep out."

Marching down the wide corridor towards them was a short, but elevated on very high heels, woman with blond hair teased up to add height, in a red and black Chanel suit, a red blouse open to show some cleavage and lots of Bulgari gold chain bracelets. "And who is this angel of God you're bring us today, Mary Rose? I hope he's available."

"Judge Natale, this is Patrick Foley, an intern for Judge Lyons of the Appeals Court."

"Joseph Lavin Lyons!?! He used to be so handsome—and thin. He was two years ahead of me in law school. Of course, I'm much younger. He was so handsome—and so shy. Now we know why.

All the girls, there were only ten of us in the whole law school then, had a crush on him. But, alas, he bowls in a different alley. And you're the intern, huh? Wasn't Monica Lewinsky an interne?"

"Yes, ma'am. I started today. The judge thought I could learn a lot by coming down here, that it would give me a practical outlook."

"You tell Judge Lyons, 'Joey' to me, that Nancy Natale still has a little shine for him, and that if he ever changes his mind, I'm in the Judges' phone book. Tell him also that the only words we want to see him write are 'Trial Judge Affirmed.' That's all he needs to know. Nice to meet you! I got a cute niece, if you're so inclined, Patrick. Bye, bye, Mary Rose. Guard this cutie. *Ciao bello.*" And off she went with a wink.

Mary Rose smiled and after Judge Natale went out the door they had just passed through, Mary Rose said, "They're not all as shy as Judge Natale."

Patrick looked at her wide-eyed. Just then Mary Rose knocked on the lintel of a slightly opened door to an office marked "Chief Justice Cesar Lopez."

"Come in," said the booming voice from inside. "How nice to see you, Mrs. Quirk!" said the man behind the very cluttered desk in the room, the walls of which were covered with multiple images of Caesar Augustus, in every media and from every angle. Malcolm X, Cesar Chavez, Bobby Kennedy and Lolita Lebrun also adorned the walls. Copies of the famous statue of Caesar Augustus in armor, holding a staff with an eagle on top, littered the desk, the conference table and the sideboard. "And who is this young man you bring us, a new assistant clerk perhaps? Does he speak Spanish?"

"*Si, yo hablo Español pero no soy un 'assistant clerk.' Yo soy un interno para el Juez Lyons en la Corte de Appelidos. Me llamo Patricio Foley.* Yes, I speak Spanish, but I am not an assistant clerk. I'm an in intern for Judge Lyons of the Appeals Court. My name is Patrick Foley."

"*Mucho gusto a conocerle*. Very nice to meet you," said the Chief Justice. "We should speak English so as not to leave Mrs. Quirk out of the conversation. Where do you go to law school?"

"I'm between my second and third year at Boston College Law School."

"And how is Judge Lyons? He sat down here for a few months. I trust it was enlightening for him. He has not overturned us since."

"Judge Lyons is very well. I just started work for him and only met him a few weeks ago so I do not know him very well yet."

"Oh, and where did you meet?" the Chief Justice asked, catching Patrick off guard.

Patrick began to feel like he was being interrogated, and with reason, but decided to tell the truth. "I wrote him asking for a position." Patrick stopped there, knowing that writing Judge Lyons was only the preface to where they met, and "not responsive," as the trial lawyers like to say.

Chief Justice Lopez let that answer slide, perhaps to return to it later. *Why does he care?* Patrick wondered.

Mary Rose Quirk, who was no dummy, and who, by the way, unbeknownst to everyone but her husband and children, understood Spanish, interjected, "I was wondering if Patrick could sit in the well with some of the judges for a couple of days. We could find him a seat at the Clerk's desk."

"If the judges don't mind, I don't either. It would be good to ask the individual judge in the session before putting Patrick in such a …lofty seat."

"Oh, of course," Mary Rose said. "We already asked Judge Natale and she thought it was a great idea."

Patrick was curious because, as far as he knew, *they* had *not* asked Judge Natale, not that Patrick thought she'd object after all that coquetterie she had just displayed. *There was a game going on between Mary Rose and the Chief Justice. She was asking his permis-*

sion and once she got it she told him she had the approval of one of the judges anyway, like his permission was a rubber stamp that she really did not need. What's up with that? Patrick thought.

"Who's her clerk today?" The Chief asked.

"Jim Hartman," Mary Rose answered.

"Well, he'll be an experience for the young man," The Chief said. "How are you going to keep Jim in line?"

"Judge Natale is very good with Jim. I'm sure that you heard of the time she hit him on the head with a law book. Jim was mouthing directions to an assistant D.A., who was questioning a cop. The defense attorney was in his seat looking horrified. Judge Natale leaned over and told Jim to stop it. When he didn't stop she bopped him with one of the Massachusetts Reports, volume number 365, I think. The experience of watching how the judge controls the trial clerk will be good for Patrick. And if one or both of the court officers falls asleep, there'll be more fun."

Patrick sat in his seat wide-eyed at the candor of Mary Rose's revelations.

The Chief Justice smiled slightly and said in his booming voice, "Well, Jim is an equal opportunity coach. He gives advice to both sides. One day when I was sitting he corrected the defendant's English while the defendant was testifying. Jim wouldn't let the defendant say 'ain't.' However, Judge O'Hara has it right. When I first arrived on the Court, I complained about Jim Hartman. Judge O'Hara said, 'Cesar, at least he's interested. We can't say that about all the people who work here.'"

The Chief Justice then turned to Patrick, coughed lightly, then said, "Mister Foley, things aren't as bad as they sound. Take all this with a grain of salt. Life at Court is not like television. Some days it's wilder."

He then rose from his chair, all five feet, two inches of him. He came around to the front of his desk and shook Patrick's hand.

"Good luck, Mister Foley. Don't forget us down here in the pits, where Justice is wrought, w-r-o-u-g-h-t.

"And Mrs. Quirk, when you have Mr. Foley settled with Judge Natale and Mr. Hartman, would you come back and see me, please? I'm afraid that Nemesis man is sending spies around again. Every time there's a sex case in the First Criminal Session, three oldtimers with rosary beads appear in the front row. It doesn't matter what kind of sex case—prostitutes caught in the back of a car, gay sex in an alley in the South End or the men's room at Macy's, statutory rape, real rape—they gasp loudly as the complaint is read and if there is any testimony at all about the particulars of the offense, they moan and bless themselves wildly. One little woman takes notes. If it bothers them so much, I wonder why they come at all. James Foley, the court officer, says that the note taker is from The Gate of Heaven Parish in South Boston and used to be his Uncle Charlie's girlfriend in the fifties. Otherwise, we know nothing about them or how they know what cases are being called when. The Defense bar is getting very upset. They say that these characters are prejudicing bail decisions—that the judges are afraid to let sex defendants out. Could it be that they have a snoop in the Clerk's office, who keeps them informed? I'm thinking of Mary Ciamelli. She has gotten strange recently. I know she is a friend of yours and that you grew up together in the North End…."

Mary Rose interjected, "I grew up with her younger sister. We all went to Saint John's School with the nuns in the North End. She wasn't like this then. I didn't bring her in here. Don't blame her on me. The old Chief Justice asked Mr. Costello to hire her and I think that the then Speaker of the House of Representatives asked him as well. Apparently the Speaker's spinster sister went bowling with Mary every Thursday night and Mary needed a job. I have never been a friend of Mary. Her mother died two years ago and she hasn't been the same since. Her sister says that Mary spends all her spare time in church."

The Chief Justice said, "Well, will you come back and see me? We have to do something. We don't need a scandal, or even a scene. I'm afraid that they're building up to something. They may be keeping tabs on the judges, making note of who's letting what criminals go. And if there's an inside source, she may be documenting matters. All we need is to be labeled 'Soft on Sex.' I can see the *Herald* headline now."

"They'd never call you 'Soft on Sex,' Chief," Mary Rose said with a smile. "Chief, I'll come back, Chief. Sorry to have jumped at the mention of Mary Ciamelli. Some people think there is an Italian conspiracy around here and that I'm the head of it. I don't like the woman. Never did. She was always so prissy. She had the best handwriting in the school—pure Palmer Method. Her 'O's were perfect. They gave her prizes, like handwriting was a big deal. We have her transcribing docket entries into the docket books in the Clerk's office. I'll bet she wishes she never won that Penmanship prize."

The Chief Justice blushed at first and then smiled. He returned to his chair behind the desk and climbed up into it. Sitting down, he looked six feet, two again.

"*Adios*, Senor Foley. *Buena suerte. Cuidale. Nos vemos. Si yo puedo ayudarle, regresa a verme*. Goodbye, Mr. Foley. Good luck. Take care. We'll see you. If I can help you, return to see me."

When they left the Chief's office Mary Rose took Patrick outside the Judges' Lobby door, into a little alcove in front of what appeared to be a closet. She stopped, turned, pushed Patrick against the door, looked up at him and said, "I assume that Judge Lyons made you take the 'Vow of Secrecy and Silence' up there in the Appeals Court. Well, it applies here as well. That little horn dog lady-killer was less than discreet in there. I'm surprised. Well, you didn't hear a thing, and if I hear that you said anything, I'll cut your tongue out and throw it to the mackerel off Castle Island in South

Boston. Now come with me. Judge Natale has begun her session and is waiting for you. Straighten your tie! Do you have a pen? We'll give you a pad. It's the least we can do for Judge Lyons. Don't say a word except 'please' and 'thanks,' especially to Mr. Hartman. You can take notes if you have to, but don't let anyone see them and be sure to take them with you. People get very paranoid around here, particularly if they have ambition. Mr. Hartman, on the other hand, is lucky he still has a job. He has been advised that he better be nice to you. Go right through that door and sit to the right of the Clerk. James Foley, the Court Officer, is waiting for you just inside the door. Are you sure that you're not his cousin? You're both good looking."

Patrick went through the door. Indeed a tall, blond, wavy-haired, handsome court officer met him just inside the door and held him back just as the Assistant District Attorney stood up and said, "I'd like to call my first witness, Trooper Horace Mulligan."

Patrick blanched. Court Officer James Foley pointed to the chair next to the clerk. Patrick proceeded to that seat as covertly as he could. He crouched as he walked in the hope of becoming invisible. He almost bumped into Trooper Horace Mulligan as he, Mulligan, walked to the witness stand.

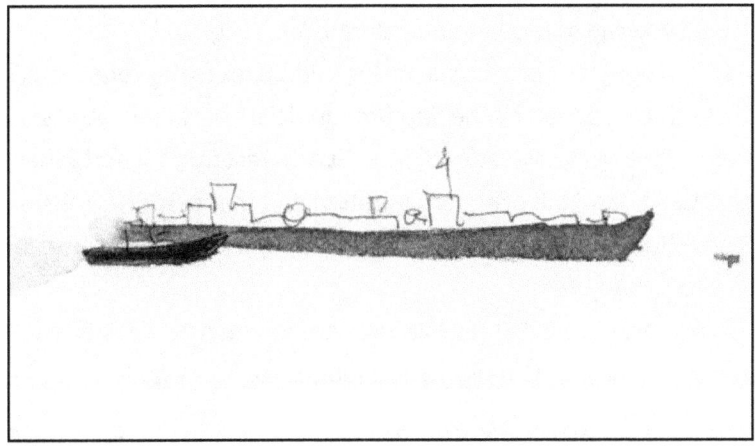

* * *

Meanwhile, back at the Appeals Court Joe was chatting with the beautiful Honorable Justice Gigi Boland in the Appeals Court's Law Library, a place that, because of the research capabilities of personal computers, even the law clerks did not often visit anymore. It was the safest place for a confidential conversation because it was usually empty. Joe and Gigi were supposed to be planning the Annual Judges Dinner for the twenty-five Appeals Court Justices. They would get to that soon enough. This annual dinner would probably be just like the one the year before, and the one the year before that, and so on back to the first annual dinner in 1973.

As a result Joe and Gigi took the time to catch up on gossip. They were appointed the same year, both were single and both lived in the City. They were pals.

Joe started, "I really would like to go to the State House for the vote on the Anti-Same-Sex Marriage Amendment. It's so close, the vote, I mean. We just might win it."

"You don't think that you'll get in trouble over that, do you?" Gigi said. "What do you care about marriage? It's such an outdated institution. Are you going to get married, Joe?"

"Not right away, but maybe. That vote is very important. I'd like to witness history."

"So you can tell your grandchildren, Joe?" Gigi said.

"Oh, Gigi! Don't be so cynical!" Joe said. " Back to the vote, there is that ethical opinion by the Supreme Judicial Court Ethics Advisory committee that says attending a GLAD[1] reception is forbidden; that GLAD is an advocacy organization and that part of its mission is to influence legislation, and that we cannot be part of those endeavors in any way."

Gigi said, "We didn't give up everything when we took this job! Did we? Didn't certain black male judges we know go to that 'Mil-

[1] Gay and Lesbian Advocates and Defenders

lion Man March' in Washington some years ago? And don't most of the African American judges, male and female, go to NAACP Legal Defense Fund dinners? A lot of my berobed girlfriends go to women's events all the time. We get invited to the Catholic Lawyers' Guild Red Mass every year. There's always a rant at the lunch after those. Doesn't old Firrfield go to the Social Justice lunches at the American Jewish Congress? When he was sniffing around me after he got appointed he even asked me to speak at one of them. They discussed pending legislation before I spoke. I thought that they weren't going to leave me any time to speak. Where do you draw the line? What's social or noble and what's political? Does the quest for your rights become political just because you don't have them yet? All these events for other minorities and for women are shows of strength to make sure the rights aren't taken away. That's just as political, isn't it?"

Joe didn't want to have to make the arguments that Gigi had just touched on before some tribunal or another. He just wanted to be able to do what he wanted and be left alone. He was tired of being a petty public figure—a "dingitary," as they say in South Boston—and subject to scrutiny every time he turned around—or over.

Over the years Joe had shared a lot with Gigi. Joe told her that Patrick Foley began working as an intern that day, although he did not tell her Patrick Foley's true birth name.

They both commiserated about how to keep earnest interns busy, that sometimes it was like throwing a stick to a dog, which kept on finding it and returning it to be thrown again. "When do we get to ponder if we have to spend our time babysitting them?" Gigi said. "I know we should be grateful, but…"

Joe told Gigi that he might have found the solution. He told her that he had sent Patrick down to the Boston Municipal Court into the welcoming arms of Mary Rose Quirk. Gigi knew Mary Rose from a committee they were both on entitled *Women in the Courts*. The Chiefest of Chief Justices was the chairperson of the committee and she got quite a kick out of Mary Rose and her candor. No fool she! The Chiefest of Chief Justices also appreciated Mary Rose's downstairs political influence with the Legislature.

Gigi asked Joe if he thought she should march in the upcoming Gay parade. All her "boys" were going and she thought it would be "amusing" if she went as well.

Joe told her that it was forbidden by the Supreme Judicial Court's Committee on Ethics and pointed her to the opinion. "Besides," Joe said, "You wouldn't have a good time. There's nothing radical about it anymore. The biggest delegations are from banks and insurance companies. Just go to the Street Dance after the Parade in the South End. The testosterone level goes pretty high there and the 'boys' take their shirts off." Had she thought about going to the Lesbian Street Party in Jamaica Plain after the Parade or the Fenway's Women's Event? The women were mostly lesbians, but she could pass if she dressed down for the night.

Gigi harrumphed in indignation, and called Joe a killjoy. She

said, "I suppose we should talk about the annual dinner. Why does it have to be so boring? "

Regarding the dinner, at the most recent bimonthly meeting of all 25 of the Justices, in this very library, the Honorable Alexander Smythe, the senior member of the Court, had suggested that this year "wives be included."

The Honorable Mildred Bailey said, "That's a great idea, Justice Smythe. I'm sure my wife would like to come, but what about the women members of the Court who don't have wives? What about poor Judge Boland and Judge Lyons who have neither a wife nor a husband?"

Judge Smythe, who had been too long at the fair five years before, scratched his head in confusion and went back to sleep.

The next proposal was from Judge Parsnip of Lenox, who said that there ought to be a vegetarian alternative to the usual roast beef. This woke Judge Smythe up. He said, "If you can't eat the roast beef, work your way around it. Better yet, eat your veggies before you come and just drink the wine. That will save us money as well. We won't have to feed you."

At last the Chief Justice saw fit to interject and said, "I am appointing a committee of three to organize the dinner, Judge Boland, Judge Lyons and myself. If there are any other suggestions, perhaps you could send them to me…in an email." Everyone knew that the Chief had no idea how to use his computer, never mind find emails, and that Miss Mary Margaret Managhan would pick them up and deep six them. She had always made the preparations for the dinner and she had no intention of not doing it again this year.

Gigi Boland then said to Joe, "We have to move the dinner. Another year at the second floor of the Parker House in the Oliver Wendell Holmes Junior Room will kill me. If we can get to the Chief with a new place, we can do an end run around Mary Margaret. She doesn't like us anyway, so we have nothing to lose. I've been typing my own opinions for years and you dictate to your clerks and then edit. Let's have the dinner at Guido's Back Bay Grille. I know the owner. He's a love."

Joe said, "I know that he's a love. I should've said 'yes' to him years ago. That restaurant is a gold mine. Did you know that he's doing a lot to defeat the Anti-Same-Sex Marriage Amendment?"

Gigi said, "I've known Guido for years. I never knew that he was a gay activist."

"Well he is, even when he doesn't know he is," Joe said. "He's very quiet about it. He gives. He gave this time."

Now that gay activism had come up in the conversation for the second time, and directly, Joe thought he could tell Gigi what was really on his mind.

He told her about the confusion over who presided at the *Williamson v. Randozza Enterprises, Inc.* oral argument and how it had prompted a full-scale multi-pronged attack from Sam Nemesis. Joe described his meeting with the Chief Justices and his hiring Dewey Battle to represent him. He got so carried away with himself that he did not notice the smile slowly appearing on Gigi's face.

When he did see her smile, he was not happy and said, "Why are you laughing at me. I thought you were my friend. I can't tell you the anxiety and discomfort this has caused me. The District Attorney and United States Attorney are in on it, for Christ's sake. Nemesis sent a copy of his complaint to them and to our Chief and Her Imperial Highness upstairs. Even if I'm able to put a stop to the complaint at the Judicial Conduct Commission and whatever the D.A. and United States Attorney might do, If It hits the papers, I'll be like Clarence Thomas—Nobody will ever take me seriously again."

Gigi continued to laugh. She said, "Alright, I'll tell you, although it may get me thrown out of the Sisterhood. It's comic around here. Last week there was a lunch meeting of the women judges and

the Honorable Mildred Bailey was complaining that in the advance sheets her name had been omitted as Presiding Judge at the *Williamson v. Randozza Enterprises, Inc.* oral argument. She thought it was a conspiracy, another instance of male chauvinism at the Appeals Court—that you and the Reporter of Decisions were in cahoots. She was going to visit Firrfield and the other judge who sat that day to get affidavits from them to the Chief Justice indicating that in fact she had presided in that particular case. You know she has ambitions and has not presided much. That's seniority. There are just enough of us ahead of her that her turn to preside comes rarely. So, she wants credit for every time she does preside. She wants to be the first openly gay person of either gender on the Supreme Judicial Court."

"Openly gay?" Joe said. "Have there been any closeted gay people up there? I remember old Harrison Lowell Benedict, who sat up there when I was a young lawyer. He looked like he had a skip to his hip, but I think it was just that he wore bow ties, had a lisp and was a birdwatcher. His wife was the 'butch' in that house. Did you ever see her?"

"I'm not old enough to remember Harrison Cabot Benedict, or his butch wife although she did look manly in a Dutch cut. And to quote Tallulah Bankhead when she was asked if so-and-so was gay, 'He never sucked my dick.' I'll never talk. I don't know which of them up there was or is gay. It's a girl thing. Mildred sees you as her rival for the next vacancy on the Supreme Judicial Court. She's never gotten over the fact that you were the first openly gay judge in Massachusetts. She's a competitor. Have you ever seen her play softball?"

"No. I haven't. And I hope I never do. The picture of her running around all sweaty is horrifying. Her rival? I'm about to retire. If the raise comes through, I'm out the door. She knows that. I think that I've been here too long. I want to live a little. I'm tired of being so circumspect. I want Angelo to marry me and take me away from all this. We can live in Fort Lauderdale in the Winter and travel in the Spring and Summer. I'd love to spend next Spring in Italy while I can still walk. You know that my left knee has been acting up again?" Joe added.

"More importantly, I have to talk to Mildred Bailey and reassure her that I had nothing to do with the mistaken entry of the Presiding Judge on the *Randozza*....I mean the *Williamson* case. It's in my interest to clear this up soon. Is she here today? Do you know? We can go see the Chief right now, if Mildred is here. I just finished telling our Chief that Mildred presided at that hearing. It would be good if he heard it from her as well."

"No, she's at home in New Plymouth with her family. She'll be back to sit on a panel later in the week. I'm on the same panel. I'm presiding," Gigi added. "Even though I'm much younger, I have seniority. It comes from having been a hot shot prosecutor at a young age."

"It comes from that and from…dating…a Governor's Legal Counsel, Gigi. Whatever happened to him?" Joe said.

"He went back to his dull but pretty wife and became general counsel of her father's software company." Gigi said. She had few secrets from Joe and his reminding her of one of them didn't bother her at all. She'd do the same to him when the opportunity next arose.

"Well, I have to decide. Should I call Mildred or wait until she returns?"

"Why not ask your crack legal team?" Gigi said. "They're smart guys."

"I can't tell you how grateful I am to you, Gigi. I've been a wreck. I saw no way out. I was preparing to throw in the towel." Joe said, as he rose to leave the library.

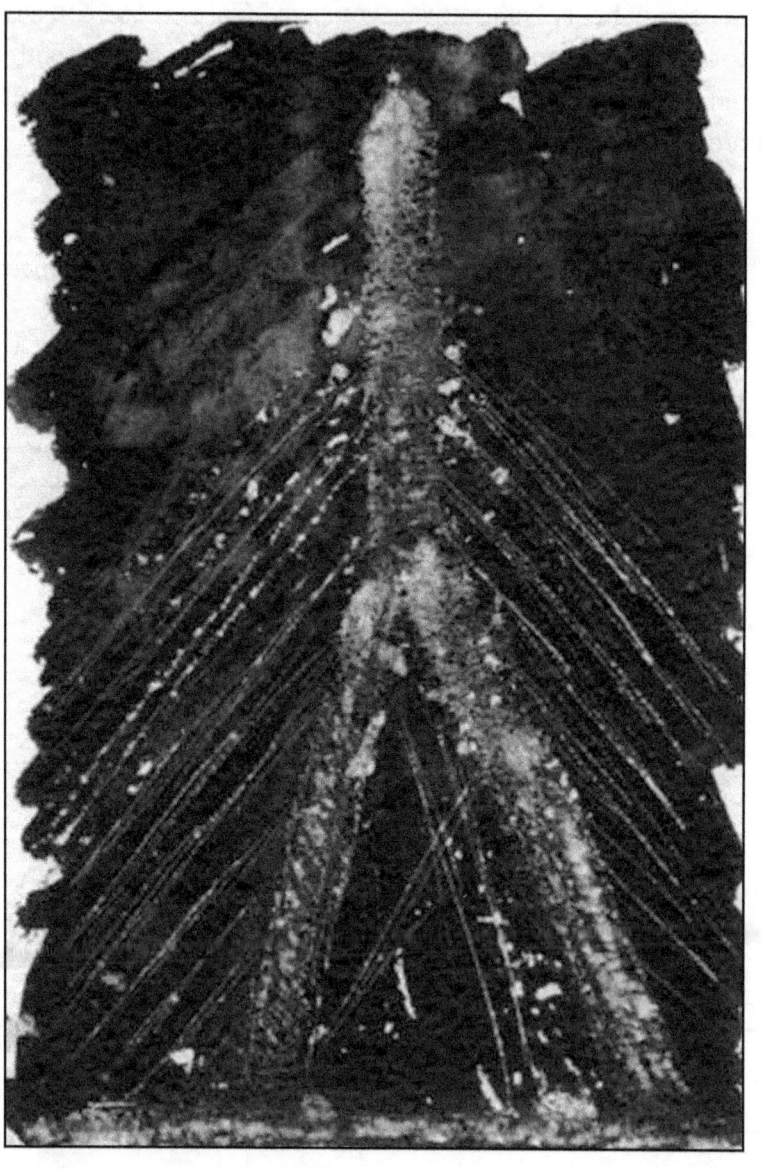

Patrick Learns a Lesson

P atrick Foley sat through the hearing before Judge Natale. He even came back on Friday to hear the rest of the testimony. He was fascinated. His curiosity was piqued by the witness, Trooper Horace Mulligan, the same State Police Officer whose conduct Patrick had earlier been assigned to examine for Judge Lyons.

This hearing in this case, *Commonwealth v. Roscoe Haskins*, was also regarding a Motion to Suppress Evidence, the same kind of motion that was in issue in *Commonwealth v. Thomas Jefferson Mobutu*, which had been assigned by Judge Lyons to Patrick Foley to research. It was a great opportunity for Patrick Foley to attend a hearing on this very subject and to discover how this most important rule of Criminal Law Procedure, "The Exclusionary Rule," works. The rule is quite simple, "Evidence illegally seized from a person cannot be used against that person in a criminal case." The hearings were usually to determine if the seizure of the evidence was illegal.

The Exclusionary Rule is a comparatively recent invention, the result of the United States Supreme Court's expansion of civil liberties to the individual states in the Nineteen Sixties. Hearings occur before a judge only. Judges at these hearings now determine the fate of most drug cases. If the judge decides the search or seizure was illegal, the defendant wins, the evidence, is suppressed, and cannot be introduced at trial. The case is over.

Conversely, if the judge does *not* suppress the evidence, the defendant has to start scrambling to work out a plea agreement. The rule also operates regarding illegally obtained confessions or admissions.

The defense in the *Haskins* case claimed that Trooper Horace Mulligan for no legally justifiable reason stopped the defendant, Roscoe Haskins, while he was riding his bicycle on Tremont Street in the South End. The defense added that then the Trooper illegally searched the defendant until he found a bag containing one half ounce of marijuana in a pocket of Roscoe's baggy pants.

Contrary to some expectations (but not those of First Assistant Clerk Mary Rose Quirk, who had told him he better behave) the courtroom clerk, Jim Hartman, was very helpful, passing papers to Patrick to read as the hearing progressed. First was the Motion to Suppress itself and its accompanying affidavit. The affidavit was in the standard form saying as little as possible except that the State Police trooper had stopped and searched Roscoe Haskins illegally while the eighteen year old, high school senior, Roscoe, was riding his bike on Tremont Street in the South End.

The police report of the incident signed by Trooper Horace Mulligan was a little more specific. It said that Roscoe was riding his bike while wearing a black hoodie on a 95 degree day, that he was continually looking back, that he was intermittently on his cell phone, that he crossed the very wide Tremont Street a number of times while in the view of Trooper Mulligan and, most damning, that at one point almost at the corner of Pembroke and Tremont Streets, Roscoe stopped in front of the Chinese Restaurant on Tremont Street, paused until someone came out of the restaurant and handed Roscoe a small package while Roscoe handed the person an unspecified amount of what appeared to be American currency.

Roscoe was then stopped at the little garden of the South End Branch Library on the corner of Tremont Street and Rutland Square. Trooper Mulligan said he feared for his safety. Therefore, he did a "pat frisk," an outer garment pat down, of Roscoe Haskins. He felt something in the left-hand pocket of Roscoe's "baggies," his oversized pants. That something the Trooper believed to be marijuana. That was what the Trooper's official police report said.

On the other hand, Trooper Mulligan's *testimony*, what he said under oath on the witness stand, particularly during cross examination by Roscoe Haskins' attorney, Ms Vivian Lee, cast the facts in a different light.

This was not Trooper Mulligan's first encounter with Roscoe. He had arrested him twice before on non-drug charges, specifically assault and battery and disorderly conduct. Both times Roscoe was found "Not Guilty." Yes, Trooper Mulligan had testified at those trials. Yes, he did often ride through the South End, although his specific assignment was to patrol the Massachusetts Turnpike for traffic violations. Yes, the Boston Police Department usually made arrests in the South End, but the State Police also had the power to do so. Yes, the previous two arrests of Roscoe occurred in the South End. Yes, it was unusual for the State Police to patrol downtown Boston unless specifically assigned to do so. No, he was not looking to get Roscoe Haskins finally on some charge or another. Yes, he, Trooper Mulligan had been the subject of harassment charges filed by Selim Shui, a friend of Roscoe's and he had been suspended without pay for thirty days as a result of such charges. No, he was not a bigot. He recognized Roscoe immediately when he first saw him on the bike back by the Villa Victoria on Dartmouth Street, even wearing the hoodie. No, Tremont Street heading south was not the most direct route to the Massachusetts Turnpike. Yes, continuing on Dartmouth Street to Tremont Street and then going north on Tremont Street would have been a more direct route to the Massachusetts Turnpike. As a matter of fact, yes, he could have gotten on the Mass. Pike from Dartmouth Street itself at Copley Square. No, he did not have a vendetta against Roscoe and his friends. Yes, it could have been that Roscoe was ordering Chinese food on his cell phone and that that was what he was picking up outside the Chinese Restaurant on Tremont Street. Yes, he did find Chinese food, #69, beef and broccoli, in the bag that Roscoe was balancing on his handlebars.

At one point Vivian Lee took a breath and went over to her table to look at some notes.

Judge Natale said, "Will there be much more cross examination of this witness, Ms Lee? This may be a good time for a recess if you have any more questions. Otherwise we can proceed."

Vivian Lee looked up and said, "No, your honor. Thank you. I rest."

"And you, Mr. Assistant District Attorney, do you have any further questions on redirect of the Trooper?" She went on, "Remember that redirect is not 'repeat,' and redirect is not the time to ask questions that you forgot to ask the first time. This is not a jury trial and I've been around, so there is nobody to perform for. What do you say, Mr. Assistant District Attorney?" Clearly, Judge Natale had forgotten the poor man's name. Thus, she addressed him by his title.

"The Commonwealth has no other witnesses, your honor. The Commonwealth rests."

"Thank you, sir. Do you wish to argue?" Judge Natale said. "This has been a short hearing. I have been taking notes, but if you wish to argue the evidence, I will certainly hear you."

Both lawyers got the hint that Judge Natale did not want to hear anything more and simultaneously they said, "No, your honor."

"The Motion to Suppress is allowed. Written findings will follow," said Judge Natale and up she rose, tapping Patrick Foley on the head with her notebook as she came to full height, 5'6" with the four-inch spiked heels. "Come with me, kid," she whispered *sotto voce*. "Thank you, Mr. Hartman, for your help today," she added in full voice.

Mr. Hartman beamed. Patrick Foley, a quick study, thanked Mr. Hartman as well. Mr. Hartman beamed even brighter. He knew that Patrick would report his good behavior to Mary Rose Quirk. Trooper Horace Mulligan left the courtroom as soon as the Assistant District Attorney said that the Commonwealth would rest and before Judge Natale announced her decision. He didn't care about the result; he got paid for time in court, win, lose or draw.

Outside the courtroom door Judge Natale looked over her left shoulder while walking unsteadily on her high heels and said to Patrick, "Walk this way." He followed her as best he could to her office door, which was not locked. *En route* they passed other judges' offices with open doors. Some of the judges looked up as he passed.

"Come in, kid," Judge Natale said. "Sit yourself down. Now what did you think of that?" she added before his butt touched the seat of the chair.

Patrick didn't know what to say. He didn't want to be presumptuous or a big shot. But he didn't want to appear stupid either. "I certainly think you made the correct decision, Judge."

"Of course I did. Now what am I going to write for findings?"

After a pause Patrick said, "You could say that there were no articulable facts justifying the stop and the pat frisk."

"Yeah, I could say that. Those are the words I am supposed to write. But I could also say the Trooper's testimony completely lacked credibility. Maybe I'll say both. Anyway, go back and tell Joe Lyons that I still have a crush on him but I married well and don't want to screw that up. He's not interested in me anyway, but at our age it's good to be desired. Will you be back here again? Did you talk to our illustrious leader?"

"I will, if Judge Lyons sends me, and I did talk to Chief Justice Lopez. He's a very interesting man."

"He's an old goat. Thank God that his term is almost over," Judge Natale said. "If there's anything I can do for you, anything you need explained, let me know. It's a great country with a great Constitution. You just saw a number of the rights in the Bill of Rights in action.

"The defendant, that little punk Roscoe Haskins, was appointed counsel, the Sixth Amendment. He didn't have to testify because he might incriminate himself, the Fifth Amendment. His right to be free from unreasonable searches and seizures was protected, the Fourth Amendment. And there may be a few more. If he had called the Trooper a name, and he should have, we would have protected his First Amendment right to Free Speech as well. This is a wonderful country, Patrick, a wonderful country. You'll do well in this business, Patrick. Now go tell Joe I still love him."

Patrick thanked Judge Natale and returned in a hurry to the Appeals Court. He rushed to Judge Lyons' office and sat on the court officer's chair outside the door. He noticed that, unlike Judge Natale and most of the BMC judges, Joe locked his office door. *Why was that?* he wondered before Joe appeared from a "very important" meeting with Justice Gigi Boland.

"Hello Patrick! How was your day down in the mines?"

"You won't believe it, but the same trooper, Horace Mulligan, who was the chief witness in the Mobutu case you gave me this morning was the principal witness in a Motion to Suppress hearing at the Boston Municipal Court that I sat in on today. Oh, before I forget, Judge Natale sends you her greetings, her love actually. They really like you down there. I spent some time with Mary Rose Quirk and met the Clerk himself. They admire you a lot."

"They do until I overturn some time-honored practice they

have down there. They're very good people, not as jaded as they pretend to be. It's the place where it's all happening—the 'Old Bailey' of Massachusetts. Mrs. Quirk holds the place together. Poor Mr. Costello is long gone. Did he think I was Judge Larkin? And did Mary Rose correct him?"

"He thought that you were Judge Lawlor and that you were appointed by Governor Paul Dever. Back to the hearing, Trooper Mulligan is such a…" Patrick started to say.

"Shhhhhh, you can't tell me anything extraneous about Trooper Mulligan. I will have to recuse myself if you do and I will have to report you as well. So, keep it to yourself. I think that I'll have to take you off that case, Patrick. No, you didn't do anything wrong. Not yet," Joe said, standing in his black robe with his hands in his pants pockets, in front of his desk in the judges' lobby looking very authoritative.

"I see that look on your face—like I'm going to spank you. Don't fret. Just remember that we judges—and juries too—have to decide each case on the record before us. I can't be hearing outside information. I can't be using outside information. Let me give you an example. Suppose that I live on the same street as Police Officer, let's call him, Veritas and I know him to be a liar. I'll just invent a situation." Joe paused to do so. "Suppose that at a neighborhood meeting concerning illegal occupancy of single family houses Officer Veritas said that there were only two people living in his house and that there were only two cars parked in his yard. Yet every morning at 6:30 A.M. when I drove to work I saw four cars parked there and five people leaving the house.

"Let's say that now Officer Veritas had been a witness in a case that has been appealed and assigned to me. Officer Veritas testified under oath at a hearing on a Motion to Suppress that Doper Daley, the man whose car he stopped for a broken taillight with Daley behind the wheel, had an open, clear, see-through plastic bag full of a 'green herblike substance' sitting on the dashboard in front of Daley and that there was no one else in the car. Officer Veritas first smelt what he believed to be marijuana before he saw it 'In Plain View.'

"Now, I, from my personal experience driving to work, even that morning, have reason to believe that Officer Veritas doesn't always tell the truth—at least when he is not under oath.

"A series of cautionary red flags should go up. I am not inclined to believe Officer Veritas as soon as I read his name. Even if I think I can separate Officer Veritas' statements made when he was not under oath from those he might make under oath, I probably still will look at his testimony with more than the usual jaundiced eye. The yellow in my eyeball may be approaching burnt sienna. And here he is, the sole witness at this hearing, not contradicted by anyone, except maybe inconsistencies of his own, more or less effectively cross examined, but believed nevertheless by the trial judge, who by the way lives in Worcester and doesn't know Officer Veritas from Adam.

"What am I, as an appellate judge, supposed to do? Should I jump in at the conference with my brother and sister judges and say, 'Veritas is a liar! We can't believe him,' and then tell them why?"

Joe paused to let this sink in. Patrick looked astonished at this exposition, shocked at its candor.

Joe continued, "What I think I should do is get out of the case right away. 'Recuse myself' are the words we use. I can't worry about the injustice that may have been done by the visiting trial judge having believed Veritas. In the balancing of things that we do up here, and that trial judges do down there, it is more important that the judge be impartial. The reason that the judge from Worcester heard the Motion to Suppress may be because the regular local judge knew that he could not believe Veritas either, and scheduled the case for the day the visiting judge was going to preside.

"Think of what it must be like for trial judges in small communities where everybody knows everybody else, Nantucket for example, where everybody may be related to everybody else. Nobody wants to talk about this issue. The show must go on. It's never discussed, although the Superior Court, like the High Court in Ireland and England, all trial courts, consisted of judges who traveled a circuit so that they would not be wed to any one place, so that they would not know the players, the lawyers, or the parties or witnesses in any particular place, so that they could not develop prejudices, maybe even prejudices based on experience.

"It's ironic that in these days of fast automobiles and better transportation, that the range of the circuit of the Massachusetts Superior Court judges has diminished and that they only preside within a small circumference of their home. In the old days, a Superior Court Judge from Wellesley, for example, might be assigned to Plymouth in the East for one month and then to Pittsfield, in the far West, the next month. Of course, they would have to stay in a hotel, usually a bad one, in the county seat where they were sitting. That created certain problems—like how did they spend their off the bench time. Sometimes the local judges entertained them—and maybe even gave them the lay of the land, but that's another lecture.

"I could go on, but you get the message. Neither I nor you can bring our personal information to the case we are working on. Did I explain that to your satisfaction, Patrick?" Joe asked.

Patrick said, "Yes, you did. Thank you very much. I had never thought about that issue before."

"But what about using my 'Common sense and Experience of Life?' Those words that judges tell juries they should employ in coming to a decision?—like that no dope smoker is going to keep the marijuana stash in an open bag on the dashboard of a wobbly old car that may have to come to a sudden stop? Not only is the grass visible but also it may fall off the dashboard and spill all over the floor.

"That, my friend, is a different thing. We ask juries all the time to use their common sense and experience of life. Judges hearing matters without juries are expected to do the same. Common sense about the dangers of balancing things, particularly 'loose, flaky, leaflike substances' on dashboards may well be just what we are looking for in juries—and judges—and by extension law clerks and interns.

Joe concluded, "So, I'm going to assign you to another case, maybe some juicy zoning case from the Berkshires, something about whether a practicing meditator, not a religious community, can build a giant four-storey statue of the Buddha by the side of Route 2, the highway on the Mohawk trail, the road that all the leaf-peepers drive in the Autumn to see the Fall foliage. He wants to put the giant Buddha just inside the Pittsfield line, at the hairpin curve where the Golden Eagle resort is now. It's a very scenic spot. 'It will ease your way around the turn,' the meditator says.

"There are great issues about *Freedom of Religious Expression, Separation of Church and State, Zoning and Private Property Rights,* to say nothing of the practical problem that concerns the State Highway Department about a four-storey Buddha distracting the view of a driver at a perilous hairpin curve in the Berkshires. We let Mitt Romney put his giant Mormon steeple up in Belmont about 150 miles back on Route 2. What do we have against the Buddha?"

Joe stopped talking to let this sink in. He put his previously gesturing hands to rest back in his pockets and began to turn away from Patrick.

He turned back and said, "Now you can call that handsome, jackbooted, jodhpured boyfriend of yours, the embodiment of the fantasies of Tom of Finland, and thousands others, and find out the skinny, the dope, on Trooper Horace Mulligan. Just don't tell me—

at least not until the Mobutu decision is published."

Patrick was astounded. He had never heard such practical, real life candor from any of his law school professors, not even the Professor of Clinical Studies, the person who guided students playing at being lawyers in certain of the trial courts. Patrick didn't realize the constraints that were put upon judges. In law school, and particularly in clinical courses, judges were portrayed as the pomposities who had to be won over by whatever legal knowledge, talents or charms one possessed.

Most of all, Patrick hadn't realized how paradoxical and contradictory it all was—the judge could not use personal information, but he could use his common sense and his experience of life. Where do you draw the line? And how many judges knew about marijuana use!?! It had not occurred to Patrick that many judges now sitting had been rebellious students in the sixties, seventies and eighties and that the "real world" and its ways weren't just invented when Patrick and his peers were born.

The Party at Ganymede Farm

Angelo had received his own invitation to the Ganymede Farm party. He didn't know who sent it. He hadn't yet met Neal Freedman and, as far as he knew, he didn't know anyone else connected to the Farm. Angelo did not worry about this mystery too much, but he remained curious, and that curiosity was one of the reasons he agreed to go with Joe to the Ganymede Farm 35th Anniversary Party.

Joe had heard stories about how fabulous, in a pastoral and bucolic way, the costume party on Saturday night had been on previous anniversaries. Attendees of earlier parties seemed to spring out of the woodwork when Joe and Angelo mentioned that they were going to Apollonia. It seems that Joe was among the last to know of this hidden Massachusetts gay treasure. Even some of Joe's straight friends from Central and Western Massachusetts had attended the Costume Ball on prior occasions. Even Joe's colleague, Justice Mildred Bailey and her partner Louise, who lived nearby, had attended the 30th Anniversary party, but they thought the theme this year—Cowboys and Indians—was politically incorrect and they were boycotting it. "We shouldn't celebrate the subjugation of our Native American brothers and sisters," Mildred told Joe solemnly.

Joe agreed, but a party was a party, and men looked good as either cowboys or Indians, so Joe and Angelo had no such scruples. They decided to wear jeans and western snapped-button shirts like they'd seen on rodeo shows on TV, pretty tame costumes. Joe hoped he wouldn't look like Gabby Hayes. Angelo, of course, could wear anything (or nothing) and look good. Joe didn't want to win a prize; he just wanted to fit in and not look foolish.

Angelo picked Joe up at 11:00 A.M. on Saturday morning, June 9th. The Saturday events included an early morning hike up a mountain which would not have interested Joe at any hour. Although they had been invited to stay at Neal's house with two other couples and one bathroom, Joe thought it would be more convenient for them to rent a motel room in nearby Grumby. Angelo selected a place called the *Travelers Inn* and reserved a room for non-smokers with a king-size bed. The man taking the reservation had an (East) Indian accent and told Angelo that the room would cost $62.00. He also gave Angelo a four-digit reservation number, as if the motel was going to be filled with people, which Angelo thought unlikely.

When Angelo and Joe arrived at the very neat but unadorned motel, right off the highway, there was one car in the parking lot. Both Joe and Angelo walked into the little office in the middle of the row of motel units. A small young East Indian woman with glasses was behind the counter in a small office area adorned with heavily tinted reproductions and busts of a contemporary (East) Indian man wearing eyeglasses. There was even a large plastic clock with his face on it. There were also garlands of paper flowers draped around the tiny office and an incense burner in front of one of the man's portraits. Joe thought this was pretty exotic for North

Central Massachusetts. He wondered what the locals thought.

Angelo said, "Good afternoon! We have a reservation for a room for tonight, reservation number 9085, with a king-size bed, non-smoking."

The woman, who was beaming at their entrance, looked up over the counter at them both, then in a sing song lilting, slightly British accent said, "Oh yes, but you will want two beds."

"No, we want a king-size bed," Angelo said.

"But you are two men?" she said.

"I know we are, but I reserved a king-size bed," Angelo said.

"It is not ready. A queen-size bed is ready. That will be cheaper, $54," she said, as if that should seal the deal.

"No thanks. We're big boys. We'll wait for the king-size bed."

During this colloquy a skinny man about 60, who Joe had seen outside in the parking lot, came into the office. He looked like an extra from *Deliverance*. He had long stringy gray hair, a railroad cap, farmer's overalls and crossed eyes. When the man bumped Joe in order to get clean towels and sheets from a closet beside him Joe realized that he was the chambermaid. He didn't say a word as he fussed about in the little space. Joe worried that he was the enforcer, and thought they better take the queen-sized bed.

Angelo either had not seen the man, or had seen him and was not so fearful. As she searched through her papers after their dialogue, Angelo said to the Indian woman, "Who is that man on the clock and in all the pictures?"

She said enthusiastically, "Oh! He is my god! These are all pictures of him," and then gave a name, which neither Joe nor Angelo, who thought of themselves as educated men, even in the mysteries of the East, recognized as a deity, or even a saint.

"Very interesting," said Angelo. "Does he have many disciples here?"

"Oh yes, we are all his disciples."

How many East Indians can there be out here in Grumby, Massa-chusetts? Joe thought. *And have they taken over entirely so that the former Yankee farmers are working for them as chambermaids? God bless America!*

Apparently, Angelo's expression of interest in the deity took the day. The woman then said, nodding to the rustic in the overalls behind them, "Ben will show you your room—king-sized bed, no smoking. Thank you very much."

They followed Ben to the last room in the line of motel rooms. In spite of the magnetized sign on the door over the room number that said, "No Smoking," it stank of smoke. *They must move these "No Smoking" signs to whatever room is available,* Joe thought to him-self. But the room was clean, had a king-sized bed with a very col-orful bedspread, and a big television. He was later to discover that there was a nice view of a marsh outside the bathroom window.

Joe remembered what a stripper in Montreal had told him about bedspreads in hotels—that they were filthy because every-body fucked on them—and he removed the bedspread.

He then said to Angelo, who was bringing in their bags, "But you are two men!"

Angelo laughed and tackled Joe onto the bed.

"Not now, Angelo, that guy may still be outside the door," Joe said.

"All the better. It'll add to the excitement," Angelo said as he pulled his shirt up over his head.

Joe said, "I need to pee. Let me go," and went into the bathroom.

Angelo said, "I'm going to call for more pillows."

When Joe returned, Angelo was naked on the stiff but clean white sheets with a hardon and a smile.

"Come here, Joe. Come over to the edge of the bed."

Joe did as instructed, and Angelo unbuttoned and unzipped Joe's pants. He then pulled them down below Joe's knees, bringing Joe's Black Watch plaid (for the excursion to the country) boxer shorts with it. Joe had a semi, which Angelo noted before putting it in his mouth. It didn't remain semi for long. Without removing his cock from Angelo's soft mouth, Joe struggled to get his shoes off and kick the pants below his feet. Then came his shirt, which he tossed wildly behind him, landing it on the garish lamp near the big screen TV opposite the bed.

Joe leaned against the side of the bed to lower himself to Angelo's mouth while Angelo pulled a pillow from behind him to keep himself raised up to meet Joe's cock without strain.

If Ben was listening outside the door, he would have heard Angelo saying, "Come to Daddy! Come to Daddy! Don't be ascared! I'll protect you. Give Daddy that big cock! Come on! Come on! Thatta boy! That's a good Irish boy! Come on my chest!" there was a 'splat,' and then, "Oh yeah! Oh yeah!"

Angelo all the while was working his own cock, and just as Joe tensed up prior to coming, Angelo did the same. They both spewed gism all over Angelo's perfectly distributed hairy chest.

Joe collapsed on the bed on top of Angelo. Angelo rubbed his head. "Nice Irish boy! Nice Irish boy!" Angelo repeated in increasing softness until they both fell asleep.

The sleep didn't last long because soon there was a knock on the door. The young Indian woman with glasses from the desk was outside with two more pillows as Angelo had requested.

Thank God (hers or theirs) that she had waited a while for the delivery. Maybe she came by earlier and heard the passion and decided to wait until things quieted down. Maybe she listened to their passion at the door.

Angelo got up, still naked, leaned around the door to hide his lower body and opened it.

"Here's your pillows. Is everything alright?" she said cheerily with the same lilt while staring at Angelo's beautiful upper torso.

"Just fine. Thank you very much," Angelo replied.

*　*　*

Angelo brought his recently purchased GPS, which he and Joe called "Blanche." Once they left the motel Blanche directed them onto the highway and further west for two more exits. They went through a town with a deserted mill and a new giant CVS store and then over a river, which was running high due to the rainy spring. Further twists and turns took them up a hill onto another road and finally to a sign that said "Ganymede Road."

Neal's directions told them that the Farm was one mile down this road. The woods became thicker and thicker, but the sun shone through the tall pines. Finally a handsomely carved wooden sign on their left said "Ganymede Farm," with a lot of numbers below, including number 75, which they knew to be Neal's address. In they went. Almost from the beginning of Ganymede Road there were a number of clearings to both the right and the left that had paper signs in front saying, "Park here for Anniversary Party." The lots were all empty at this time, 2:00 P.M. in the afternoon, seven hours before the start of the dance at 9:00 P.M. Joe thought they ought to park while they still could, but the more adventurous Angelo decided to see how close to Neal's house and the party itself he could get before having to park. "We can always come back," he said to Joe.

As they drove slowly down the road two men on horseback crossed the road from a path on the left to one on the right. "Jesus, that's the Lone Ranger and Tonto!" Joe said. "Hi Ho, Silver!" Indeed the men were dressed as the Lone Ranger, including the black mask, and Tonto in Indian gear. The horses were authentic as well—a big white horse like Silver for the masked man and Tonto on a Pinto that looked just like Scout. "*Kemosabe,*" Angelo said, even though his only knowledge of the pair was from Saturday morning reruns in the Eighties.

Further down the road a group of Indians in breechcloths was sitting by the side of the road as an older gent carrying a staff stood in front of them pointing up into the trees.

As they passed slowly one of them yelled, "Aaaangelo!" and Angelo stopped the car. He and Joe got out and went over to the group. The older gent with the staff, in a fuller Indian costume of buckskin pants, a shirt and a headband, did not seem to welcome this interruption, but he stopped talking nevertheless. One of the more handsome "braves" jumped up and ran to Angelo.

"Angelo, it's me Rob, Rob from the gym in Malden. I'm so happy you could make it. This is Neal Freedman," he added pointing to the older man who appeared to be acting as the teacher. "You must know him. He was one of the original communards here and is the last one left. I live here with my boyfriend, whose previous lover was an original as well. Is this your 'old man'?" Rob said, nodding to Joe.

"Yeah, Rob, this is my partner Joe Lyons."

"Joe Lyons? Joe Lyons? I am your classmate Neal Freedman. How nice to meet at last."

Joe said, "Thank you so much for inviting us. You do look a bit familiar, maybe from the IAB[1] Pool." They both laughed. I'm very happy to meet you. As Joe and Neal Freedman reached out to shake hands the other "braves" of all shapes and sizes stood up as if they were witnessing the meeting of the Pilgrims and Chief Samoset in Plymouth in 1621.

Neal said, "Go down to the first house on the left. That's my place. We'll be down soon. We were having a nature walk and are now strategizing what we can do when we go to the State House in Boston for the Anti-Same-Sex Marriage Amendment vote next Thursday. I know you can't get involved in politics, but we'll just be a minute. We have to decide if we want to dress like this or in our civilian clothes. Rob thinks we ought to dress like this."

---

[1] Indoor Athletic Building

"Well, Rob certainly would attract attention," Joe said with a big smile.

"Angelo would look good as an Indian too, even though most of them were hairless," Rob said. "I've seen Angelo in the locker room. He's got that hirsute, tawny thing down. Don't shave for us, Angelo."

Angelo, well into the spirit of the whole day, ripped open his Western snap-buttoned shirt and gave them all a display of the grizzly torso that Rob had described. There were lots of "Ooh, Babies" and "Oh, Daddies" from the assembled "braves."

Angelo said, "I don't think I can get the day off on Thursday. It's the day of the MassCas, you know, the standardized State tests in English and Math. We all have to be at school to cheer on our little darlings. Joe will be near the Statehouse, however, and I have a friend in the Senate President's office. He's going to keep us informed as the day goes on. There's a veritable daisy chain of phone callers. How are you guys getting there? Are you taking a bus?"

"We're going in Rob's truck—twelve of us. That is if we can fit." Neal added, "Meet us at my house. Go to the pool. The water is beautiful. Rob and the boys cleaned it this morning. It's just below my house. Follow the path. It's right next to the dance tent. I think they are still setting up. Maybe you can help them down there. Stay for dinner at my house. There'll only be twenty of us!"

* * *

Joe and Angelo did go for a swim and, true to form, Angelo took off his bathing suit before jumping in the deep end of the pool. This started a flurry of other stripteases, some quite dramatic. One man kicked his bikini up into a tree. It also made Angelo some new friends, none of whom he desired like they wanted him. As usual, very few of the men there understood Gerontophilia and they each thought they had a chance with Angelo. Joe, although secure in the knowledge that he was Angelo's heart's desire, with the midday bang in the motel to prove it, was still a little uncomfortable with all the attention that the naked Angelo received. However, he felt too old to gambol in the water with Angelo. *Let Angelo play with the other boys*, Joe said to himself.

Down the road from Neal's house, on a rise above the pool, the Lone Ranger reappeared and perused the crowd until his masked gaze fixed on Angelo. After an indecent amount of time staring at the naked Angelo, he smiled and rode away into the woods. "Who is that masked man?" There is something familiar about that guy, Joe said, but he couldn't put his finger on it. The hat and the mask, as well as the outfit, a perfect replica very well made, disguised the man underneath.

There were twenty men for dinner at Neal's house and they all crowded into the open first floor. These guys were so friendly— none of that citified attitude and reserve. Even the New Yorkers, in their more glamorous cowboy outfits, as if designed by Marc Jacobs or Michael Kors, were attitude-free. Of course, they were friendlier to Angelo than to Joe, but one short, muscular, dark Latino man without body hair except for a thin black treasure trail from his navel down to the skimpiest of breechcloths, sidled right up next to Joe and, while snuggling his leg against Joe's, engaged Joe in a discussion of the Law of Search and Seizure. He wasn't a lawyer, but a journalist and it turned out that he regularly covered criminal trials.

This guy was so attentive that Joe found himself moving away from him further down the couch. Joe felt compelled every once in a while to give an affectionate pat or two to Angelo, who was sitting in front of him on a hassock, entertaining a worshipful claque. Joe also frequently referred to "my partner, Angelo," hoping that Cochise would realize that Joe was taken, even though, underneath it all, Joe wouldn't have minded if Angelo and the rest of the men in the room disappeared for a bit while Joe rubbed his tongue all over that very smooth body next to him.

Except for the roast chickens, all the food was grown in Neal's garden. There was steamed cauliflower, corn on the cob, braised Chinese cabbage and a salad of Arugula and watercress. Neal even made two blueberry pies and the New York contingent brought an enormous cheesecake from Zabars.

People ate hastily because most of the men had yet to put on their costumes. Joe and Angelo had nothing else to add to their basic, subdued gay cowboy drag. It didn't have a lot of flair, but it was thematic. They simply borrowed the cotton dinner napkins and tied them around their necks to add a bit of pizazz. They promised Neal that they'd return them, ironed.

A procession of men left Neal's house to walk to the dance while similar groups came down from the other houses in the compound. There were only creosote torches every twenty feet or so for lighting and Joe feared that he'd fall down. He hung on to Angelo, who willingly supported him. The music had started and beckoned them. Local people, old hippie farmers by the looks of them, some gay men, a couple of cowgirls and a string of almost naked (and chilly) Indians, some guys in tutus, and some young children, who could have belonged to anybody, were already dancing in the tent.

Outside the tent, where Joe stopped to get a cold drink out of a cooler, Joe found himself next to Jeanine, a woman from Grumby and her partner, Noreen. He asked Jeanine if she knew about his motel and its East Indian owners. "Oh yeah," she said, "I'm a visiting nurse. All the motels are owned by Indians. There are probably fifteen of them living at that place. We've got everything here now —Latinos, Vietnamese, Indians. It's not like the olden days when there were just French Canadians, like my people, Poles, Irish and a few old swamp Yankees. I still love it here and wouldn't live anywhere else."

"How is it being gay here?" Joe asked.

"I mind my business and they mind theirs," she said taking another swig of beer. "I've been here all my life and my parents and grandparents before me. Nobody's going to mess with me."

"What do you think is going to happen on Thursday with the Gay Marriage vote?" Joe asked.

"Our Rep and our Senator are going to vote against the Amendment. They're good people. They may even be here tonight. All the local pols come to this party. It's good for votes. I don't know what Billy Meadows in the next district is going to do. People have been talking to him. He sometimes comes to this party, with his wife, of course. They ride their horses down here after parking the trailer up in the first lot. They always come in costume. But I don't think he'll be here this year after voting for the Anti-Same-Sex Marriage Amendment on the first vote. He'd better not or someone might knock him off his high horse. I don't trust him. I never did. He's a spoiled brat, if you ask me—too rich and too good-looking. I think he's a closet case."

Joe said nothing. He didn't mention the events in the "Staff Only" room at Guido's Back Bay Grille.

It was getting a little edgy out in the yard and Joe could smell marijuana. He looked into the tent through the big opening in front of him. Angelo was dancing in the middle of the breechclothed Indians who were dancing around him tugging at his snap-buttoned shirt. Angelo was showing his hairy chest. Gradually the Indians pulled away from Angelo, all except one, a tall man who had on a whole deerskin suit. Joe recognized him as Richard, a gym buddy of Angelo's and the former boyfriend of a friend of Joe's. Richard was safe. He was in his early forties, about the same age as Angelo and skinny—not at all Angelo's type. Richard was a good dancer, however, and Joe realized that there were at least two, if not three hours of this party to go. Joe had two options; he could stand on the sidelines like an old fart, or he could dance himself. He hadn't danced in about ten years and even then it was for only one or two songs.

I'd better try it now. It's going to be pretty boring if I don't, Joe thought. So, out he went onto the parquet dance floor. He was embraced by both Angelo and Richard. The three of them danced for four or five songs together, sometimes sandwiching one or the other, usually Angelo, in between. Richard had some pretty wild steps. At a break in the music Richard explained that he had three older sisters, and that they had told him that he would never get a girlfriend unless he learned to dance. "They taught me to dance, but I still don't have a girlfriend," Richard laughed.

Joe took the break as an opportunity to go through a small opening on the right side of the tent to go outside to pee. *We're out here in the woods, for crying out loud,* Joe thought. *It's easier than going halfway up the hill to the Porta Potties.* Joe was twenty feet from the tent and he couldn't see anyone around, but his eyes hadn't entirely adjusted to the dark. He looked up at the stars, pulled out his wanger and began to pee. He walked forward slowly as he looked up. He hadn't seen stars like this in years. Suddenly he bumped into something hairy and warm in front of him. There was a loud whinny. In fright Joe jumped back, as well as a 66 year old man could, shook his dick dry, and zipped up his fly. As his eyes adjusted Joe realized that he had bumped into a horse, Silver to be specific. The whinnys came from Silver and Scout, who along with Silver was tied to a tree. *Where were their riders,* Joe wondered?

It didn't take long for him to find out. On the side of a tool shed a few yards to Joe's left and down a few more feet, Joe espied Tonto leaning with his back to the shed and his pants down. The Lone Ranger was shirtless on his knees before Tonto revealing a very buff, shaven chest. Joe tried not to be intrusive, even turning away for a bit. But there was something about that chest that looked familiar. *Could it be?* Joe looked back. *There was also something familiar about Tonto. The hair is longer, but I think that's..... No, I must be having hallucinations. How would those guys have ever met? Florida is a thousand miles from here. That can't be Billy Meadows as the Lone Ranger and Carlos Colorado the Cuban refugee from Haulover as Tonto?*

I better get out of here before they see me. Jeanine just said Billy sometimes comes to this party. Maybe they want me to see them. I can't see his face with the mask and hat still on, but the other guy certainly looks like Carlos—a little more flesh on the bones, but I'm sure that's Carlos. Oh shit, how am I going to explain Carlos to Angelo? I never said anything about him before. I'd better get out of here.

Just then Joe heard the familiar cackle, "Ha Ha Ha Ha" coming from the tent and he hotfooted back into the tent. He looked around and indeed there he was, Tom Murphy, dressed as Hopalong Cassidy, all in black. Tom was bouncing along to the music in a circle that included Angelo, now shirtless, and skinny Richard, also without a top, and Patrick Foley dressed like the palest Indian who God ever created, like a settler boy kidnapped by the Iroquois, or a Circassian among the Turks. Rod, the Trooper boyfriend, in contrast, was the darkest. He wore a very skimpy suede breechcloth, and for some reason explained only by lust, his State Trooper boots and harness. They were quite the group. Joe was relieved to see Tom Murphy, although he wondered why Tom had said nothing to him about coming. Patrick Foley's and Rod's presence was also a surprise. Joe hoped there'd be a break in the music so he could tell Tom what he'd just seen, and be able to ask him what to do should Carlos recognize him in the presence of Angelo.

There was no break. Joe threw himself into the dance again. Angelo snuggled up behind him and Richard faced him in the front, but only so he could reach around Joe and rub Angelo's hairy chest. Next to them Patrick and Rod and Tom made a similar sandwich with Tom as the filling and Rod behind. That lasted for three songs. Then they all disassembled and Joe looked over at the small opening he had just reentered. In the doorway, now dressed, were the Lone Ranger and Tonto, Billy Meadows and Carlos. Joe elbowed Tom Murphy and nodded in the direction of Billy and Carlos. Tom looked over as well, looked back at Joe and held up his hands as if to say, "What am I supposed to be seeing?" Joe nodded Tom back and mouthed, "Take a good look."

Tom did, and after a few seconds stopped dead. His eyes widened and he looked back at Joe. He nodded Joe through the big opening with a sideways pull to his head, like the men of the Aran Islands do as a greeting. Tom headed to the outside. Joe followed. Once outside they walked away from the wallflowers looking in or drinking by the open side of the tent. Tom walked over to the pool and sat down in one of the deck chairs. Joe sat opposite him.

"I don't fucken believe it! I don't believe it!" Tom said. "I saw them on horses as we drove in a little while ago, but I thought they were just part of the local color. Where do I start? What is Billy Meadows doing here?"

"Well, he lives nearby." Joe said. "It seems he often comes to this party, but usually with his wife. A local woman just told me that."

"What's he doing with Carlos? How did Carlos get up here? We just left him in Florida a few weeks ago."

"I have no idea. Maybe Billy is trying to make a statement. Maybe being seen shirtless in the 'Staff Only' with his hand down Guido's pants has liberated him in some way. Maybe he'll vote against the Anti-Same-Sex Marriage Amendment now."

"That's a lot of 'maybes,' Joe. Maybe he's on drugs," Tom said. "I wonder if I can talk to him. Our last conversation wasn't very satisfactory."

"When was that? You never told me that you talked to him," Joe said.

"There's a lot you don't need to know, Joe. I talked to him just after you saw him on the floor *in fragrante delicto*. Isn't that how you guys in Criminal Law say it?"

"Not to be a pedant, but we say '*flagrante*', Tom, with an 'L.' *Fragrante* is good too, however, especially if Billy was wearing cologne."

"Fuck you! You stay away from him. He's trouble and likes making trouble. Let's go back in. I'll try to get him out here. That may mean you'll have to entertain Carlos, however. Are you up to that again?"

"Carlos never laid a hand on me, Tom. Nor did I touch him. I'm clear on that," Joe said

"Yeah, yeah, sure," Tom said as he headed back to the tent.

As Joe looked in the tent for Angelo, and Tom looked for Billy Meadows, a procession consisting of two Dale Evans, three buffalo, one Princess Summer Fall Winter Spring, John Wayne with a mask, Gabby Hayes (or maybe just the farmer next place over,) five big ladies in granny dresses and bonnets, the Shawmut Bank Indian, a couple of oldline Mormon women with the upsweep from the place in Texas that was raided, men in tidy whities underwear and cowboy boots, one guy who was getting long in the tooth but came every year as Marilyn Monroe, no matter what the theme, two people as one horse, two cows, innumerable Indian braves in skimpy breechcloths, three Indian braves in tutus, as well as three Indian chiefs of indeterminate sex with big headdresses passed by for the judging for the best costume.

However, in the center of the floor there was Angelo, shirtless with his hands over his head, bouncing up and down like the disco god of all time while Billy Meadows the Lone Ranger, Richard and Carlos/Tonto were shimmying down to the floor around him. "There he is," Tom said, pointing to the four of them. "And you better go save your boyfriend."

Carlos and Richard rose up and began doing something Latin, perhaps a Salsa or was it a Samba? Before Joe and Tom could move, Carlos spotted them in the entrance way, dropped Richard on the floor, in the middle of a dip, and ran through the processional march to embrace Joe with enthusiasm excessive certainly in New England, and probably *de trop* and *demasiado* anywhere in the Western world.

"Ay, *maduro mío, Salvador de mi vida*. Ay, my old man, Savior of my life," Carlos kept repeating while kissing Joe's face all over.

Joe could see Angelo, mouth agape, stopped dead in the middle of the dance floor looking at them. The Lone Ranger was still mimicking obscenities in front of Angelo in tune to the music, "Stop in the name of Love" by the Supremes—a message to them both perhaps. Joe tried to push Carlos away and was even successful for a minute, but Carlos then went to his knees and clutched Joe's legs.

Tom cut through the processional and approached Angelo and The Lone Ranger. He pulled the Lone Ranger/Billy Meadows up and whispered something in his ear. He then whispered in Angelo's ear. Angelo rushed over to Joe. Billy and Tom went out the side door (from which Joe had exited earlier to answer the call of nature when he saw Billy and Carlos holding up the woodshed.)

Angelo gently pulled Carlos off Joe. Carlos kept repeating, "*Este hombre es un Salvador! Yo me estaba ahogando! El me salvo mi vida! Es un santo!* This man is a savior! I was drowning! He saved my life! He's a saint!"

Angelo, who had Latino fourth grade students in Revere (or 'Rayvayray' as they pronounced it) and knew a few words in Spanish said, "*Yo se, Yo se.* I know. I know. *Calmate.* Calm down!"

Carlos began to kiss Angelo, much to his chagrin. "*Su papi es un santo. El es un angel de Dios. El me salvo mi vida! Que Dios les bendiga ustedes dos!* Your papi is a saint. He is an angel from God. He saved my life. May God bless you both!"

Just then they heard the sound of hoofs. The Lone Ranger/Billy Meadows, still masked and now fully dressed with his shirt back on rode up behind them on Silver, holding a rein from Scout as well. "Carlos, come on, *Kemosabe, Vamonos.* Let's go."

Carlos, who knew which side his bread was buttered on that day, jumped on Scout and the two of them rode off up the hill. "Hi Ho, Silver!!" rang out as they mounted the hill.

Gigi's Solution

On Tuesday, June 12, 2007, two days before the vote on the Anti-Same-Sex Marriage Amendment, Judge Mildred Bailey strode into the Courthouse like a fury carrying a bulky LL Bean green cloth briefcase under her arm. She bounded up the stairs, taking them two at a time. Mildred was followed by five-year-old twin Latino boys from Guatemala, both named *Luis*, and another woman who looked a lot like Mildred, named *Louise*. Louise was wearing a large "Marriage Equality" button as were the two boys. Both Mildred and Louise were about five-foot two-inches tall, lean, with mousy grey hair in a no-care Beatles bob. Louise was dressed in a khaki, boxy pantsuit and wearing sensible brown tie shoes. Mildred was wearing a similar gray pantsuit and the same brand shoes in black. Mildred was headed for the Chief Justice's office, having called him from Route 2 to request an important meeting.

Mildred and Louise, and the two boys lived in New Plymouth, a Massachusetts town about 75 miles and an hour and a half away from Boston. The town center of New Plymouth was up on a hill and very pretty. It had a green and some houses facing the green.

There had once been a school there and some of the school buildings were still in use, one as a theater. The Hessians had passed through during the Revolutionary War and there was a monument attesting to that fact. New Plymouth is adjacent to the Quabbin Reservoir and there are a couple of side roads that lead down from the main street to overlooks of the mammoth man made in the 1930s inland sea, which provides water to Boston and 41 other communities in Eastern Massachusetts.

There were people living in town with the names of some of the original settlers, but mostly there were descendants of French Canadian, Polish and Finnish farmers. Other people arrived there in the seventies, or later like Mildred and her partner, now wife, Louise Applethorpe, a social worker for the Department of Mental Health.

Louise was carrying a CD in a plastic case in her left hand as she ran up the stairs behind Mildred. The first person Mildred encountered, once at the Appeals Court second floor of the John Adams Courthouse, was *not* Court Officer O'Brien, one of whose few tasks it was to make sure that no "stranger" snuck into the Judges Lobby, the holy of holies. Mr. O'Brien had his favorites, like Mary Rose Quirk of the BMC, for whom he opened the door, but he was supposed to keep everyone out but the judges, their law clerks and interns unless specifically told otherwise by a judge—or Miss Managhan, with whom he was having a cup of coffee in the robing room around the corner.

The first person who Mildred Bailey ran into was the Honorable Gigi Boland, enrobed as if ready to do court business. She, like the other judges, never used the robing room, which had been the creature of some architect's imagination after watching one too many episodes of *Rumpole at the Old Bailey*. Miss Managhan had appropriated the room as an auxiliary office and was just waiting for the right time to scrape "Robing Room" off its door.

"Hi, Milly, what's the rush? You look winded. What's up?" Gigi said. "Oh, Louise, how nice to see you! Did you come into town to go, uh…shopping? There's a wonderful sale at Bonwit's. And the kids!!! Oh, aren't they beautiful! They really aren't both called 'Luis,' are they? Louise, tell me that Mildred has just been joking."

"That's not a joke, Judge Boland," Louise said sternly. "We didn't think it was our place to impose Anglo names on them. We want to treat them equally and we want them to appreciate their own culture."

"Oh, then you're going to Jamaica Plain," Gigi said. "I know the best Burrito place there and it's open very late."

"No, we are *not* going to Jamaica Plain." Mildred said impatiently. "I needed to bring Louise with me. She told me something last night that will blow this male chauvinist plot out of the water."

"Which male chauvinist plot would that be, Milly?" Gigi asked, leaning back on her high heels and touching her cheek with an index finger. "You've detected so many that it's hard to know where to begin. I hope this one doesn't involve moving the ladies room again. I just got used to powdering my nose next to a urinal ever since you so astutely pointed out that there were an excess of toilet fixtures for men up here."

"No, Gigi, this is the plot to deprive me of credit for presiding over the *Williamson v. Randozza Enterprises, Inc.* case."

"Oh that!" Gigi said. "You might want to talk to Joe Lyons about that. He has something to say about that mistake."

"Does he acknowledge that it was a *mistake* to deprive me of credit as the Presiding Justice? Or was it a plot? Did he have a hand in it with the Reporter of Decisions? I certainly suspect that he did. Gay men, straight men, they're all part of the patriarchy. Look at the Catholic Church! If Joe will admit his error, I'll talk to him. Otherwise, I have nothing to say to him," Mildred said firmly.

"Darling, I haven't been inside a Catholic Church since my mother's funeral. I'm sure that you're right about the Catholic Church, although how would you know, being brought up as an Ethical Culturist in Manhattan? It's like Joe says about sex with women, 'There's nothing there for me.' Let the priests play their silly dress up games, himself with the white dress and red shoes leading the way like Judy Garland in *The Wizard of Oz*. They can't bother me. Now listen to me! Joe Lyons had nothing to do with the error in the report of the *Williamson v. Randozza Enterprises, Inc.* decision. As a matter of fact, you, Mildred, may be the cause of the error. You did not enlighten the record as soon as you sat down. You did not say, 'Let the record reflect that Justice Mildred Bailey is now presiding in the *Williamson v. Randozza Enterprises, Inc.* case.' You could have directed the Clerk to say it, if you were too shy. What was the Clerk doing? Falling asleep with the boredom of it all? There is a job to do when you're the presiding judge. It is an honorific with duties—not many, but you're in charge and if anyone is not doing her job, shame on her! Now get over this silly seventies self-pitying Feminist talk."

Louise looked on as close lipped and determined as Mildred. She hadn't listened to a word of Gigi's oration, or if she heard it, it went right through her, so invested was she in her righteousness, her conspiracy notion and her heroic role as the solution of the injustice.

"It's all here," she said waving the CD in Gigi's face. "I got it all. Milly never knew that I had a little camera hidden inside my Guatemalan weavers' cooperative book bag and that I filmed the entire hearing from the time Milly and Judge Firrfield and Judge Parsnip came out from behind the drape right to the end of the argument. I even have footage of the Randozzas as they left the courtroom. At least I think that it was them. I heard the handsome older woman say, 'Let's go, Dino,' to the younger man. Isn't Dino Randozza a gangster? His mother is lovely."

Gigi replied, "Oh great, Louise, don't you know that it is illegal for you to film a court proceeding without the permission of the

Court? How are we going to use your video? Wait a minute! Don't you sometimes film for the Quabbin Local News station? Don't answer yet! Could it be that you were filming this very pertinent hearing about the swindling of an investor in a nonexistent condominium project on Revere Beach for the Quabbin Local News in North Central Massachusetts? Or was it a local interest story because of New Plymouth's favorite jurist, the Honorable Mildred Bailey? Who bought that camera, anyway, you or the News station? Think about this, girls!

Gigi continued, "Why don't you and Milly go into her office and when you come out we can work on the best tactics for the resolution of this mistake. I'll give the Luises some lovely French chocolates while you're in there and I'll read them something manly, like Ernest Hemingway. They'll have a good time with me. They always do. Luis Uno can look at the latest *Paris Vogue*. He always likes that. He loves me. Look, he's in my office now trying on my pink Pashmina shawl. Luis Dos is constructing a house with the Massachusetts Reports. What lovely children you have! How do they survive in the country?! "

With that Gigi turned perfectly on her Loboutin clad heel, deftly not stepping on her train, like Madame de Pompadour at her formal presentation to Louis XV of France, and returned to her office. Mildred glared at the thoroughly bewildered Louise and gave her a very strong nod towards Mildred's office, to which they retired with the twins, who Louise had pulled away from the delights of Gigi's office.

Gigi went to Joe's office, which was opposite her own, to tell him to be ready to go see the Chief Justice and to assemble his evidence. She also wanted to bring him up to speed about Mildred and Louise. She hoped that Mildred would have the sense to lock Louise and the Luises in her office before she picked up Joe to go see the Chief Justice.

Joe said, "A fat lot of good a videotape is going to do us. The Chief doesn't have a video player and if he had one, he wouldn't know how to play it. He'd have to get Miss Mary Margaret Managhan to turn it on."

"Well, you know how to play it and to pause it too, I'm sure. In fact, I know. I saw you coming out of that gay bookstore in the South End at night with your baseball cap pulled down, sunglasses, and your collar turned up carrying *Jerking my Way through College, Bum Boys of Brazil, Italian Stallions at Play in the Barnyard* and *The Sound of Music*. So you can just put your technical knowledge to good use in your own defense. And if you can't do it, I'm sure that Mildred knows how to work the machine after showing her boys endless reruns of *Billy has Two Mommies* and Al Gore's *An Inconvenient Truth*.

Gigi continued, "Be nice to Mildred. In spite of overwhelming evidence to the contrary, she still thinks the original mistake was a conspiracy. Rather, Louise thinks that, and you just know that she's been haranguing Mildred for the past two hours in the car all the way from New Plymouth. So, it's not going to be easy to move Mildred into a more conciliatory mood. She's a smart woman, however, as we have seen as her colleagues, and she is capable of change—unlike us thick Micks. We do not have to tell her why this is important to you. God knows, enough people in town know the hot water this case dunked you into. We don't have to tell everyone. You can tell her later if she asks. She's no fool and obviously knows that you recused yourself on the *Randozza* or *Williamson* case, whatever you want to call it. It doesn't take a rocket scientist to deduce that If you thought that you had to recuse yourself and then were listed as being the presiding judge on the case, something is amiss and you might be in trouble. Mildred doesn't have to know the particulars—like you got off the case because you wanted to get in the sack and get banged by Dino Randozza again."

"Gigi, how do you know who was going to be banging who—whom?" Joe said.

"Joe darling, this is a small town. Who wouldn't like to get banged by Dino Randozza? Unfortunately he doesn't swim in my pool," countered Gigi.

Just then Mildred Bailey appeared in the hallway. She peeked in at the two of them in Joe's office and then went into Gigi's office. Gigi followed. She shut the door with a wink at Joe across the hall.

Mildred said, "This is our story. Louise was making the video for the Quabbin Public Television. It was supposed to broadcast a few days after the oral argument, but the presence of a black bear in the town Common for three days usurped the time. They seemed to think that bear was more important. Everyone in town was out there with their video camera. So, they had a lot of footage and it could be perceived as a community project. Later, the fact that I presided was no longer timely. That's what I can tell the Chief if he asks. Now how are we going to do this?" Mildred asked.

"Well," Gigi replied. "The Chief doesn't have a video player in his office. There are two in the law library. It's now 1:00 P.M. The secretaries and court officers will no longer be watching the soap operas. I think it's Erin's birthday. You remember Erin. She works the phones, but rarely answers incoming calls. She is usually talking to her mother who works at the Land Court, where nobody calls. The 'staff,' as Miss Managhan calls them, are all out at Sam LaGrassa's Deli for Pastrami sandwiches in honor of Erin. We can go to the library and you can play the tape. I'll call down the Reporter of Decisions. Once he sees the tape he can begin the process of amending the record *sua sponte*, all on his own. That's easy these days. It can be done in two minutes electronically. The report of the case has not been published in book form yet.

"Once the record is amended you will have been given your due. Then we can get back to serious business, like where to have the annual Judges Dinner and what food to serve. We have to get out of the second floor of the Parker House, Milly. The Oliver Wendell Holmes Junior Room just doesn't hack it anymore. Joe and I have some ideas about where to go, but first things first. Joe has already agreed to go with you to see the Chief Justice in the Law Library to tell him that it was you who presided at *Williamson v. Randozza Enterprises, Inc.* I'll walk down and get the Chief. Miss Managhan, Cerberus at the Gates, won't dare to stop me. Besides she may be at lunch with the other 'Misses.' I think that the second Tuesday of the month is their day for lunch. They go to Dini's to get schrod. You two go to the Law Library and get the video player and the video-tape ready. We won't have a lot of time. I'll take care of Mary Margaret and the Chief Justice. I'm very good with old men—and O.K. with termagants. 'This isn't my first rodeo,' as Joan Crawford said to the Board of Pepsi Cola."

*   *   *

To their surprise, Joe and Mildred found Miss Mary Margaret Man-aghan in the Law Library watching *The Days of Our Lives* on one of the two court-owned televisions stored there.

When Joe asked if he and Justice Bailey could have the Law Library to themselves, Miss Managhan replied pitifully, "But it's one of my stories!" as if that explained something. At first she was quite resistant to leaving. Although the show ran at 11:00 A.M. every day, Pearl Chin, a recently hired typist, taught Miss Managhan how to tape it so that Miss Managhan could watch it at her pleasure, which was usually at 1:00 P.M., the hour when all court sessions, both trial and appellate, traditionally adjourned for lunch in Massachusetts. Miss Managhan knew that nobody would be around to bother her at that hour and, more importantly, nobody would know about her secret addiction.

However, Miss Managhan dropped her resistance to clearing out after she realized that because she had a tape, which she could watch at any time, this interruption was not going to be a total loss.

That was a good thing because Joe was just about to drop his last bomb and tell her that, despite all the evidence to the contrary, she was sitting watching a soap opera in what purported to be the Law Library, the place where people were supposed to do legal research.

But then Mildred Bailey, never one of Miss Managhan's favorites, in an attempt to add *gravitas* to their need to use the Law Library for a meeting, just as Miss Managhan was reaching the door, told Miss Managhan that the meeting was going to be with the Chief Justice.

"A meeting with the Chief Justice!?! Who authorized such a meeting? I know nothing about such a meeting! You didn't arrange it through me!! The Chief should be having his lunch in his office. Jimmy O'Brien would have brought him lobster salad from Dini's Seafood Restaurant by now. Wait a minute! Is it Tuesday? Oh, then it would be the chicken soup and the pastrami with cole slaw on rye from Sam LaGrassa's Deli. Do you realize how disruptive of this Court and its administration your behavior is!?! You new judges always think you know better!" (New judges, indeed! Joe and Gigi had been on the Appeals Court over 16 years: Mildred Bailey had almost the same amount of time. Miss Managhan was about to end her fifty-first year in the Massachusetts court system. She came over from the Superior Court with the first Chief Justice.) "We have a way of doing things here and we've had it for years. You new people want to disrupt everything!" and out stomped Miss Managhan, carrying her precious tape of *Days of Our Lives* in her right hand, as well as the television clicker in her left.

At the same time at the door to the Law Library the Chief Justice stepped in warily. He heard Miss Managhan's voice as he approached arm in arm with Gigi Boland and recoiled. Gigi had also heard Miss Managhan, so she held on to the Chief Justice tightly and gabbed away senselessly, in hopes of diverting the Chief until she brought him safely to their destination.

"And you," Miss Managhan said to the Chief Justice on her way out the door, "Your head is turned by the first pretty face you see. It's a wonder you ever got anywhere without the likes of me to keep you on course. You're worse now than when you started up here. There's no fool like an old fool! I'll talk to you later."

Miss Managhan knew that there was another TV and video player in the closet of the small Single Justice Courtroom. She had put it there for just such an eventuality—the day when some self-important judge wanted to do research or have a meeting in the law library. Unbeknownst to anyone, that week she had already chased out two law clerks who were so bold as to enter the Law Library to do legal research for their judges between 1:00 and 2:00 P.M.

The Chief Justice, visibly shaken by Miss Managhan's assault, was deposited in a chair at the head of the table by Gigi, who still held his hand. "Joe, go get the other TV from the other side of the library. The clicker is behind the top row of the *Federal Digest* on the right. I hid it there two months ago. I sometimes come in here to watch *Oprah*, later in the day. Mildred, don't just stand there looking shocked! Will you give Joe a hand, please! Thank you both very much."

The TV and the clicker were produced. Mildred was instructed to put the DVD into the machine. Having two kids, she knew how to perform such feats. Gigi sat at the Chief's left side holding his hand and murmuring sweet nothings. "Are you comfortable, Chief? Would you like some water? Thank you so much for coming! It is really very Important that you see this."

Once everything was ready, Gigi stood up still holding the Chief's left hand. "My dear, Chief Justice, you know that there is a concern about who presided at the *Williamson v. Randozza Enterprises, Inc.* case last year? I needn't get into the details. Well, today we have incontrovertible evidence that it was Judge Bailey and not Judge Lyons. Mildred, will you begin the tape, please? This DVD…" Gigi began.

"What's a DVD, Gigi?" the Chief Justice interrupted.

"It's a new name for a tape, newer technology," Gigi said.

"Thank you," the Chief replied, although he still looked quizzical.

"This DVD will show that Judge Bailey presided and that Judge Lyons was not on the bench or anywhere in the vicinity," Gigi said even though she had not yet seen the DVD herself. Cautious lawyer that she was, she realized the risk she had just taken.

The tape began. You could hear the Clerk, Angie Buttinsky, calling the case before you could see her all dolled up in pink in her platinum splendor, beringed and bejeweled, her pink-covered Barbara Cartland romance laid out open and upside down to the right of the papers she was clearly reading from.

"The Court next calls the case of *Williamson v. Randozza Enterprises, Inc.* Will the lawyers please come forward? The rules of this Court allow you each ten minutes of argument. If the Court allows, more time may be allotted."

"Please begin, Mister Ladzio, for the Appelant, Randozza Enterprises," said Mildred Bailey as the camera struggled to catch her. There was Mildred finally in all her glory, moving up in her chair, which had not been adjusted to her height after Joe Lyons' previous occupancy before the recess. Poor Mildred kept on sliding back in the chair, but she used her elbows on the bench to pull herself forward, and hopefully up, so she could be seen and be seen looking like a presiding judge—and even perhaps a Chief Justice some day. As the tape was playing Mildred remembered that she had been thinking, *The next time I do this I have to remember to get the bloody Court Officer to adjust the chair for me. Why didn't he do it this time? He saw me behind the curtain leading the other two judges. He must hate women in authority. What an incompetent!*

The DVD continued. Mildred didn't have a lot to do, except keep Firrfield in line. He was about to deliver the third lecture in his Portia Law School course on *Bills and Notes*, the one on Mortgages, when Mildred got a kick from Judge Parsnip on her other side and interrupted, "Thank you very much, Justice Firrfield. How fortunate we are to have you on this panel with your expertise on this subject." Mildred was no fool. She had seen her confreres use just such a technique to silence the voluble Professor/Justice Firrfield.

Precisely as the Appellant's lawyer finished his argument and sat down, about 16 minutes into the DVD, after Justice Firrfield's comments about *Perkins on Mortgages*, just as Mildred Bailey, was about to call the Appellee, there was a knock on the door to the Law Library. Without anyone responding to the knock, in walked Court Officer O'Brien, carrying a brown paper bag.

"Jesus, Chief, I didn't know where the hell you were. What are ya doin' in here, having an orgy? Miss M&M &M [Miss Managhan] finally told me where you were. She's got a hair across her ass today. When I couldn't find you in the office, and asked her where you were I got the silent treatment, the famous 'Irish chill.' Finally she said, without even looking at me, 'Look in the law library,' like I'd know where that was. I never knew this was the law library. I thought it was the TV room. Will you be out soon? I want to watch the Red Sox this after....Oh, here's your change. They didn't have chicken soup, so I got Navy bean," and he dropped a few bills and some coins in front of the Chief Justice and left.

Mildred had stopped the DVD and Gigi turned on the lights. Gigi thought a bit and then said, "I think that it's important that you have your lunch Chief. We'll just continue the DVD with the lights on while you eat. Why don't you start with the soup first?"

The Chief nodded in agreement. As he put the pastrami sandwich to his mouth Mildred started the tape. There were no interruptions of the Appellee's lawyer by the judges on the panel—not even Justice Firrfield. Then the tape showed the adjournment of the session, the retreat of Mildred Bailey, and a bouncing around as Louise was adjusting herself to turn around to take pictures of Giussepina and Dino Randozza leaving the courtroom. Dino was looking up at the bench until he saw the camera when he put his hands over his face.

Joe had a twitch to his sphincter when he saw Dino.

Gigi said, "Well, Chief, thank you for your time. I'll just sit with you while you finish your lovely sandwich. That coleslaw looks delicious too. How was the soup? Perhaps we can figure out what to do next to resolve this matter. Judge Bailey and Judge Lyons have to return to their offices now. We can talk to them later." Gigi glared at Joe and Mildred with her best schoolteacher furrowed brow look as she nodded up and down and then towards the door.

Gigi knew that the Chief needed some womanly guidance and that he, temporarily at least, had burnt his bridge to his usual female support, Miss Managhan. Gigi wasn't going to leave him alone to feel too insecure. Besides Gigi hadn't told Mildred Bailey how important this was for Joe, the trouble that Joe was in as a result of this mistake in the record regarding the identity of the Presiding Justice in *Williamson v. Randozza Enterprise, Inc.*, although by now Mildred may well have put things together on her own.

Impressed by Gigi's skills thus far, Mildred and Joe left the Law Library, looking at each other quizzically. Mildred thought, *what is there to strategize about? There I was in the middle chair, and I did a pretty good job as well*. Joe trusted that Gigi would convince the Chief of the best way to get the word out to the Commission on Judicial Conduct, the District Attorney, the United States Attorney, and Sam Nemesis that Joe had not sat on a case where he had a conflict of interest, a conflict the nature of which was so delicate that it could ruin Joe's reputation and career.

The Chief and Gigi remained huddled in the Law Library for a while. When they came out Gigi walked behind the Chief smiling and holding a one-page statement, which she had typed on the computer in the Law Library.

Usually, the Chief's correspondence and pronouncements were typed by Miss Managhan on an old IBM Selectric. The Selectric was one of Miss Managhan's few concessions to 'modern times,' which for her ended about 1966. Who was going to force her onto a computer? This was probably the first document of the Chief Justice's that was ever typed by somebody other than Miss Managhan.

What the Chief and Gigi (mostly Gigi) decided was that the Chief Justice would write each of the other investigators, the Commission on Judicial Conduct, the District Attorney and the United States Attorney. The text of the letters was what Gigi had just typed (and drafted). The Chief Justice would tell them that he had seen, and was in possession of, a videotape that provided incontrovertible proof that Justice Mildred Bailey, *not* Justice Joseph L. Lyons, presided over the case of *Williamson v. Randozza Enterprises, Inc.* He would invite the Chair of the Commission, the District Attorney and the United States Attorney (no stand-ins) to view the tape at the Appeals Court at their pleasure.

The Chief would not respond to Sam Nemesis directly because, among other things, Sam had not written him about the matter. He would let the Commission, the District Attorney and the United States Attorney deal with Sam. Sam would scream for a while; he'd make threats, but it was unlikely that he would go to the Press or that they would listen to him. Surely Sam had read *Murphy v. the Boston Herald*, the case where a jury awarded a judge three-plus million dollars for being libeled by the newspaper. Sam would not even have the leg up that the newspaper had in that case—the Constitutional protection of Freedom of the Press. And the newspapers and other media were a little gun shy after that verdict against one of their own. They didn't want to risk liability and were not likely to want Sam's story. Rihanna, Chris Brown and Lady Gaga were of much more interest to their declining readership anyway. Or so they thought.

"The less contact the Court has with Sam Nemesis, the better," is what the Chief told Gigi while they were cloistered in the Law Library. Gigi told him he was a very wise man.

Duplicate copies of Louise's *Williamson v. Randozza Enterprises, Inc.* tape would not be made or distributed, but the letter did not specifically say that. Gigi would keep the one they just saw "For the Court." The Chief Justice would call her Imperial Highness upstairs, tell her what he had just seen and invite her to a viewing of the tape. She would undoubtedly decline, in favor of a television appearance.

"There is no need to keep this thing going any further," the Chief said to Gigi sternly as he got up to leave the Law Library, like he had thought of this scheme all by himself.

That Gigi was a genius.

The Vote

On Thursday, the 14th of June, the day of the vote of the Constitutional Convention (both houses of the Legislature) on the Anti-Same-Sex Marriage Amendment, Joe woke up early and thought twice about how, or whether, to go to work. Finally he decided, *I'm not going to be further inconvenienced by the bigots. I have lived in fear of them all my life.* And Joe didn't just mean the haters who would be standing outside the State House that day. He was thinking of the pious types who said that supporting gay rights was "political" and forbidden for judges while supporting other people's civil rights was humanistic and encouraged.

It was a warm day so Joe put on his best lightweight wool blue suit with a faint white stripe—Navy blue would have been too serious for daytime, even this day—a handsome striped shirt and a lavender tie, the latter being clearly a political statement, but let someone call him on it. Just let them dare! He walked out his front door up Beacon Street to the State House. The gays were on the State House side in front of the gates barring the stairs up to the State House itself.

On the other side of Beacon Street, the Boston Common side, were the opponents dressed uniformly in dark green "Let the People Decide" tee shirts. Joe thought that he saw Michael Nemesis on that side as well as Marie Ciamatti from the BMC Clerk's office. Joe was too busy to look too closely. He just wanted to get through the crowd. Joe heard later that some of the young men with the most scurrilous and graphic signs were ringers, Russian illegal immigrants imported from Springfield and paid to be there. The supporters of the amendment, the "Antis" stood in front of Saint Gaudens' beautiful *bas relief* monument to the "Negro Regiment" in the Civil War, sometimes called the "Shaw Monument" after the Boston native son, the white colonel, of the regiment. It is probably the best piece of public sculpture in Boston.

They ought to turn around and think about the fighters for equality they are standing in front of, Joe thought. *But they are a dreary lot and would never get the irony,* Joe figured.

On the gay side, in front of the gates, was a hodgepodge of old and young—"Raging Grannies" from Northampton and skinny gay boys in tight pants from Dorchester. Joe saw a few of the Ganymede Farmers as well as old friends from GLAD, the Gay and Lesbian Advocates and Defenders. Some muscle boys were flexing on the steps and "Dykes on Bikes" rode by and revved their engines. The gay politicos, who had brought gay marriage this far, were inside the Statehouse cornering legislators and shoring up their supporters.

In contrast to the dour supporters of the Amendment across Beacon Street, the "antis" were gay in every sense of the word. They wore all the colors of the rainbow and more, sang songs and carried homemade banners and signs. One sign showed the Cardinal Archbishop of Boston strangling the Statue of Liberty and pictorially noted the Church's previous support of slavery, opposition to women's suffrage and now denial of equality to gay people.

The whole circus was grand! Joe was delighted as he worked his way through the gay crowd. He had a big smile. *That wasn't forbidden as an expression of political support*, he told himself. Not yet, anyhow. Joe even stopped to say hello to a few older lesbian lawyers from GLAD who he knew from his pre-judicial political days. Although he hoped the *Herald* wasn't watching, *screw them if they are*, Joe thought recklessly.

Joe didn't want to leave the gates and the crowd and the excitement. He remembered being in equally festive demonstrations which had much less chance of success. But Joe knew he couldn't linger and that he had to move on, if only to go to work and he edged his way through the crowd. Toward the outside of the crowd he was recognized and some of his fans gave him a cheer, "Hurray for Joe Lyons!" Joe smiled, waved a fist in the air and walked even faster. He hoped the Commission on Judicial Conduct couldn't hear that. Their headquarters was just a few doors away in the Congregational Church building on Beacon Street next to the Athenaeum.

Joe arrived at his office, sat down at his desk and tried to read. He was too distracted. *This is too much excitement*, Joe thought as he got up to pace his tiny office.

Angelo, who knew how much this battle meant to Joe, and also knew how impotent Joe felt by not being able to participate, had arranged for a friend named Chris, a legislative aide, to call Joe when the vote came down. All morning Joe alternated between the briefs for cases he had heard earlier in the month and Boston.com, the *Boston Globe* website, on his computer hoping for some news. Fox News Boston headquarters had recently moved to the corner of Beacon and Park Streets, looking over to the State House gate.

Joe didn't leave his office for lunch. He didn't dare go out. Something might happen. He couldn't just go back and stand by the State House and watch. If he went over there, he knew that he would jump in and that would clearly piss off the Judicial Conduct Commission, to say nothing of Sam Nemesis and the Fox News viewers.

For the first time in his judicial career he asked his clerk to pick him up a turkey on whole wheat and a Diet Coke. He hated it when judges treated their clerks like hired help, but the enormity of this issue made him do it this one time. The clerk knew of Joe's anxiety, she shared it in fact, thought nothing of the request and was happy to oblige. She told Joe that she would take a peek at the State House goings-on herself and report back to Joe.

Finally, a little after one in the afternoon, Joe's friend Vinny, an artist, writer and musician called. He had called the night before and told Joe that he was going to the State House early in the morning. He said he had to be there for this moment in history.

"We won!! We won!! 151 to 45!!" Vinny knew all the details. "Morrissey from Quincy voted for us and so did Wallace from South Boston. Jimmy Vallee switched. He said he read the Goodridge opinion and people shouldn't vote on other people's rights. Can you hear the noise? They're singing the *Star Spangled Banner* outside. Do you believe that!! Gay people have been beaten up by the system for years and now when we get equality we sing the *Star Spangled Banner*!! How patriotic is that!! I'm so happy to be gay! I gotta go. I love you, Joe!"

"Wait a minute, Vinny! How did Billy Meadows vote?" Joe asked.

"He took a walk. I don't know what happened, but he wasn't there. Somebody must have talked to him. God knows, we all tried to talk to him. He wasn't talking to anybody from either side in the last week or so. I don't know what happened to him, but I'm glad it did."

Joe put his head down and wept at his desk. Then he stood up determinedly, put on the jacket of his suit, adjusted his tie and left his office. He headed to the Courthouse back door, back towards the State House. This was history! He was going to watch it. *Screw the Supreme Judicial Court Ethics Committee and the Judicial Conduct Commission. Just let them dare! Would they have forbidden blacks to watch the reading of the Emancipation Proclamation? Now that the "political issue" has been decided why can't I celebrate? I'm a citizen!*

By the time he arrived at the back door of the Old Courthouse Joe was running. He went left over to Beacon Street, past the Athenaeum and stood with other onlookers at the corner of Beacon and Park Street, right in front of Fox News. Joe still didn't dare cross the street and get closer to the gates of the State House. There were too many cameras there now.

The Governor came out of the Statehouse with the Speaker of the House, the President of the Senate, the gay State Senator Jarrett Barrios, gay Representatives Liz Malia, Sarah Peake and Carl Sciortino and others who had worked on this issue, as well as some who had not, but wanted to bask in the victory, and they all walked down the State House steps. The big wrought-iron gates at the bottom of the steps were opened so the dignitaries could talk to the crowd.

From across and up the street Joe couldn't hear what the "dingitaries" were saying, but he could hear the cheers of the crowd. He remembered his first inkling of Gay Liberation with his friend Rudy and The Student Homophile League in the late sixties. Joe and his friends thought the idea was so impossible that it was ridiculous. He remembered the two brave South End women who started the Daughters of Bilitis in Boston thirty some years before. He remembered when there were not any gay political organizations in Boston. He remembered that 20-plus years before, even when there were gay political organizations, you couldn't get a politician to come to a gay political event. A gay endorsement was thought to be the kiss of death. At best the candidates sent surrogates, but they really didn't want any gay support to be known. Joe started to tear up again.

He remembered that this political neglect of gay civil rights in Boston first broke in the mayoral campaign of 1984, when Ray Flynn, now the most Catholic conservative of any Boston politician, told the Boston Lesbian and Gay Alliance (BLGPA), "I know you're going to go for Mel King [an African American candidate who had not been not afraid to seek gay support], but think of me next." Ray Flynn won and filled City Hall with gay people. He loved activists; he did not seem to care what they were being active about. He even pushed through the City Council an ordinance prohibiting discrimination on the basis of sexual orientation and appointed Joe to the newly created Boston Human Rights Commission, which was to enforce the anti-discrimination ordinance that included gay men and lesbians in its purview. Joe served on that Commission until he was made a judge in 1989.

Joe thought, *this is a victory for me too. I've been gay longer than most of these people. Why can't I join the celebration? The vote's been won. What might I do now that can be interpreted as trying to influence anyone? How can they call this 'a political issue?'*

And, all of a sudden, as if propelled by a higher power, Joe crossed Beacon Street on the diagonal, in his handsome suit and purple tie, stopping the already slow-moving traffic. He picked up a sign leaning on the fence, which said, "It's Wrong to vote on Civil Rights" on one side and, "We're Queer, We're Here, Get Used to It!" on the other. Bouncing the sign in the air, Joe pushed his way to the cheering crowd in front of the open gates. "Let them try to punish me for this!!" he said to the Universe. He almost knocked down a State Trooper on his rush to the center of the crowd. *Could that have been Trooper Mulligan?* passed through Joe's mind quickly as he moved forward.

Joe hadn't felt so empowered since the Gay March on Washington in 1987, before he was appointed a judge, when he walked by the White House with the delegation from the state of his birth and with his cousin Lizzie shouting, "Rhode Island, Rhode Island, lavender and pink. We're not as small as you might think!"

The Fox TV camera and a news commentator followed Joe across

Beacon Street and even picked up his shout on their microphone waving above, "Attaboy, Deval! Thanks, Sal! You got it, Therese!" Another man in a dark suit and a striped tie followed them, taking notes.

*   *   *

Later in the day, well after the Celebration and after Joe had returned to his office and basked in joy and glory on the phone and with his more liberal colleagues, Joe walked by the again closed gates of the State House on his way home. He could still feel the excitement. The area had been pretty well cleaned up, but Joe espied a rosette of rainbow colored bunting, a relic of the celebration earlier in the day, stuck in the privet just within the wrought iron fence protecting the front lawn of the State House. Joe picked up the rosette, smiled, and put the rosette through the buttonhole of the lapel of his suit's jacket. He straightened his shoulders and picked up his pace to his apartment building a little way down Beacon Street.

At the concierge's desk, Larry, the doorman, while barely lifting his eyes from that morning's *Herald*, said, "You gotta visitor—Mr. Bruno." Joe could hear the television while putting his key in the lock to his apartment. When he entered there was Angelo naked, face down on the Islamabad rug, a tapestry pillow propping his elbows, with his beautiful, muscled back, hairy bum and long extended legs facing Joe.

"Now from the State House: At 1:10 P.M. today the crowd went wild as the House and the Senate, in Constitutional Convention combined, defeated the proposed Anti-Same-Sex Marriage Amendment." There were shots of the crowd scene. "The Governor, the Speaker of the House, the Senate President and other legislators took the extraordinary step of coming out the front doors of the State House, opening the State House gates, and speaking to the crowd of jubilant gay opponents, as well as the defeated proponents of the Amendment across the street."

On the television just as the Governor began, because of his height and white hair as well as the good blue suit and lavender tie, one could clearly see Joe, the Honorable Joseph Lavin Lyons, bobbing a sign up and down that said, 'It's Wrong to vote on Civil Rights' and from behind, "We're Queer, We're Here, Get Used to It." The commentator said, "Well there's an enthusiastic older man! I wonder who he is." As the camera closed in on the Governor one could hear Joe's voice saying, "Attaboy, Deval! Thanks, Sal! You got it, Therese!"

"That's you, Joe!" Angelo said, belaboring the obvious. "You lucky bastard to have been there! Oh ,Joe, this is such a great day!" And then Angelo tackled Joe down to the floor where Angelo began, with Joe's willing assistance, to remove the suit, shirt and tie so recently memorialized on the 24-inch screen.

Joe had a delayed moment of fright when he realized that his burst of exuberance had been televised, and that because of his age and his adult attire, never mind his exhortations to the dignitaries and to the crowd, he stood out among the more youthful, more casual throng. He realized that the reticence and restraint that judges had better quickly learn upon appointment had been shattered by this impulsive act earlier in the afternoon. One part of Joe's brain was assessing the possible consequences of his impulsive behavior with his Chief Justice and the Commission on Judicial Conduct, even as Angelo Bruno lowered his lovely head onto Joe's Brooks Brothers blue and white checkered boxer shorts. That fear-filled part of the brain quickly shut off and Joe lifted his bum a tad, let Angelo remove the shorts and then gave Angelo that which he so eagerly had been seeking.

The television news continued in front of them. When it reached the weather fifteen minutes later, Joe, now on his stomach, Angelo above and behind him, reached up and shut the television off. Angelo rode Joe hard, pushing him into the corner of the couch, where they both gave it up together. Spent, Joe and Angelo collapsed on the floor and Angelo rolled off Joe. They lay together silently on their backs on the beautiful rose, cerulean blue and moss green rug looking at the ceiling, waiting for it to open and heaven to appear.

Finally Angelo broke the silence and said, "What a great day, Joe, and to think that you were there! You lucky guy! I was teaching multiplication to the fourth graders when the principal came to the door window and gave me a 'thumbs up.' In spite of all my complaints about her, Joe, she's a good woman. Hey, why did you call me to tell me to come over tonight? Was it to tell me about the celebration and your part in it, and so we could watch it on TV together? If so, we missed most of it and now we'll have to wait until the Ten O'Clock News. I didn't see anything after your handsome white head bouncing that sign in front of the Governor. You're something once you let yourself go, Joe, as we just proved once again," Angelo smiled lasciviously. "That's what I love about you—all the Catholic, Harvard, New England restraint and then the burst of Irish madness. I love you, Joe."

Angelo paused, then said, "Joe, do you want to get married?"

About the Author

For seventeen years Dermot Meagher was a judge of the Boston Municipal Court, the oldest trial court in Massachusetts. Before that he was an assistant district attorney, a bail reformer, a court reformer and he taught Criminal Law and Procedure to police officers. He also had a private law practice at various times. When he was appointed in 1989 he was the first openly gay judge in Massachusetts. He has been active in a number of gay political and social organizations, including the Gay and Lesbian Advocates and Defenders (GLAD), the Massachusetts Lesbian and Gay Bar Association and the Aids Action Committee.

He is the author of *Lyons and Tigers and Bears: A Judge Joe Lyons Mystery, Judge Sentences: Tales from the Bench* and co-author with Robert Coles, M.D. and Joseph Brenner M.D. of *Drugs and Youth*.

Dermot Meagher graduated from Harvard College, Boston College Law School,The Kennedy School of Government and was a Fellow at the Harvard Law School Center for Criminal Justice.

He is also an artist and shows his drawings, paintings and prints at the Schoolhouse Gallery in Provincetown as well as other venues in New England and Florida.

Praise for Dermot Meagher's
Judge Sentences: Tales from the Bench

The stories in *Judge Sentences* are short, each involving a case or character, observed from the point of view of the judge; not the cartoon version of judges seen on daytime television and crime shows but a workaday judge in the daily grind of a big urban court system. Again and again in these stories one gets the sense of a deeply humane man trying to thread the law through the needle of human misery. The judge is empathic but not naïve. He is worldly but he is never cynical—he is what used to be called *civilized*. I loved the stories and I am inspired by Judge Meagher, as a lawyer and as a human being.
Michael Nava, novelist and attorney

Dermot Meagher has given us a great read. The Daumier-like scenes he paints in his courtroom are fabulous, rendered with wit and compassion. Like Doritos, you can't consume just one. Nothing feels forced in this book. The man writes like a dream.
Sam Allis, *Boston Globe*

Meagher's writing is insightful and compassionate; the muscular prose laced with an attractive self-deprecatory wit. Keenly and sympathetically observed, the characters and their stories, like life in the courts, are never tidy, frequently carrying a disquieting, thought-provoking edge. An excellent, absorbing read.
Lavanya Sankaran, author of *The Red Carpet*

Beautifully written and irresistibly entertaining, *Judge Sentences* reveals the working of a busy urban court through the eyes of a very perceptive and very humane judge. Meagher has a flair for the understated insight, and a profound understanding of human nature. His self-deprecating sense of humor, compasion, and intelligent shine on every page.
Helen Fremont, author of *After a Long Silence: A Memoir*